UNCOMMON
WRATH

UNCOMMON WRATH

HOW
CAESAR
AND
CATO'S
DEADLY RIVALRY
DESTROYED
THE ROMAN REPUBLIC

JOSIAH OSGOOD

BASIC BOOKS

New York

Basic Books
Hachette Book Group
1290 Avenue of the Americas, New York, NY 10104
www.basicbooks.com

Printed in the United States of America

First Edition: November 2022

Published by Basic Books, an imprint of Perseus Books, LLC, a subsidiary of Hachette
Book Group, Inc. The Basic Books name and logo is a trademark of the Hachette Book
Group.

Print book interior design by Amy Quinn.

Library of Congress Control Number: 2022940722

ISBNs: 9781541620117 (hardcover), 9781541620100 (ebook)

LSC-C

Printing 1, 2022

CONTENTS

INTRODUCTION

"TWO MEN OF EXTRAORDINARY EXCELLENCE"

A S THE SUN ROSE OVER ROME ON DECEMBER 3, 63 BC, THE
consul Marcus Tullius Cicero summoned the five conspirators. Just hours before, Cicero had completed a sting operation
through which he had obtained letters that clearly implicated the
men in a plot to overthrow the government. He also sent an official
to confiscate weapons from one of their houses. There the official
found a huge quantity of swords and daggers, all newly sharpened.
It was time for the conspirators to answer for themselves before the
Senate.[1]

One of the five could not be found, but the other four obeyed
Cicero's summons. He put them under guard and took them to the
Temple of Concord, where the Senate was meeting that day. One
by one Cicero interrogated them in front of all the assembled senators. The man at whose house the swords and daggers had been

1

found—himself a senator—claimed that he was merely a collector of fine weapons. Still, as Cicero brought out the letters, unsealed them, and read them aloud, none of the men tried to deny what was clear to everyone: they were in league with Lucius Catiline.

Catiline was a politician with bitter grievances. Though he belonged to one of Rome's oldest families, earlier that year he had, for a second time, failed to win election to the top office of consul, held annually by two men. He was on the verge of bankruptcy and could not afford to wait and try again the next year. In early November, he fled Rome and assumed command of an armed uprising in northern Italy. The five conspirators left behind within the city walls were under orders to prepare the way for Catiline's return by assassinating leading political figures and torching parts of Rome.

An army was already on its way to confront Catiline, but the Senate now had to decide what to do with the men under arrest. They reassembled two days after the interrogation to settle on a plan. As members of the body stood up in succession to state their views, two proposals gained favor. One was to put the conspirators to death at once. Not only would this protect the city from efforts underway to rescue the detainees; it would scare off wavering supporters from throwing in with Catiline. The other scheme was to imprison the conspirators for life in the towns of Italy and to confiscate their property. The advantage of this plan was that it recognized the heinousness of the conspirators' actions while also acknowledging the right enjoyed by even the humblest Roman citizen not to be executed without a trial.

It was Julius Caesar who put forward the second proposal. Though a member of one of Rome's ancient patrician families, the thirty-seven-year-old senator had built his political career by championing the interests of the people. He believed he had much to gain if he stood up for citizens' rights while still taking a firm stance against the conspirators. As more senators spoke after Caesar, it seemed as if his view was going to prevail. But then the debate unexpectedly took a turn.

Marcus Porcius Cato, a recent addition to the Senate and five years younger than Caesar, rose and gave what proved to be the speech of his life.

"Wake up, before it is too late," Cato told the senators. "We are surrounded on all sides. Catiline and his army press at our throats. There are other enemies within the walls and even in the heart of our city."[2] The Senate had to act at once. "Other crimes you may prosecute after they have been committed. But if you do not take care to stop this one from happening, once it does take place, you will appeal to the courts in vain. In a captured city, there is nothing left for the vanquished."[3]

There was only one choice. The conspirators had already confessed their guilt. And so in accordance with ancestral practice, they should be executed at once.

As Cato finished speaking and sat back down, the senators broke into applause. Many stood up to say they agreed with Cato. Cicero called for a vote, and Cato's motion passed overwhelmingly. Caesar's proposal had been crushed.

The words just quoted from Cato's speech come not from a direct transcript—one was made at the time but has not survived—but rather from a historical work written about two decades later: *The War Against Catiline* of Gaius Sallustius Crispus ("Sallust," in English), a senator who had served as an officer under Julius Caesar but then withdrew from public life.[4] The debate over what to do with the conspirators represents the climax of Sallust's work, and it is a surprising one. Over many pages, Sallust re-creates a version of Cato's speech and also a version of Caesar's. While the earlier pages of *The War Against Catiline* focus on the corrupt but charismatic leader of the conspiracy, the book reaches its greatest moment of tension not in its depiction of a rebel on the march but in the dueling rhetoric of two senators. It is as if Sallust is signaling to readers that Roman history somehow changed in the course of that debate in

A posthumous portrait of Caesar discovered on the island of Pantelleria in 2003.
Credit: akg-images

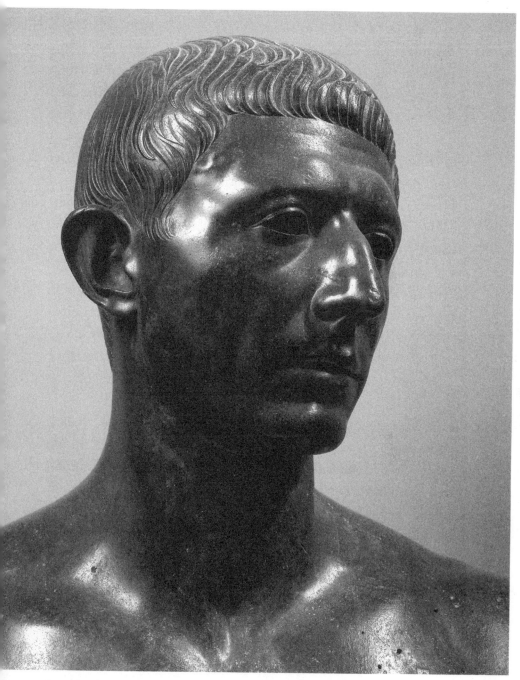

A posthumous portrait of Cato discovered in Volubilis (Morocco) in the 1940s.
Credit: G. Dagli Orti /© NPL—DeA Picture Library/Bridgeman Images

December of 63 BC. Caesar was already a major political figure.
Now Cato was too.

Surprising as Cato's triumph over Caesar is, even more unexpected is the reflection Sallust then offers. "Reading and listening
about the many splendid deeds that the Roman people have done
at home and on campaign, by land and by sea, a desire came over
me to examine what it was in particular that allowed such great un-
dertakings," he writes.[5] As he considered the matter, it grew clearer
to him that the excellence of a few citizens was what had made all
the successes of earlier days possible. But with greater power came
wealth, and wealth corrupted the citizenry. Romans grew lazy. "As
if worn out from giving birth, for many stretches of time Rome
went without producing a single man distinguished by excellence."

The age of Catiline was an age in which virtually everyone in
public life was bent on trying to capture the Republic for himself—
but for Sallust there were still "two men of extraordinary excellence": Cato and Caesar. "And since they have appeared in my story,
I am resolved not to pass them over in silence, but to describe, to
the extent of my ability, the nature and character of each."

They were roughly equal in "birth, years, and eloquence," Sallust
writes, and both achieved greatness, though for different things.
Caesar was celebrated for acts of kindness and generosity, Cato for
the integrity with which he lived. Caesar was distinguished by mild-
ness and mercy, Cato by his austerity. "By giving, by supporting, by
pardoning, Caesar won glory, Cato by never being lavish." Caesar
"yearned for a great command, an army, a new war where his excellence could shine. Cato's desire was for self-restraint, for morality,
for austerity above all." Though their characters were dissimilar, Sallust saw Caesar and Cato as personifying some of the traits that had
propelled the Roman Republic to unprecedented power centuries
earlier: generosity and toughness, a desire for fame and self-restraint.

It is a poignant verdict—poignant not just because of Sallust's assertion that great men had become so rare in Rome, and by the time
Sallust wrote both had passed on. What made the collision of these

two men truly affecting was the fact that, despite their "extraordinary excellence," they had fought one another for years like a pair of gladiators. Without either of them fully intending it, they became locked in political dispute, they exchanged insults and threats, they rallied behind them crowds of citizens and the Senate and then finally entire armies until the whole Mediterranean world was engulfed in war. Even as Sallust wrote, years after Cato and Caesar were gone, their heirs and successors were still murdering each other.

The two men's quarrel began in the year of Catiline's conspiracy, in 63, and they never stopped brawling after that. When Cato tried to block Caesar from passing legislation in the popular assembly, Caesar's followers lobbed rocks at Cato and even lifted Cato off the ground and carried him out. In his capacity as consul, Caesar tried to throw Cato into jail. Cato, in turn, gave speeches warning of new plots by Caesar to seize power. During the long war that Caesar fought in Gaul, Cato even claimed that Caesar had broken a truce and should be turned over to the enemy for punishment, to avoid a curse falling on Rome. Caesar, when he learned of the proposal, sent a letter to the Senate that was full of slanderous attacks against Cato. After the letter was read out, Cato stood up and denounced Caesar again. "It is not the children of Britons or Celts you have to fear," Cato said, "but Caesar himself."[6]

In personality, the men were opposites, and that fed into the dispute. A disciplined politician and general, Caesar also had an appetite for sensual pleasure. He took pride in his handsome looks, the daringly loose clothing he wore, his seduction of the wives of Rome's most powerful senators. To Cato, who wandered around Rome in dingy clothing and barefoot, who hid books of Stoic philosophy in his toga to pull out and read in spare moments, Caesar's luxury was horrifying. It could not be dismissed; it had to be denounced.

Cato's austerity and his unbending, anger-filled opposition to anyone he considered corrupt brought him into conflict with Caesar's most important characteristic: his obsessive need for recognition. Pride like Caesar's was not unusual among the senators of Rome, who strove to make names for themselves. But to an unhealthy degree, Caesar's self-worth became wrapped up in the recognition he received—or did not receive. The ancient biographer Plutarch tells the story of how when Caesar was crossing the Alps to take up an administrative post in Spain, he came to a small village with a handful of people living in hard circumstances. His companions jokingly asked, "Can it be that even here there are fierce rivalries over office and struggles for supremacy and jealousies of one powerful man against another?" Caesar replied, deadly serious, "I would rather be first here than second in Rome."[7]

Roman politics was rife with struggles between powerful figures. But special circumstances allowed this feud to become legendary. One was the sheer political talent of both men. Each excelled, for instance, at public speaking. Caesar could stir large crowds in Rome to support legislation he was proposing and could mobilize men to come to his defense when he felt threatened by enemies. Cato also performed well before mass audiences. He had an almost magical ability to calm angry mobs. He was especially effective in the Senate, as the debate over the Catilinarian conspirators showed. Cato could prick senators' consciences like no other. Another talent he and Caesar shared was for striking alliances with important politicians. Though Cato denied it in his own case, both men contracted marriages for themselves and members of their families to maximize their power. Each of them was manipulative. Caesar knew just how to play himself up as the innocent victim of senatorial plots. Cato obstructed public business in ways that nearly forced his opponents to respond violently and discredit themselves. In differing ways, each man was a master of accruing and deploying power.

The fuel that inflamed the political duel into a full civil war was in the two men's competing visions for the Republic and the followings each attracted. Each of them encouraged an us-versus-them mentality that made politics highly partisan. The need to stop the other side became paramount. If Caesar is allowed to keep fighting Gaul, it will be the end of the Republic. If Cato defeats this proposed legislation, it will be the end of the Republic. Out of the fear of some perceived threat or a desire to overcome opposition at a particular moment, politicians on both sides broke the usual rules of politics, resulting in louder denunciations, more feverish worries, and even nastier partisanship.

In the eyes of Caesar and his supporters, conservative senators had for too long run the Roman state to suit their own interests. Senators, they felt, disregarded the needs of ordinary citizens, whether those leading precarious existences in the city of Rome or the peasants who formed the backbone of legions. To the indebted and the desperate, the Senate seemed cruel. Caesar insisted that Romans should enjoy the splendid amenities befitting a world-class city. He wanted to take ordinary soldiers and make them great. He singled them out for recognition in the pages of his famous war commentaries, but he insisted that they held the potential for even greater things. Together they could expand the Roman empire, establish new colonies, and bring in new wealth for everyone—not just a handful at the top.

Cato countered that Rome's real problem was corruption. He was convinced that money corroded politics. To win ever more competitive elections, candidates increasingly courted voters with direct bribes. And to fill campaign coffers or settle debts or pay for lavish villas, the politicians, when they went off to overseas governorships, ripped off Rome's provincial subjects. Governors provoked unnecessary wars to pull in plunder. Like Caesar, Cato had many problems with the senators of his day. Yet unlike Caesar, Cato, along with a circle of like-minded politicians, saw the Senate as the main bulwark against generals accruing too much power. For Cato, Caesar's growing cult of personality was just the latest example of this alarming tendency.

There were precedents for the grand duel between Cato and Caesar. Groups of senators, similar to those of Cato and his circle, had banded together before against any man they thought was becoming too big and cultivating the people too much. Cicero and his allies took on Catiline—before Catiline turned to conspiracy. In the early years of Cato's and Caesar's political careers, a faction of senators drawn from Rome's noble families tried to counteract the growing power of the great general Pompey. Before that, many nobles pitted themselves against another great general, Caesar's uncle Marius. A rivalry between Marius and another politician, Sulla, led to a long civil war in the 80s BC.

Caesar and Cato envisioned futures for Rome that could not coexist—an empire wielding its power for the people versus a Senate protecting the people from all-powerful empire builders. Their quarrel illustrates the clash of two important viewpoints and, in doing so, it exposes challenges the Republic was facing. Each side identified real problems. Remote as the toga-clad Romans might seem to us, their questions are ones that challenge democracies today: How do democratic states promote prosperity? How do they hold free and fair elections? How do they confront the rise of a demagogue?

But the quarrel of Caesar and Cato was not just an intellectual exercise. It led directly to the outbreak, in 49 BC, of a great civil war in which tens of thousands of soldiers died. The violence and upheaval brought an end to republican government in Rome and ushered in the rule of emperors, all of whom called themselves "Caesar." Amazingly, that title, in various forms such as Kaiser and Tsar, stayed in use through World War I.

In the chain of events leading up to the outbreak of armed conflict, Caesar and Cato's hatred and suspicion of one another, and the ways they and their allies acted on those feelings, were critical at every stage. At the key moment, when Caesar's long war in Gaul ended and he was ready to return to Rome, mutual distrust and loathing blocked all compromise. Caesar himself, in the history he wrote of the civil war, acknowledged the role played by the quarrel. In January of 49 Cato refused to agree to a plan to send a delegation to Caesar to try to prevent war. "Cato was goaded on," Caesar wrote, "by his long-standing enmity with Caesar and resentment over his election defeat."[8] The belittling mention of Cato's defeat (in a run for the consulship, several years earlier) shows that the enmity was mutual.

War broke out not because of enduring hatreds in large swathes of the populace. It broke out because of the fighting between politicians. Years of demonization and threats, of violence and obstruction, by Caesar, Cato, and their respective allies, meant that each side feared to back down. Each had taken actions the other side could not forgive. One aggression justified another; force could only be met by counterforce.

It would, of course, be an oversimplification to explain the terrible civil war that broke out in 49 purely as the result of the political and personal feud between Cato and Caesar. Other individuals played their part, most of all the general Pompey, who went from being a friend, ally, and even son-in-law of Caesar to his most formidable military antagonist. Ancient writers actually attributed the outbreak of the civil war more to the breakdown of Caesar's relationship with Pompey than to the feud with Cato.[9] Still, important as the role of Pompey and others was, we have to keep in mind that, immediately after Cato's death, friends and relatives of his began producing a flood of eulogies and memoirs that did not always respect historical reality. Cato became an iconic figure, the last free Roman, whose efforts to save his country were no less noble for their failure— actually, more noble. As he was turned into the unblemished hero of a lost cause, his role in the buildup to civil war was downplayed. "The winners had the gods on their side, the losers Cato," as the poet Lucan summed it up.[10]

To understand how the Roman Republic came apart, even this particularly notable feud must be weighed against underlying weaknesses in the state that led to war. To be sure, the Rome of Caesar and Cato was not the "House Divided" of Abraham Lincoln's 1858 speech, a nation torn apart by slavery. Both the antebellum US and the Roman Republic were slave societies, but unlike in the US, nobody in Rome, aside from those enslaved, even questioned that institution. Even so, there were strains on the house of the Republic. Many Italians outside the city of Rome had only recently won full Roman citizenship, after a bloody rebellion that broke out in the year 91 BC. The terms of their enfranchisement proved contentious. Those Italians shut out of the settlement clamored for rights to be extended to them, causing political figures like Caesar to champion them, partly in hopes of winning their support. The city of Rome itself—with a population perhaps approaching a million, exposed to fires and to floods of the Tiber River and to chronic problems with the food supply—became increasingly unruly. Desperate men picked up stones and threw them at politicians who seemed uncaring. Some city dwellers joined gangs for hire.

As the house came under stress, a flaw in its design seemed to become apparent as well. By tradition, it was the Senate—the council of several hundred men who had held political office—that set the Republic's foreign policy and controlled its finance. But there were also several different assemblies of free male citizens who were able to legislate on any matter they wished, and from the later second century BC onward they had been encroaching on the Senate's prerogatives. Some disgruntled senators refused to accept this trend, which led to arguments, physical confrontation, the occasional murder, and then—during the childhoods of Caesar and Cato—the civil war between Marius, Sulla, and their respective supporters.

Huge armies squared off against each other. At the war's culminating battle, fought just outside the walls of Rome near the Colline Gate in November 82, the victor, Sulla, took six thousand Italian soldiers captive and had them butchered in the city. He also put bounties on his enemies and displayed their heads in public, as if they were trophies. Though only a teenager, Caesar was dragged into this awful struggle because of family connections to Sulla's chief opponents and was forced to go into hiding. Cato, although never directly threatened, is said to have recoiled when he went with his tutor to Sulla's house and saw men's heads being carried out from there.

Both Caesar and Cato were shaped by this war. The peril Caesar had been in left him with sympathy for Sulla's victims and the downtrodden more generally, as well as an obsession with his own personal safety and standing. Cato, for his whole life, feared another general entering Rome in arms, as Sulla had.

Civil war, and the brutality of Sulla's victory, wrought incalculable damage on Rome.[11] In his hour of victory, Sulla pushed through a set of reforms that tried to restore power to the Senate, but he did so in a way that failed to build consensus. After his death, key laws of his were struck down. Sulla had confiscated large tracts of land in Italy on which he settled his veterans. This left gangs of struggling men roaming around the countryside for years afterward. Some joined armed uprisings, like the rebellion of the gladiator Spartacus in the later 70s BC and then the movement that Catiline headed up ten years afterward. A willingness to resort to violence was doubtless Sulla's worst legacy.

Historians explaining how the Roman Republic fell typically emphasize structural factors such as the conflict over where power should lie and the instability in the countryside.[12] But to blame only such seemingly impersonal forces would be to go too far. A republic is, after all, a man-made object. If we follow Lincoln's metaphor and accept that a republic is a kind of house, we must acknowledge that responsibility for its maintenance lies with the politicians and the citizens who elect them. A house can be strengthened by its owners, or it can be neglected. Structural problems can be identified and fixed, or ignored. A house can be vandalized, even by those who live inside.

So it was with the civil war that broke out in 49—it was unnecessary. It was not, to borrow another phrase from the 1850s, an "irrepressible conflict," where large numbers of Romans lived in fear of one another and compromise was impossible. Compromise should have been feasible as Caesar prepared to return from Gaul. Compromise was a part of Roman political tradition. Even after Sulla's civil war, peaceful compromises were reached between Pompey and the Senate. Moreover, in the year 49, many politicians, not to mention thousands of men and women in the city of Rome and the towns of Italy, saw that going to war was folly. They could not have known what all the consequences of war would be, but the earlier Sullan conflict had shown that it was likely to be devastating.

These consequences weigh heavily on Caesar's and Cato's shoulders. Actions they took on the eve of war and also years earlier both created their impasse and won them each enough allies that they could drag all the Roman world into a fight. Their feud may not have been the sole reason for the war, but it would not have been the same war, with the same devastating ramifications, without the two men's mutual enmity to stoke the flames. Even after they had died, their memories inspired a younger generation to continue the fight. In bitterness, both sides—Caesarians and Catonians—demanded revenge.

It was, as the historian Sallust implied, a tragedy with two heroes. Both Caesar and Cato were flawed men of immense talent. They were masters of political stunts. The wild accusations, the awful rudeness, the never-ending schemes to mortify one another were provocative, sometimes funny. There is frankly something delicious about their world, with all its intrigue, the swirling gossip, and the skill with which politicians, these two especially, created their personas. Yet we have to reckon with the terrible outcomes of their fighting that nobody, including themselves, wanted. The story of Cato and Caesar, in the end, speaks most to the ravages of partisanship.

Politicians can and must argue with each other all the time. But regularly staking out extreme positions, while perhaps rewarding for an individual politician's career, threatens to devastate the political system overall. Mutual denunciations and threats, satisfying in the moment, make each side warier and less reluctant to work with the other. Deadlocks ensue, and to break them leaders take actions that further erode trust and even peaceful shared governance altogether. Leaders recklessly issue ultimatums that limit the options for everyone. They might even resort to physical violence. Polarization does not have to end in civil war. But a major civil war starts with it.[13]

So it was in Rome. Neither side wanted war. Both got it.

CHAPTER 1

COMING OF AGE IN CIVIL WAR

A LARGE CROWD WAS GATHERING IN THE FORUM, THE VAST OPEN square in the center of Rome. Amid the temples and colonnaded halls built by the Republic's leading men, much of the crowd would have milled at ground level, but some probably climbed onto the temple steps or perched on building balconies for a better view. The funeral of Julia, the widow of the great general Marius, was about to take place.[1]

It was 69 BC, about two decades after a quarrel between Marius and his rival Sulla had precipitated Rome's first civil war. Marius had died just two years into the war, but his and Julia's young son had kept up the fight until he was defeated in a siege four years later. Young Marius's head had been one of those displayed by Sulla in the Forum, just where his mother's funeral was now set to start. "First learn to row, before you try to steer," Sulla is said to have joked when presented with the head.[2] In his desire for revenge, Sulla also dug up Marius's ashes, flung them in a river, and tore

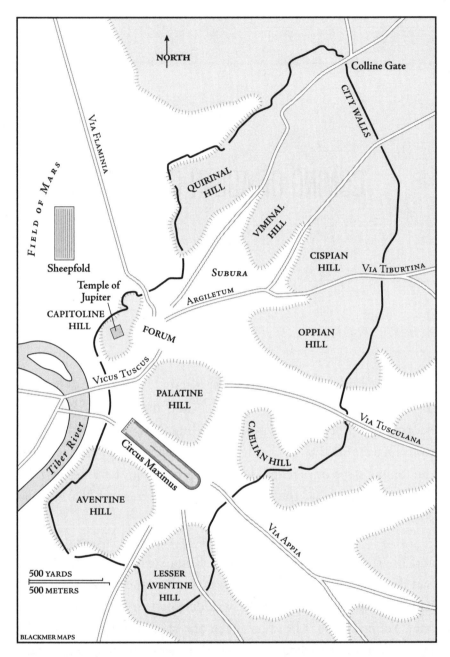

Rome, ca. 100 BC, showing the hills, the walls built in the fourth century BC, and a few major roads and sites. On the Field of Mars, a low-lying floodplain of the Tiber, young men did military training, and one of the popular assemblies, originally military in character, met in a large, uncovered enclosure divided into aisles, known as the Sheepfold. The Circus Maximus was a chariot racetrack.

A marble relief shows a Roman funerary procession. The deceased rests on a couch carried by eight bearers and is accompanied by musicians and mourners.
Credit: L'Aquila, Abruzzo, Italy, Luisa Ricciarini/Bridgeman Images

down all the statues and monuments erected in honor of Marius's victories. For years, the family was consigned to an official oblivion.

Funerals of the great men of Rome had long been one of the city's spectacles. The body of the deceased was placed on a couch, which was carried on a litter into the Forum, accompanied by musicians and mourners. Ahead of the litter strode actors hired to portray the ancestors of the deceased who had held political office. The actors wore wax masks that represented the faces of the dead with uncanny realism. They also put on the dress appropriate for the rank of those they impersonated—a toga with a purple-lined border for a consul, for example.[3]

Grand funerals for the women of political families were a newer development. Women could not hold office themselves—they could not even vote in elections—but over time they had become more prominent in public life. They visited the temples to worship the gods, they attended games, they intervened with male politicians on behalf of the people. Women's funerals honored their place in the community and also gave male relatives opportunities to promote themselves and their families.

It was Julia's ambitious nephew Caesar, about thirty years old by then, who organized the festivities on this occasion. The Julii were, like the few other surviving patrician families of Caesar's day, ancient, but they had left little mark on history. As Caesar grew up, he would have noticed that the wooden cupboard in the family house where the masks of office-holding ancestors were stored had few recent additions. To compensate, the family insisted that they were descended from the goddess Venus and her son Aeneas, the prince of Troy whom the Romans claimed as their founder. At the parade in 69, Caesar was also able to include, alongside masks of Julii, those of the Marcii Reges, the family of Julia's mother and Caesar's grandmother Marcia. They, too, were patrician and claimed descent from one of the kings who ruled Rome before the foundation of the Republic, Ancus Marcius.[4]

The climax of the public funeral was a eulogy, delivered from the high speaker's platform at the edge of the Forum known as the Rostra. It fell to Caesar to speak, and as was typical for such addresses, he talked about his family's ancestry. "The family of my aunt Julia is, on her mother's side, descended from kings," he began impressively. "On her father's side, it is linked to the gods."

He must have let that sink in before elaborating, "This is because the Marcii Reges, which is the family name of Julia's mother, go back to Ancus Marcius, and the Julii, the clan of which our family is a branch, go back to Venus."

"And so," he went on, "in our family is found the sanctity of kings, who have supreme power among men, and the holiness of gods, who hold under their sway the kings themselves."[5]

Caesar's rhetorical education was on full display. The Julii did not have the ancestral exploits that many other noble families could brag of, yet you wouldn't know it from Caesar's audacious remarks. But for the crowd gathered that day, Caesar pulled off something far more impressive still. In the parade, he included not just masks of the Julii and Marcii but also those of Marius and Marius's son, both of which Sulla had banned from public display. For years, the

Roman people had not even been able to look at a statue of Marius. Now they shouted and clapped with joy. It was as if their old hero, the man who had saved Rome from the German invasion, had come back to life.

As the funeral for his aunt showed, Gaius Julius Caesar, born in 100 BC, had an unusual double heritage. On the one hand, he was a patrician Julius, but on the other, his most important relative was Marius, one of the greatest gate-crashers in all of Roman political history. Though the Julii had languished for centuries, they remained noble—meaning that ancestors in the male line had held high political office. As a noble, Caesar would have been expected to compete in elections and try to rise up the ladder of magistracies, from the lowest rung of quaestor, a financial position, all the way to the consulship at the top. He would also have been expected to perform military service and risk his life in battle to earn a reputation for valor.[6]

In the decades before Caesar's birth, the fortunes of the Julii had started to show modest improvement. One sign of this was the marriage of Caesar's paternal grandfather into the more illustrious family of the Marcii Reges. Caesar's own father had married Aurelia, a member of a highly successful family of the plebeian nobility. Originally, the so-called plebs had been the common people of Rome, and the term could still refer to the masses. But over the centuries, as many of the original patrician families died off, some plebeian families had climbed the ladder of office and attained great power. Aurelia, who was herself probably the daughter and granddaughter of consuls, had knowledge and connections to help her son as he tried to make his political career. She supervised his childhood education and for years after that watched over his interests. In later times, she became a byword for the strong Roman mother. Her own husband's career stalled at the praetorship, the office just below consul, and he died when Caesar was fifteen.[7]

As important as Caesar's noble ancestry was his relationship with Gaius Marius, who for many years was the leading man in Rome. Marius was what the Romans called a "new man," the first in his family to hold office. Not a single mask adorned his house, though Marius made up for this by bragging that his masks were the medals he had earned in war, as were the scars on the front of his body—the only acceptable place for a Roman to incur war wounds.[8] Marius came from a little town in the rugged mountains southeast of Rome. Courageous and hardworking, he had caught the attention of a prominent noble who took him to Spain. When he killed one of the enemy before his commander's eyes, his reputation took off.

Marius used connections with the nobles when he needed to, but it was by attacking the nobility that he won political dominance. In 119 BC, he held the office of tribune of the plebs. Ten tribunes were elected annually, and by tradition they were supposed to represent the interests of ordinary citizens. They had direct control of one of the popular assemblies, the Plebeian Assembly, in which all male citizens except patricians could vote.[9] In this assembly Marius introduced legislation designed to ensure the secrecy of voting. This threatened the control of the nobles over the votes of poorer Romans, and one of the consuls persuaded the Senate to come out against the law and to summon Marius to the Senate to explain himself. The Senate, which was dominated by the nobles, could not pass laws but rather issued decrees that were supposed to be authoritative, like the decree instructing Cicero to execute the Catilinarian conspirators in 63. When Marius appeared in the Senate, far from backing down, as a new man should have, he threatened to have the consul dragged off to prison, something he could do as tribune. The Senate gave in, and Marius's law was passed.

Marius's election to the consulship about a decade later infuriated the nobility even more. For years, a war had been dragging on between Rome and a king of northern Africa named Jugurtha. A talented military commander, Marius went to serve on the staff of one of the generals the Senate had placed in charge. Through his accomplishments there and his willingness to share in the war's hardships, Marius won over the soldiers, and they soon wanted him to assume supreme command. When Marius asked his commander for permission to return to Rome to stand for the consulship, the noble sneeringly replied that Marius might be ready when the commander's own son, a very young man, was. But Marius was granted permission to return to the capital, and he made hay of his exploits. By linking ongoing military failures in Africa to the haughtiness of the nobility, Marius turned his status as a new man into an asset and was able to win election as one of the two consuls for the year 107.[10]

Marius immediately had the Plebeian Assembly vote him commander of the war against Jugurtha, overriding the Senate's normal prerogative to make such assignments. Mustering a fresh round of troops, he allowed even those without property to serve. By tradition, citizens were supposed to provide themselves with their own arms and armor to fight in the legions and so had to demonstrate some wealth. The requirement was sometimes waived, but Marius ended up removing it permanently.

With his enthusiastic new army Marius successfully ended the war and was awarded a triumph, the Republic's supreme military honor. Jugurtha, wearing a single gold earring, all that remained of his once great wealth, was dragged in chains through the streets of Rome and then thrown into prison for execution while Marius, crowned with a laurel wreath, rode in a chariot drawn by four horses. To the further frustration of Marius's enemies, on the same day as the triumph, January 1, 104, Marius embarked on his second consulship.

He turned his attention to another lingering conflict that the noble leadership had seemed powerless to resolve. Several years before, thousands of Germanic warriors from northern Europe had begun a migration toward Italy and in 105 had inflicted a grave defeat on the legions, among the worst in all of Roman history. No one seemed to have the skills and luck to defeat the barbarians—until Marius.

From 104 through 100, the new man held an unprecedented series of five consulships in succession as he beat back the blond giants. Among the people, Marius was hailed as the savior of Rome. Offerings and libations were made to him as if he were a god. Marius, in turn, worked hard to reward his soldiers for their part in the victories. He provided lands for them to farm. To Italians who served in his army he granted Roman citizenship with unusual generosity.[11]

Caesar would find his most important political model in his uncle Marius. Both championed the same groups: ordinary Romans, Italians, and common soldiers above all. Marius's bold generalship and his willingness to stand in the front line of battle inspired Caesar as well.

Still, good as Marius had been at taunting the nobles, he was not much of an orator, and Caesar looked elsewhere as he refined his political skills. In this domain, Caesar tried to copy a younger kinsman of his father's from another branch of the Julian family, Caesar Strabo. Strabo was one of the best speakers of his day, famous for an ability to skewer opponents with jokes. Once when another orator who flailed his arms too much as he spoke was up on the Rostra, Strabo cried out, "Who's that talking from a boat?"[12] Another time, Strabo was arguing with a rival and suddenly said, "I will now show you what kind of man you are." "Show me, please," the rival said. Strabo pointed with his finger to a German shield hanging nearby—displayed in honor of Marius's victory—on which was painted an absurd-looking man whose tongue was hanging out of his mouth.[13] The crowd burst into laughter. Caesar preferred to leaven his speeches with Strabo's wit rather than bludgeon like Marius.

Marcius Porcius Cato, born in 95 BC, also belonged to a noble family but one with a different profile from that of the Julii. The Porcii were, in Roman terms, much newer. Their roots lay in the Sabine territory in the hills northeast of Rome, and they had not gained

citizenship until long after the expulsion of the kings and the establishment of republican government. They farmed and fought well
as soldiers but never held political office until their fortunes were
transformed in the later third century BC by one of the most extraordinary characters in Roman history, Cato the Elder.[14]

Cato the Elder was another of the rare new men who made it
to the heights of power, pioneering techniques that Marius would
later use to good effect. He championed traditional Roman values
of hard work, austerity, and a willingness to make any sacrifice for
the public good, and he attacked noble senators for failing to live up
to those values. With his sharp tongue, he cut others to the quick
and never lost a chance to demonstrate his toughness. Even as a
general, he carried his own armor, like an ordinary soldier, and he
made do with the same food they did. He drank only water, except
in a raging thirst, when he would call for a little vinegar. A tough
old animal skin was his blanket. While the other commanders of
Rome's overseas provinces used public money for lavish accommodations, Cato spent barely anything. He made his circuit of the cities on foot, followed by just a single slave. Prosecuting others for
embezzlement was a favorite pastime. Romans chafed under Cato's never-ending crusades against luxury, but they took pleasure in
watching how rudely Cato treated almost everyone—the grandest
senators, foreign kings, and especially the Greek doctors in Rome,
who Cato claimed were all murderers.

When Cato looked through the masks of the ancestors, it must
have been the one of his great-grandfather, Cato the Elder, that
stood out. The elder Cato became the chief model for the younger,
who by his late teenage years was already garnering attention by
emulating the censor's famously austere lifestyle.[15]

But in Cato's cabinet of masks there was a gap where his father's
should have been. He had died when Cato was still a very young
child, without having reached high office. The father did hold a
tribunate, during which he challenged Marius; in the developing
struggle between the Senate and the Plebeian Assembly, he stood

with the Senate.[16] Cato, as he started to forge his political identity, would hew to that line also, in keeping with his reverence of the past. As so many senators would bear in mind later on, during the worst crisis the Republic had ever faced, Hannibal's invasion of Italy, it was the Senate that kept its nerve and ensured Rome's survival.

Soon after the death of his father, Cato lost his mother, Livia, as well. Cato, his younger sister, and two older half siblings from Livia's first marriage—a brother and a sister—were taken in by Livia's brother Drusus, who lived in a large and fashionable house on the Palatine Hill, the city's most desirable address for politicians because of its proximity to the Forum.[17] But soon Drusus was also dead. As tribune in the year 91, he tried to enact an ambitious program of reform with the ultimate goal of bolstering the authority of the Senate. His plans aroused controversy, and as he returned home one evening with a crowd of supporters, he was fatally stabbed by an unknown assassin.

Cato, his sister, and his half siblings probably stayed on in Drusus's comfortable house, with an aunt or grandmother to keep an eye on them.[18] The older half siblings, Servilia and her brother, Servilius Caepio, seem almost to have become surrogate parents for Cato. Asked as a little boy whom he loved most, Cato answered, "My brother." After him? "My brother." And after *him*? "My brother."[19] The questioner finally gave up. Cato became devoted to the good-natured Caepio and even as a young adult could barely eat or go down to the Forum without him.

Cato also forged a bond—not atypical for a Roman noble—to a slave, his tutor, a kindly Greek named Sarpedon. Sarpedon was exceptionally patient with Cato, who demanded to know the reason for everything and kept asking, "Why?"[20] Although another tutor would likely box a child's ears for such impertinence, Sarpedon tried to answer Cato's questions. Sarpedon grew fond of the boy and accompanied him into his teenage years.

Cato's early biographers insisted that even as a child he gave signs of his later well-known tendency to think things through for himself and to act independently.[21] Cato once attended a birthday party where the boys entertained themselves by going off to a separate part of the house and pretending to put each other on trial, with full prosecution speeches and punishments for the convicted.[22] At this party, a good-looking younger boy was put on trial, an older boy led him away to a room and locked the door, and the younger boy then called out to Cato for help. Cato fearlessly rushed past those guarding the room, rescued the child, and led him home, seething with anger. The good-looking boy had been at risk not just of violent sexual assault but also of a permanent stain on his honor. With this episode, Cato's biographers were saying, even at a young age Cato showed willingness to take action if he thought wrong was being done. Children can harbor a strong sense of justice. Cato had it his whole life.

Living relatives and dead forebears shaped who Cato and Caesar became, but the dominant figure of their early lives turned out to be Sulla.

With his blond hair and piercing blue eyes, unusual features in Rome, Lucius Cornelius Sulla stood out. He was born, like Caesar, into a patrician family that had sunk into obscurity. There were few masks for him to display, and also little money. Shockingly for a patrician, Sulla shared lodgings in an apartment house with an ex-slave, and he passed his time among actors and entertainers. Thanks in part to an inheritance from a wealthy prostitute who had grown fond of him, he was able to embark on a public career, and he joined the staff of Marius during the war against Jugurtha. It was Sulla who, through negotiations with Jugurtha's father-in-law, had actually captured the king after a daring mission. Sulla engraved the exploit on his signet ring, and Marius forever afterward resented how the young man seemed to have upstaged him in ending the long war.[23]

The two men came to open blows in 88. Though about seventy years old and quite fat by then, Marius was determined to secure command of the war against Mithridates, an eastern king who had recently invaded Roman territory in Asia Minor and presided over a grisly massacre of Romans living there. Marius was not only hoping for one last triumph to cap his already extraordinary record. He could finally exact revenge on Sulla, who was serving as consul and had been assigned command by the Senate in the traditional way. But Marius had grown old. Romans looked on with pity as they saw him go down to the Field of Mars each day and try to keep up with the young soldiers during military exercises. Many thought the arthritic old man should return to the hot baths on the Bay of Naples, where he had a villa.[24]

Drawing on techniques he had used before, Marius had the Plebeian Assembly pass a law awarding the command against Mithridates to himself. In response, Sulla took an unforeseen step that set him apart from all his contemporaries and was to be a turning point in the Republic's history. He marched on Rome with an army. Romans climbed onto their roofs and threw stones and tiles at Sulla's forces as they entered the city. Not to be stopped, Sulla shouted orders to set the houses on fire and grabbed a blazing torch himself. Marius gathered what armed men he could and tried to fight Sulla in the streets but, badly outnumbered, had to flee Rome. The next day, Sulla summoned the Senate and had Marius and his prominent supporters declared enemies of the state.

With his command of the war against Mithridates reinstated, Sulla soon went east in search of a glorious victory. In his absence Marius returned to Rome and established control of the city. Mad with rage at what he had endured, he ordered the band of slaves that made up his bodyguard to slay anyone he deemed an enemy. Headless trunks were tossed into the streets. Marius was elected to an unprecedented seventh consulship in 86 BC but died just a couple of weeks into his term.[25]

The death of the bitter old man came as a relief to the city of Rome, but it did not end the ongoing conflict. Political allies of Marius, including his consular colleague Lucius Cornelius Cinna,

could not reach any kind of settlement with Sulla, who wanted revenge on his opponents. Cinna made preparations to resist Sulla
militarily but was stabbed to death in a mutiny of some of his soldiers. Die-hard supporters of the Marian cause desperately looked
to Marius's young and inexperienced son, who, against the wishes
of his mother, Julia, was elected to a consulship.

What the young Caesar thought at the time about his uncle's
rampage or his cousin's doomed command is unrecorded. We are
only told that Caesar was nominated by Marius and Cinna to fill a
newly vacant priesthood of Jupiter.[26] Only a patrician could hold the
post, and like other religious offices it came with great distinction.
Unusually, though, this particular priesthood also imposed many
taboos on its occupant. The priest of Jupiter was forbidden to mount
a horse or spend more than a night away from Rome or gaze upon a
dead body.[27] For anyone familiar with Caesar's later record of conquest, the thought of him assuming this post is unfathomable. Even
so, at the time, the Julii apparently saw the priesthood as an opportunity to win glory.

For Caesar the post carried consequences. While still a boy, he
had been betrothed to Cossutia, the daughter of an equestrian.[28]
Originally Rome's cavalry, equestrians in this period were men of
substantial wealth who did not serve in political office but filled important roles as military officers, government contractors, and jurors
in criminal trials. Cossutia lent no social distinction to Caesar, but
she did bring a large dowry that could support his household as he
embarked on a political career. Compared to other noble families,
the Julii were less well off, which probably explains the desirability
of the match. Yet the priest of Jupiter could only marry a patrician.
This meant Caesar had to break off the engagement with Cossutia. It's possible that, given her family's lack of luster, this was not
such a great blow to Caesar. After all, in her place he was to marry
Cornelia, the daughter of Marius's patrician associate Cinna. The
young couple appear never actually to have been inaugurated as
priest and priestess, perhaps because the chief priest, an opponent

of Cinna, refused to give the required consent.[29] Thus, in the end, Caesar ended up avoiding all the inconvenient ritual restrictions but managed to gain the cachet of a patrician bride even so.

In the east, meanwhile, Sulla won several impressive victories over the forces of Mithridates, enough to merit a triumph, but he then made a peace with the king so he could return to Italy and have his revenge on the Marians. He landed in southern Italy in 83 and by November of the following year had taken back Rome. To reestablish control, he relied on terror, far beyond the norms that Romans were accustomed to. Six thousand men taken captive in a battle just outside the walls were marched into the city center under guard. Sulla summoned the Senate to meet at a nearby temple, and at the very moment he started speaking, executioners began slaughtering the six thousand. As their shrieks filled the air, Sulla calmly told the senators not to be concerned; it was only some criminals being reprimanded.[30]

As murders continued, one bold senator finally begged Sulla to allay public anxiety and give an indication of who else was to be punished. Sulla consented and started posting lists of citizens who were named outlaws; rewards were offered to anyone who murdered a person listed. The property of the proscribed was confiscated, and their sons and grandsons were banned from ever holding public office. Some were added to the list and killed just for their wealth, and a dark joke of the "three men walked into a bar" variety circulated: one was killed by his mansion, one by his estate, and one by his baths.[31]

Sulla had himself appointed dictator. The office, last used 120 years before, had traditionally been assigned for a limited term as a way of efficiently managing military crises. Sulla intended to hold the job for as long as he wished, and he wielded his extraordinary power to pass whatever laws he pleased to reorganize the government. He stripped the tribunes of many of their powers and decreed that no law could be passed in the Plebeian Assembly without the approval of the Senate. There were to be no more struggles like the fight over the Mithridatic command in 88. Sulla also rewarded his partisans. Italian communities that had supported the Marian side saw their lands confiscated and turned over to Sulla's veterans. Sulla even felt free to marry women against their will to his favorite officers.

Among the most impressive supporters who flocked to Sulla when he landed in Italy in 83 was Gnaeus Pompey, a young man of extraordinary ambition and ability who would come to play a major role in the conflict of Caesar and Cato, siding first with one, then the other. Just after Sulla's return, through force of personality as well as family connections, Pompey raised a private army of three legions and racked up a string of victories over several of Sulla's opponents. As Pompey marched with his sleek new army to meet Sulla, Sulla paid him the extraordinary compliment of getting off his horse and saluting Pompey as imperator, a title normally bestowed on a victorious commander by his own troops.[32]

Now master of Italy, Sulla, who was besotted with Pompey's talents and perhaps his handsome looks too, sought to draw the young man closer. Together with his highly distinguished wife, Metella, Sulla urged Pompey to accept the hand of Metella's daughter from a previous marriage, a woman named Aemilia. Pompey felt he had no choice but to comply with the dictator's wish, but even the ambitious Pompey must have found the situation troubling. Not only would he have to divorce his current wife, Antistia, but Aemilia was also married at the time—and pregnant. She would also have to divorce.[33]

The wedding ended up looking less like a celebration than like yet another of the creepy stunts Sulla was so fond of. Aemilia was presented to Pompey heavily pregnant. His ex-wife, Antistia, had only recently suffered the loss of her father, killed in the Senate house in a purge organized by the younger Marius, and of her grief-stricken mother, who had taken her own life. Now Antistia was losing Pompey. And it was all for nothing, since shortly after moving in with Pompey, Aemilia died giving birth to the child of her previous husband. Shocking as the whole episode was, it was not atypical of the disasters the Roman ruling class suffered in those years. Yet the nobles did not withdraw from politics. Almost anything beat lives of quiet obscurity.

As Sulla's viciousness peaked with the slaughter of so many citizens, Caesar was coming into full manhood. He was tall, with a fair complexion, shapely limbs, and keen dark eyes. He paid attention to his appearance, carefully shaving his face—and, it was said, other parts of his body too. His dress was remarkable. Beneath his toga flowed a tunic with unusually long, fringed sleeves that reached his wrist. The belt on it was barely tied at all.[34]

Upon Sulla's return to Rome, Caesar's position became precarious. While political office was still many years off, as a nephew of Marius and son-in-law of Cinna, Caesar would have been considered a future leader of the Marians, which is to say of all the groups in Roman society that chafed under senatorial dominance, such as the struggling Italian peasants. Sulla, determined to prop up the nobility and the Senate, wanted to be sure that there would be no resurgence of the Marian cause. To ensure that Caesar's connection to Marius was entirely severed, Caesar would have to divorce Cornelia. Sulla might initially have presented this as an opportunity for Caesar and offered him a prestigious new match, as he did for Pompey. But Caesar already had a wife of the highest social distinction, Cornelia, with whom he appears to have been very much in love. Furthermore, in killing the younger Marius and desecrating the tomb of the elder, Sulla had attacked members of Caesar's own family. Angry and defiant, Caesar refused to give up his wife.[35]

The consequences for him were severe. Caesar was stripped of the opportunity to fill his priesthood, of his dowry from Cornelia, and of the property he had inherited from his father. Convinced that his life was in danger, he fled Rome in disguise and went into hiding in the mountainous country northeast of the city. Each night he secretly moved to a new house but was caught when, having fallen ill and suffering from a fever, he had to be carried by a litter. A group of Sulla's soldiers was combing the district—probably looking for men on Sulla's list of the condemned. Caesar only escaped by bribing their leader with a substantial sum. Though no ancient account explicitly says so, it appears that Caesar was among those proscribed; even if not, he would have feared being killed.[36] It was a lawless time.

Back in Rome, friends and family tried to intervene with the dictator on Caesar's behalf. One group to speak up for him were the influential Vestal Virgins, the six priestesses who tended the flame of the hearth goddess, Vesta, the extinction of which was thought to endanger Rome. They had probably gotten to know Caesar when he was nominated priest of Jupiter, and they would certainly have known Aurelia. Two of Aurelia's kinsmen also spoke up for Caesar. Reluctantly, Sulla capitulated. Caesar's later biographers assigned various remarks to Sulla for the occasion: "Be on your guard against this badly-belted boy. . . . In Caesar there is more than one Marius."[37] One has to wonder whether these warnings were only "remembered" by critics and admirers of Caesar after he established himself as a popular politician some years later. It is not a stretch, though, to suppose that Sulla, looking at the unusually independent young man before him, with his loose belt and defiant gaze, had a sense of the course Caesar's life would take.[38] The same fiery daring that burned in Sulla also burned in Caesar.

Almost singlehandedly this eighteen-year-old had stared down a dictator. If they had not before, the Marians would look to the courageous young man as a future leader; the groups Marius had rallied would be Caesar's natural base in politics. The danger Caesar had lived through branded him with a sense of the injustice of many of Sulla's acts. In the years to come, Caesar would stand up for Sulla's victims, especially the sons of the proscribed, who were banned from holding political office.[39] He would sympathize far more easily with the needy than the affluent. He would not let Sulla's political

successors ruin lives the way the dictator had tried to destroy his
with Cornelia. Caesar's brush with Sulla left him with a hatred for
civil war, but it also hardened him. Committed as he was to justice,
he also came to think that he could only rely on himself. To survive
and flourish, he needed to acquire more power than anyone else.

Cato had a very different experience of Sulla's dictatorship. Sulla,
an old family friend, actually showed some warmth to Cato. Once,
the dictator was putting on a festival known as the Trojan Game, in
which boys of the nobility executed elaborate equestrian maneuvers.
Two boys were selected to serve as leaders. As one, Sulla appointed
a son of his wife, Metella, whom all the boys accepted because
of her great influence. When Sulla appointed as the other leader
a cousin of Pompey, for some reason the boys were unhappy and
would not practice with him. When Sulla asked whom they wished
for instead, they all cried out, "Cato." Cato it was.[40]

Sulla invited Cato and Sarpedon into his house one day and con-
versed with them, a kindness he showed to few others. Sarpedon,
worried about his pupil's safety, insisted they keep returning to pay
their respects, even though the house was like a scene from the un-
derworld, with men regularly being led there and tortured. Cato,
appalled when he saw the heads of some of the proscribed being
taken away from the house, asked Sarpedon why nobody killed
Sulla. Sarpedon answered that nobody had had the opportunity.
Cato replied, "Well, why haven't you given me the sword to kill him
and free the country from slavery?"[41] When Sarpedon heard this
and saw the look of anger on Cato's face, he was so frightened that
he kept a careful watch on Cato afterward.

It is hard not to wonder if this story was recast after subsequent
events. When Cato was first elected to political office in the 60s
BC, he demanded that anyone who had killed men on Sulla's pro-
scription lists should return their rewards to the treasury.[42] New details of Cato's encounter with Sulla might have been "remembered"

then—just as they possibly were about Caesar once his political career was well underway. But a thirteen-year-old boy could easily
make a threat to stand up to a tyrant, however unlikely he might
have been to succeed. The rhetorical education of Roman children
teemed with tyrants who needed to be denounced—and killed. The
threat would be natural for a boy like Cato, with his strong sense of
justice.

Over the next few years, as he grew into manhood, Cato's distinctive personality showed through unmistakably.[43] Quite unlike
Caesar, with his elaborate grooming, Cato was developing a taste
for austerity. When, for instance, his beloved older half brother,
Caepio, took to wearing perfume, as young Roman men sometimes
did, Cato refused to use it himself, even though he copied Caepio in
other ways.

Around the age of twenty Cato established his own household,
where he could impress visitors with his self-control. He rejected
fancy foods. He drank sparingly (notoriously, this was later to
change). At any hour of the day, he would walk the streets rather
than take a carriage. While others embraced a new fashion for a
particularly vivid shade of purple on the tunics under their togas,
Cato rejected it for a duller shade. More startlingly, he would even
go out in public barefoot and without a tunic at all. Like Caesar,
Cato drew attention to himself through dress, but while Caesar
wanted to appear stylish, Cato's look was that of a Roman from
hundreds of years before, the sort you would only see in the ancient
statues littering the city. The tough men of old didn't need soft un-
dergarments, nor did Cato.[44]

Cato's attire helped him win publicity and could remind voters
of his powerful ancestor, but like the rest of his lifestyle, it was not
merely a stunt. Soon after moving into his new house, Cato invited a
Stoic philosopher, Antipater of Tyre, to stay with him. It was a common practice for Roman senators to have an in-house philosopher
to assure them of their outstanding virtue and coach them through
moments of disappointment. Cato had a deeper commitment to

Stoicism, with its stern commands to shun materialism, to strive only for a life of virtue, and to judge weak any man who wallowed in luxury or even the occasional indulgence. Cato especially enjoyed "justice when it is rigid and does not bend to clemency or favor."[45] He wanted to be above blame himself and was all too ready to look down on others for their failings.

Unlike many moralists, though, Cato was no hypocrite. He pushed himself as hard as he pushed anyone else. He was desperate to stay true to his commitment to justice. Stoics trained themselves to suppress emotion as much as possible, but throughout his life Cato was always livid when he perceived unfairness. He roared like an angry bull at others' misdeeds. Years after Sulla's dictatorship, he seethed with hatred for how unscrupulous men had taken the chance to enrich themselves.

Cato's first marriage engagement showed the lengths to which he could take his anger. Betrothals were highly legal affairs in which the prospective bride and groom and their families ratified a contract. Cato had selected for his wife a woman named Aemilia Lepida. Originally she had been betrothed to Cornelius Scipio Nasica, a noble with a far more distinguished ancestry than Cato's. Scipio had changed his mind, but then, before Lepida married Cato, Scipio reconsidered yet again and was able to win her back.[46]

Cato was furious. He even contemplated taking legal action. When friends barely dissuaded him from taking this unprecedented step, he found revenge by writing scurrilous poems about Scipio. Cato's inspiration was the archaic Greek poet Archilochus, who, after being jilted, retaliated so forcefully in his verse that his fiancée and her father both reportedly hanged themselves. While Cato seems to have spared Scipio the obscenities Archilochus was famous for, his revenge was unworthy of a Stoic. Cato's manhood had been insulted, but more than that it was a sense of injustice that made him snap. He ended up marrying a woman named Atilia, who came from a less distinguished family than Lepida's. She was, according to the biographical tradition, the first woman he had sex with—if true, another sign of his intense desire to lead a temperate life.[47]

Strong feelings and opinions may be common in young men, and the sons of Roman noble families were encouraged to act aggressively to win fame. Caesar and Cato stood out in their adolescence, as they would later in life, for their vehement commitment to justice and personal integrity: for all their differences, they had this in common, and it helps explain why they would stand apart as the two great figures of their generation. Caesar defied Sulla, Cato tramped about Rome shivering in the cold. The danger Caesar experienced in civil war gave him a sympathy for innocent victims. Cato was more embittered against those who had profited illegally. Both shared a horror for the disaster of civil war, strong even for members of their generation.

Having passed all the laws he wished to, Sulla gave up his dictatorship, held one last regular consulship in 80 BC, and left Rome for good, spending the last couple of years of his life cavorting on the Bay of Naples with the actors and actresses whose company he had always enjoyed most. He also was working on his lengthy memoirs, in which he cast himself as a favorite of the gods who enjoyed victory after victory.[48] Even though there was widespread revulsion at his cruelty, and new unrest cropped up after his death, his supporters in the Senate managed to hold on to power in Rome for the next decade.

To go anywhere in politics, Caesar and Cato needed to devote these years of their lives—Caesar's twenties, Cato's late teens and early twenties—to establishing their reputations and training themselves as soldiers and public speakers. They had to be careful around Sulla's old friends, Caesar especially. But they never forgot what they had lived through and seen.

CHAPTER 2

MAKING NAMES FOR THEMSELVES

I N MANY TIMES AND PLACES THOSE ASPIRING TO A POLITICAL CA-
reer have found it useful to serve in the armed forces. In Rome
it was mandatory. And so after his brush with Sulla, Caesar left
for military service on the staff of Marcus Minucius Thermus, then
serving as governor of Asia. Thermus was a partisan of Sulla, and a
tour with him, especially if it was successful, offered Caesar the further opportunity of improving his relations with the men in charge
of the Republic.[1]

In Asia, Thermus had been entrusted with the task of subduing Mytilene, an ancient Greek city-state on the island of Lesbos
that had joined the rebellion of King Mithridates of Pontus against
Rome about a decade earlier. Mytilene's impressive walls and extensive fleet—along, perhaps, with some strategic alliances with local
pirates—had allowed the city to hold out against the Romans in a
lengthy siege.[2] Thermus was determined to end it.

The east at the time of Caesar's first visit, ca. 80 BC. Macedonia, Asia, and Cilicia were provinces under Roman governors, and the other territories shown were held by kings more or less friendly to Rome.

As part of his preparations, he sent Caesar to collect ships from King Nicomedes of Bithynia, a large and wealthy state on the coast of Asia Minor, kicking off a scandal that would dog Caesar for the rest of his life. In the east, the Romans commonly kept men like Nicomedes in power, in exchange for which the kings maintained order and offered support in wars. Apparently Caesar spent longer than was expected at the king's court, and he returned for a second visit later on. While Caesar might have had good reasons for dallying—it was typical for Roman nobles, even at a young age, to cultivate friends and allies across the empire—enemies of Caesar spread a more salacious story. The handsome young Roman, they said, was having an affair with the old king.[3]

Sex with another male in and of itself was no slur on a Roman man's masculinity. Most important was that his own body not be penetrated, and the accusation held that Caesar had been in the passive role; he had become the "Queen of Bithynia." Stories circulated of Caesar riding in Nicomedes's litter, serving as a cupbearer at the king's banquets, even being dressed in purple and escorted by attendants to the royal bedchamber, where he was laid down in a golden bed for his deflowering.

Little or any of this may have been true. Similar smears were commonly directed against young Romans on the make, especially if they were good-looking, and were dragged out for years afterward. The stories do at least give a sense of the luxury of Nicomedes's court, which must have made an impression on young Caesar. In later years, he was to become an avid collector of gems, statues, and paintings. He could determine the weight of pearls, it was said, just by holding them in his hand.[4]

Caesar was fortunate in that he could brag of a real accomplishment to set against the gossip. After returning from Nicomedes's court, he took part in the final, successful assault on the long-recalcitrant Mytilene and for his part in it was decorated by Thermus with a civic crown. A much-prized honor, the crown was given only to those who had saved a fellow soldier's life in battle. It entitled a wearer to various privileges back in Rome—including the right to wear the crown itself, made of oak leaves, at ceremonial occasions.[5] Years later, Caesar was to appreciate a similar crown of laurel that he was allowed to wear at all times, not just for its distinction but also because it masked his receding hairline.[6]

With Mytilene finally vanquished, Caesar transferred to the service of Publius Servilius Vatia.[7] A pillar of the Sullan regime, Vatia had held the consulship of 79 BC and was now tackling a longstanding problem made only worse by the war with Mithridates: the infestation of the coasts of Asia Minor with pirates. But shortly into this new tour, Caesar received urgent news from Rome. Sulla was dead, and the seething discontent against him and his policies, suppressed for several years, was bursting into the open. There was even talk of denying him a funeral in Rome, although that was quashed when his faithful lieutenant Pompey had Sulla's body brought to the city on a golden bier.

Caesar returned to Rome at once. Despite his youth, his relationships with Marius and Cinna would make him a powerful ally for the forces trying to undo Sulla's measures. Though he was invited to join the revolt, and the brother of his wife, Cornelia, did join, Caesar ultimately stood back, correctly determining that it would fail.[8] One of the consuls of 78, Quintus Lutatius Catulus, with help from Pompey, took vigorous measures to suppress the uprising. The dictator's injustices still rankled with Caesar, but he was not prepared to throw away his career in a futile attempt to remedy them. Caesar was learning how to choose his moments.

Caesar turned twenty-two the year Sulla died. Almost a decade still remained before he could hold the quaestorship, the first rung on the ladder of political offices that brought membership in the Senate. In advance of that, it was essential to make a name for himself in Rome, not only to ensure electoral success but to begin building the influence that, along with actually holding office, brought power and glory to a Roman politician. The civic crown was a start, but it would take more.

Looking back later at his own early days in politics, Caesar's near-contemporary Cicero recalled a humbling moment.[9] Cicero had won election to the quaestorship and been sent to Sicily as his area of responsibility. Rome was suffering a scarcity of grain at the time, and Cicero compelled the Sicilians to send additional supplies to the city, in the expectation that he would win acclaim for his efforts. After sailing back from Sicily at the end of his term and landing at the busy harbor of Puteoli, Cicero nearly fainted when he was asked what day he had left Rome, and whether there was any news from there. With gritted teeth he replied that he was just back from his province. "Yes, of course," his questioner replied, "from Africa, if I'm not mistaken."

Irritated though he was, Cicero claims that he found the experience valuable: "I became aware that the people of Rome have rather deaf ears, but sharp and sensitive eyes." He went on to explain, "I stopped thinking of what men would hear about me; I did take care that every day after that they should see me personally. I lived in their gaze. I kept close to the Forum. Neither my porter nor sleep denied anyone from having access to me."

The Forum was where news was made. This was because much of the city's politics took place there. It was in the Forum that a magistrate could convene a meeting on whatever topic he wished—a new legislative proposal, the progress of a war, the latest bribery scandal. Up onto the lofty speaker's platform, the Rostra, he would climb to address crowds that might number in the thousands. So loud did the people roar on one occasion, it is reported, a crow flying overhead dropped dead, as if struck by lightning. It was in the Forum that magistrates lined citizens up to vote on legislation. Tensely would the magistrate wait as the ballots were cast and counted; passage of a controversial bill was like victory on a battlefield. In the

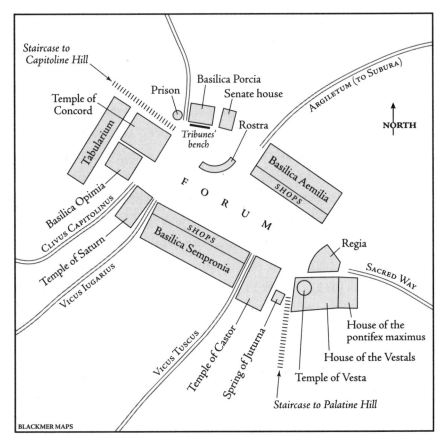

The Roman Forum, ca. 75 BC. The crossroads of the city, the Forum was also the center of politics. In this large open area citizens carried out business and socialized. They also watched games and plays, mourned at funerals, heard speeches from politicians, voted on legislation, and protested. The surrounding temples displayed works of art, served as repositories for valuables, and in some cases hosted meetings of the Senate. The Temple of Saturn functioned as the treasury. The exact sizes and locations of some buildings are conjectural.

Forum, too, religious festivals and funerals were staged, sometimes with lavish entertainments—theatrical shows, gladiatorial matches, wild-beast hunts.[10]

Citizens came to the Forum to hear debate, to vote, to worship, to mourn, to be entertained. Even on ordinary days a pageant of politics unfolded. Through the Forum senators swaggered, trying to draw attention with their purple-trimmed tunics and togas and the large retinues of supporters that accompanied them. To the Forum came candidates for office, with clever slaves at their side to whisper

The triumph was among the greatest spectacles to behold in republican Rome. This marble relief, from the Temple of Apollo Sosianus, shows a tree-trunk trophy and prisoners on a litter about to be hoisted by muscular attendants (left) and oxen being led for sacrifice (right).
Credit: akg-images/De Agostini Picture Lib./G. Nimatallah

Gladiatorial games were another of the city's spectacles. This coin shows a match in progress.
Credit: Courtesy of the American Numismatic Society

A wild-beast hunt unfolds on this coin. A lion is speared in the foreground. Behind, another man attacks a panther, and a wounded boar is also shown.
Credit: Courtesy of the American Numismatic Society

the name of everyone's hand they were shaking. In the Forum the ten tribunes of the plebs sat on their tribunal, ready for citizens to make appeals for help.

For a politically minded young man not yet old enough to run for office, spending time in the Forum was of the greatest benefit. There he would watch how more experienced politicians and candidates conducted themselves. He would also start building up his own retinue of followers—by greeting citizens, inviting them to his house for a meal, or doing small favors for them. When even the humblest Roman boy came of age, he would put on the toga of manhood and walk to the Forum with family and friends at dawn. It was the great man's duty, if asked, to join the procession, even from the outermost edges of the city.[11]

Upon his return to Rome, Caesar appeared often in the Forum to try to charm ordinary people.[12] Beyond such daily interactions there was one especially good way to grab attention, and Caesar seized that too. Those accused of major criminal offenses in Rome, including murder, treason, electoral malpractice, and extortion in the provinces, were tried at standing courts held in the open air of the Forum. The praetors, magistrates just below the consuls in rank who presided over the trials, would sit on elevated wooden platforms along with juries numbering as many as seventy high-ranking Romans. There were no public prosecutors; rather, the praetor and jury would choose a well-trained speaker to stand up and make the case. Young men not uncommonly applied for the privilege to do so, eager for the publicity they could earn.[13]

Criminal trials were great events, almost a form of theater. The defendant—often a major politician—might speak for himself and would certainly call on his most eloquent friends to support him. His relatives sat beside him on a bench below the tribunal, dressed in rags and smeared with dirt to arouse pity. Especially exciting was the onslaught of the prosecutor's speech. What evidence would he produce? What scandals from the defendant's earlier life? No argument was inadmissible. Gossip picked up on the street corner could be cited as evidence, as could eyewitness testimony.

A starring role in a trial was an irresistible opportunity for Caesar, and in 77 he secured the right to prosecute Gnaeus Cornelius Dolabella, who had recently returned from the governorship of Macedonia and been awarded a triumph by the Senate. Whatever his military talents, Dolabella pretty clearly had been guilty of abuses in his authority—a common problem among provincial governors during and after the years of Sulla's domination. Caesar was able to make his case not only by using ample evidence of wrongdoing handed over by the Greek cities but also with his own thorough training in rhetoric. A forceful orator, Caesar prided himself on the clarity of his language. "Avoid a strange and unusual word as you would a reef," was his advice to speakers. He had a talent for witty epigrams, and his delivery was marvelous. He spoke in a high pitch and with impassioned gestures that thrilled his audiences.[14]

Speaking on behalf of Dolabella were the two leading advocates of the day, Quintus Hortensius and Gaius Cotta. (So small was the ruling class of Rome, Cotta was himself a kinsman of Caesar's mother's.) Dolabella also spoke in his own defense, gleefully raking up stories of Caesar's visits with Nicomedes. It was likely at this trial that the salacious tales about Caesar took root in public consciousness.

Caesar ultimately lost to this older and more experienced team, but he acquitted himself well. He published his own speeches from the trial, which gave them an audience beyond the crowd gathered in the Forum. This amounted to a success in what was surely his main goal: to establish himself as a public figure in Rome.

The following year, the Greeks enlisted his help in another case. This time it was a civil suit for recovery of property, launched against Gaius Antonius, a brutal officer of Sulla's who had plundered Greece during Sulla's war against Mithridates. When judgment went against Antonius, he appealed to the tribunes of the plebs. Although Sulla had curtailed the tribunes' right to initiate legislation, he did let them keep their traditional power to veto the actions of other magistrates, including the praetor handling Antonius's case.

It was for situations like this, as far as Sulla was concerned, that tribunes existed. At least one of the tribunes agreed to support Antonius, and so the Greeks' claims were dismissed. Many in Rome were disgusted, not so much out of sympathy for the Greeks but at Antonius's brazen move: to have a judgment thrown out like this was unusual. There was nothing Caesar could do, and while he would have preferred a victory, he at least gained some additional goodwill.[15]

Caesar needed to consider how to spend his next few years. He was in his mid-twenties and had begun to establish a good reputation, the Nicomedes affair aside.

About four years thence, he would be eligible to stand for the post of military tribune. Not a political magistracy, it was still a significant office that involved administering the yearly draft as well as commanding in the field. Twenty-four military tribunes were elected each year. Caesar could be confident in gaining one of the positions when the time came, but meanwhile he craved some further distinction, ideally one he would not have to share with twenty-three others.

To keep on prosecuting risked making him look like the sort of speaker who spent all his time in the courts, going after anyone he could—a lawyer for hire. Also, while it was acceptable for a young man who aspired to a political career to carry out a prosecution or two, the longer Caesar persisted, the more he risked acquiring enemies and alienating too many members of the small ruling class. Though Cicero was right that visibility in Rome was important for a young man in politics, a dashing military exploit, like Sulla's capture of King Jugurtha, could catapult a reputation. Caesar had won the civic crown, but he might do more.

Once again, it seemed opportune to leave the city. Caesar decided to travel east. Ostensibly his purpose was to spend time on Rhodes studying with a master of public speaking there, Apollonius

Molon.[16] Caesar certainly would have enjoyed the bracing intellectual life of that beautiful island, not to mention its splendid artistic heritage. But already familiar with the politics of the region from his earlier visit, he probably sensed that he would also have the chance for some military adventure. His friend Nicomedes had just died and, having no legitimate heirs, had bequeathed his kingdom to Rome. The Senate promptly agreed to accept the legacy, and not simply because Bithynia would make an attractive addition to the empire in its own right. Tensions between Rome and King Mithridates had been flaring up, and the senators did not want Mithridates to snatch Bithynia first. War with Rome's old foe was likely to break out, and Caesar would be there to join it.[17]

Yet opportunity came sooner than expected. On his way to Rhodes, Caesar was captured off the coast of the small Aegean island of Pharmacusa by one of the many bands of pirates that were so active at the time. For nearly forty days he was held in captivity on a ship along with the physician with whom he was traveling and two slaves; meanwhile, the rest of his party was off raising the ransom the pirates had set. Allegedly Caesar scoffed when the pirates set the ransom at 20 talents. He insisted that he was worth more and promised they would get 50.[18] That was equivalent to 1.2 million Roman sesterces, or three times the wealth required to qualify as an equestrian in Rome.

Throughout his life, whenever he was attacked, Caesar struck back. In the interest of advancing his political career, he made an exception, suppressing at least temporarily his feelings against Sulla and Sulla's friends. But on these pirates he could exact immediate revenge. As soon as the ransom was delivered and Caesar was freed, he sailed to the nearby harbor of Miletus, raised a small fleet, and set back out. Caesar had warned the pirates he would return. Even so, they were caught off guard when he sailed up to their ships, which were anchored off the same island where they had been before. After a fight, he took most of the pirates into captivity. He journeyed to the governor of Asia to ask that the pirates be crucified, the standard punishment for outlaws in the Roman world. As it happened, the governor was in the midst of organizing the new territory of Bithynia, and Caesar's visit may also have had the goal of helping some of the late Nicomedes's relatives. For whatever reason, Caesar and the governor clashed, and the governor refused to make an immediate decision on the fate of the pirates. Outraged, Caesar returned to his captives and had them killed anyway. It was the first sign of a ruthlessness that others who later crossed Caesar would come to know. His brutality notwithstanding, Caesar's actions were well calibrated to add to his popular appeal. For years, pirate fleets had been growing in size and spreading havoc further and further afield. Romans fumed that these brigands drunkenly caroused on every coast of the Mediterranean.[19] In taking revenge on the band that had kidnapped him, Caesar knew he would gain recognition when word of what happened made it back to Rome. The story was Forum gold.

By the time Caesar finally made it to Rhodes to begin his planned course of study, hostilities broke out between Mithridates and Rome. When allies of Mithridates launched an attack in Asia Minor, Caesar crossed from Rhodes and recruited troops from the local communities, just as he had done to take on the pirates. With these forces, he drove out Mithridates's prefect and prevented nervous allies of Rome from defecting. Though not so memorable as his revenge on the pirates, his actions had the potential to spawn yet another tale to impress people back home.[20]

Caesar's second sojourn in the east was proving more fruitful than even he might have hoped. He was acquiring not just a dashing reputation but also firsthand familiarity with military and imperial affairs that would commend him to citizens and politicians back in Rome. His profile in the city was growing, as was shown by exciting news he received while still overseas in 73 BC. He had been elected pontiff, one of the city's most distinguished priesthoods.[21]

Romans were zealous in the worship of their gods. Only with the gods' support would Rome and its empire stay rich and powerful, and so the gods needed to be cultivated assiduously, with bountiful sacrifices, opulent temples, festivals, prayers, and more. Positions in the major priesthoods went to the most powerful members of society, the men of the great noble families. One did not have to be old, however, to gain such a position. When a vacancy opened, it sometimes would go to a young noble, especially if his family had had a tradition of service in the college.

There were several priestly colleges in Rome, each of which cultivated distinctive expertise. The augurs, for instance, specialized in divining the will of the gods through observation of the flight of birds, thunder and lightning, and other natural phenomena. The pontiffs oversaw the worship of the gods and controlled the city's sacred spaces as well as the calendar with its many festivals. In addition to fifteen pontiffs, the college included the Vestal Virgins, who tended the perpetual flame of the hearth goddess, Vesta, in her temple near the Forum, as well as the so-called *flamines*, male priests assigned to the worship of an individual deity. Among the latter group was the *flamen* for Jupiter, the position Caesar had been nominated to back in the 80s but had to give up.[22] The fact that it was the other pontiffs who elected Caesar in 73 sheds great light on how well his strategy over the preceding few years was paying off.

The college was made up almost entirely of nobles who had supported Sulla, men like Servilius Isauricus, on whose military staff Caesar briefly served, and Quintus Catulus, the consul of 78 who had suppressed the rising after Sulla's death. They never would have allowed Caesar to fill the spot freed up by the death of his mother's kinsman Gaius Cotta if they thought he was a new Marius, threatening the privileged position of the nobility. Caesar's behavior had assured them he could be trusted not to rally the people against the Senate, as Marius had. Their confidence, as later events would show, was misplaced, but for his efforts Caesar had won a rich prize.

He sped back to Rome and was inaugurated in his new office, which fortunately had none of the taboos associated with the priesthood of Jupiter. At subsequent elections, he presented himself as a

candidate for the military tribunate and with great support from
the voters handily won one of the twenty-four positions.[23] Nothing
is known of the service Caesar performed in that office, suggesting
that it was adequate but not exceptional, perhaps simply for lack
of opportunities. It hardly mattered. A near decade of sometimes
frantic effort, from the storming of Mytilene to his entry into the
pontifical college, had raised his stature.

For all of Caesar's brilliance, his entry into public life followed a
conventional trajectory. Cato's was a different story.

A man whose hard face rarely broke into a smile, Cato was not
inclined to walk around the Forum charming citizens. While he
had commanding features, especially a large aquiline nose, he was
not renowned for his looks.[24] As for trying to buy goodwill with
meals or relying on slaves to remind him of voter's names: that was
cheating, or so Cato thought.[25] One should be elected purely for
what one had to offer the Republic as a whole. Cato was diffident,
too, about performing services for other politicians or aspiring politicians, unless he thought it was for the public good. He bristled at
the thought that he could be bought by favors.

It was fortunate for Cato that he already had been elected to a
priesthood by his early twenties. His spot was on the Board of Fifteen for Sacred Actions, a group whose main responsibility was to
consult, at the request of the Senate, a collection of Greek prophecies known as the Sibylline Books.[26] The person whose position
in the college Cato filled is unknown; perhaps it was a distant relative, which would explain his selection at a young age. It spared
him having to canvass senior members of the priestly colleges later.
So prestigious were the priesthoods that his appointment meant he
gained an enormous advantage in elections.

Still, Cato needed to make a name for himself, and he came to see
that it was precisely his unusual behavior that could set him apart.
And so he played it up. Dressing as if he had been born centuries

earlier not only paraded his reverence for tradition; it caught "the sharp and sensitive eyes" by which he needed to be seen.[27]

For his oratorical debut he wanted something equally arresting. Cato had received a thorough training in rhetoric and practiced the art assiduously—one of the clearest signs that he did wish to excel in politics, if on his own terms. Yet, as he told a friend, he only wanted to stand up and speak if he had something important to say. One might have thought that a criminal prosecution would appeal to him, just as it had to his great-grandfather with his never-ending battle against corruption. Perhaps aggrieved parties shied away from turning their affairs over to so odd a young man.

Opportunity struck in the form of a complaint from the tribunes of the plebs. In the northwestern corner of the Forum stood the Basilica Porcia, a large hall built by the elder Cato when he was censor back in the 180s BC. The tribunes found it a comfortable spot to sit and make themselves available for consultation by citizens who sought help in private legal proceedings. With their powers curtailed by Sulla, this apparently was a more important part of the tribunes' job. But a pillar, they complained, blocked their seats, and they wanted it taken down. Cato, however, determined to stop the tribunes from taking over his ancestor's building as if it were theirs, went to civil court to get an injunction against them. This gave him the chance to deliver a speech in the Forum denouncing the proposed renovation.[28]

It might seem remarkable that the removal of a single column could cause such a controversy, but this was surely Cato's goal. While a high-profile prosecution would grab attention, making a big fuss over one pillar was in its own way just as newsworthy. It helped, of course, that the pillar stood in such a conspicuous building and could be gestured at during the debate, whether by Cato and the tribunes or by ordinary citizens discussing the matter among themselves. The dispute was perfect for putting the young man on the map, regardless of whether he won or lost.

As it turned out, Cato's vigorous speech so impressed listeners that he ultimately prevailed over the tribunes after all. The oddly dressed youth had an appealingly direct, even blunt, style. Enamored as he was of Stoicism, he understood that dry or ruthlessly logical oratory would not move audiences. He occasionally lightened his tone with flashes of humor and acknowledgments of his own eccentric personality. Another strength was his voice. In the years to come, it would prove one of his greatest assets in politics. It was loud enough to be heard by even a large crowd, and strong enough that it did not easily wear out. Cato could speak all day without getting tired.

The Forum crowd would be keen to hear at least a little more from Cato, but there were limited opportunities for him to speak until he held a magistracy. Also, he needed to spend some time away from Rome developing skills as a soldier. Here, too, he would end up behaving unconventionally, in part out of conviction but also with an eye to standing out.

His first service was with his beloved older half brother, Caepio. Caepio had been elected as one of the military tribunes for the year 72, at a time when Rome was facing an unexpected crisis. The previous year, a breakout from one of the prisonlike gladiatorial schools of southern Italy, led by the legendary Spartacus, had erupted into a full-scale rebellion of thousands of slaves. Two separate Roman armies, under the command of praetors, were badly defeated, prompting the Senate to send both the consuls for that year into the field. Caepio was assigned as an officer in the army of one of the consuls, Gellius Publicola, and Cato gladly volunteered to join Caepio.[29]

Cato was disappointed in how the war proceeded. Both consuls sustained defeats, and for a time it looked as if Spartacus would march on Rome, as Hannibal nearly had done. Still, Cato tried to show discipline and bravery. He embraced the rigors of camp life, as if he were Cato the Elder brought back to life. And when Consul Gellius proposed that Cato receive decorations for his valor, Cato said he had not earned them and refused to accept them, in another move worthy of his great-grandfather. Anyone else, certainly Caesar, would have grabbed the award. Perhaps Cato was priggishly suggesting that his own standards were higher than anyone else's, including the consul's.[30]

Several years later, Cato won election to the military tribunate himself and was sent to help command an army in Macedonia. It was to be his first great journey overseas, and he took with him an entourage of fifteen slaves, two freedmen, and four friends. One of the friends was Munatius Rufus, who, in an illuminating if perhaps slightly idealized memoir published after Cato's death, recorded their eastern tour in some detail.[31] The two were so close they even shared a bedroom, although there is no indication they slept together. Cato appears to have been entirely faithful to his wife, Atilia, during their long separation.

After arriving at camp in Macedonia, Cato worked hard to develop his skills as a commander. His approach mirrored his emerging thoughts on politics. He spent no time toadying to the top leadership but rather tried to inspire the men under his supervision. Anything he asked them to do, he did himself. He dressed, lived, and marched as if he were an ordinary soldier. He gave explanations for each of his orders and reinforced them with rewards as well as punishments. Just as in Rome he professed to care about the Republic more than his own advancement, so in Macedonia he put the army ahead of himself. But again, he must have known that his unconventional behavior, which extended even to refusing to ride on horseback and walking with the ordinary troops, would make him stand out. Sternness and self-control enjoined a certain kind of respect.

Although Cato apparently had no great military exploits on this campaign, other adventures ensued. Granted leave for two months, he decided to visit Pergamum in Asia Minor, one of the most beautiful cities of the east. Dramatically set on a lofty hill, Pergamum was a showcase of innovative architecture that far eclipsed anything to be seen in Rome. The kings who once had ruled the city had crammed it with ancient masterpieces of Greek art while also commissioning impressive new sculptures. A jewel of the city was its library, which boasted two hundred thousand volumes. Whereas other visitors came to gape at the art, Cato had a different mission. Athenodorus Cordylion, one of the most eminent exponents of Stoic philosophy, lived in Pergamum, and Cato wished to befriend him. Athenodorus was a man after Cato's own heart, severe and uncompromising. As director of the Pergamene library, he had ordered unwelcome passages to be removed from the writings of older Stoics. He made it a point to resist friendships with anyone in power, even kings. After meeting Cato, however, Athenodorus concluded that he was dealing with a different kind of Roman. He agreed to travel with Cato back to camp and ultimately to Rome. It filled Cato with pride that while other Romans hauled back paintings and statues as mementoes of their eastern travels, his catch was a distinguished philosopher.[32]

After his year's service as military tribune ended, Cato decided to stay on and see more of Asia Minor. Although the region was notorious for its temptations—Cicero called it the *corruptrix provincia*, "the province that depraves"—Cato's goal was not to visit the fleshpots but to examine conditions in a vital part of the Roman empire after so much unrest had occurred in recent years.[33] He also wanted to pay a visit to an old family friend, Deiotarus of Galatia. Like Nicomedes, Deiotarus was one of Rome's client kings who ruled a small territory in the highlands of central Asia Minor. He lent valuable aid to the Romans in the wars against Mithridates and also shrewdly cultivated powerful Romans to increase his power.[34]

Cato's way of touring differed from that of any other well-off Roman. Naturally he insisted on walking, even as the rest of his party rode. At daybreak each morning he would send ahead his baker and cook to the place where he intended to spend the night. They were to enter the city without a fuss and find an inn for Cato, if he did not already have a family friend or acquaintance with whom to stay.

If there was no inn, they were to ask the city magistrates for accommodation and cheerfully accept whatever was offered. The lack of fanfare made the magistrates assume that it was nobody important coming, and so Cato would often arrive to find that no lodging had been prepared. To make matters even worse, when Cato did appear he would sit silently on the piled-up baggage, as if he were a nobody. Then came the inevitable explosion: "Oh you wretched men! You must change this terrible way of welcoming visitors. Not all who come to you will be Catos."[35]

Equally strange was Cato's behavior on the visit to Deiotarus. The evening that Cato arrived, the ruler plied him with gifts. This was standard in the court of an eastern ruler, but Cato looked down on it as bribery and left in a huff the next morning. When he reached the nearby city of Pessinus, an even larger pile of gifts was waiting for him, along with a letter from Deiotarus, begging him, even if he did not wish to take anything, to at least permit his friends to do so. Cato still would not yield. To accept one bribe, he thought, opened the way for others. And accepting a payoff not only compromised the integrity of one's decisions; it placed demands on provincial populations that led to resentment, just as excessive requests for accommodations did. The concern was not an abstract one: a key reason Mithridates's first great rebellion had succeeded was the mounting frustration at the perceived unfairness of Roman rule. All the gifts went back to Deiotarus.

Serious-minded as Cato was, the tour inadvertently ended up having comic moments. When Cato was entering the city of Antioch, on foot, he saw large crowds on either side of the road: young men in military cloaks, children, and even magistrates or priests dressed in pure white and wearing crowns.[36] Cato, who thought the welcome was intended for him, was irritated with his slaves for not having put a stop to it. He ordered the rest of his entourage to get off their horses and walk with him. The elderly man in charge of the festivities bustled up to Cato and, without greeting him, said, "Where have you left Demetrius?" This Demetrius, a freedman of Pompey and now one of Pompey's most influential advisors, was actively being courted in the east because the seemingly endless war against King Mithridates had just been turned over to Pompey.

Cato's friends were seized with fits of laughter, while Cato himself simply exclaimed, "What an unfortunate city!" But later he also laughed over how he had been confused for the attendant of a former slave.

All in all, the tour was successful for Cato, even if he had not earned glory in war, as Caesar had. Cato had enhanced his reputation in other ways, seen something of the empire, and developed his thoughts on leadership and governance. As he stepped onto the boat for Italy, however, he clutched one grim memento of his stay, an urn with the ashes of his half brother, Caepio.

When Cato had been on campaign in Macedonia, he had received word that Caepio, while traveling to Asia for some assignment, had fallen sick in the small town of Aenus on the northern shore of the Aegean Sea. The weather was stormy, and no ship of suitable size was sailing, but still Cato clamored onto a little vessel with only two friends and three slaves. They barely escaped drowning and landed in Aenus—only to find that Caepio had just died. Cato, forgetting every tenet of Stoic philosophy he had ever learned, grieved uncontrollably. Wailing, he hugged Caepio's dead body. He arranged for a lavish funeral and had a statue of Caepio made of fine Thasian marble set up in the marketplace of Aenus.[37]

The departure from Cato's usual austerity and restraint was striking. But as Munatius no doubt wanted to explain to readers of his memoir, there was a side of Cato that was easy to overlook. Beneath Cato's carapace of inflexible opposition to pleasure and inappropriate requests lay softer feelings. There was his love for Caepio. And later in life, when civil war broke out, Cato wept in grief when citizens killed each other in battle.[38]

For Munatius, Cato's grief did not detract from his thorny reputation but enhanced it. The hard line Cato took with others, whether fellow politicians or even friends and companions, was not the spiky weed of some misanthropy. It was the flower of a rare devotion to justice. Back in Rome, as soon as Cato held his first magistracy, that dedication would bloom in unexpected ways.

Still, the way Cato scolded kings and berated town councilors suggested that, high-minded as he was, he enjoyed confrontation and would seek more of it.

CHAPTER 3

POLITICAL AMBITIONS

NOBLE BIRTH OPENED UP THE POSSIBILITY OF POLITICAL CA-
reers for Caesar and Cato, and through their soldiering and
speaking they readied themselves. Now came the next stage: holding major offices and showing what they aspired to do with power.

In 69 BC, Caesar held the quaestorship, the first rung in the ladder of magistracies. This was the start of the climb up, but if we are
to believe his ancient biographers, he wanted far more than that. As
dictator, Sulla had raised the number of men holding quaestorships
each year to twenty. Two supervised the treasury in Rome; most of
the rest were sent to provinces to help the governors with the public
accounts and other tasks. For his sphere of responsibility Caesar
was assigned Spain. As he dutifully toured the province to preside
over the dull judicial hearings that were a quaestor's duty, he came
to Gades. There, in the city's great temple of Hercules, he noticed a
statue of Alexander the Great. He let out a sigh, "disgusted with his
own laziness: at the age at which Alexander had already conquered

the whole world, he himself had done nothing worth remember-ing."[1] He immediately asked to be released from his duties so that he could return to Rome and exploit the greater opportunities there.

This story, as handed down in ancient biographies and histories of Caesar, has often been described as apocryphal—invented later, perhaps by admirers of Caesar or perhaps by critics who thought his ambition had become inordinate. Either is possible. After Caesar rose to power, his early political career was both exaggerated and smeared, and so later accounts must be read with some caution.[2] What is certain is that, after his less controversial military service in the 70s BC, Caesar became more ambitious and daring, and more than once in the 60s he took gambles for big prizes. Flaunting his relationship with Marius, in one bold act after another he broke with Sulla's vision for Rome and showed that he thought power should rest not with the Senate but with all the people—with the many, not the few. The patrician transformed himself into a populist.

From his first departure to the east until his election to the pontif-icate in 73, Caesar had steered clear of political controversies. He had sailed right around the growing storm of those years: the strug-gle over the power of the tribunes of the plebs. But he had to keep watch over it because it was engulfing politics more and more.[3]

The struggle dated back to Sulla's dictatorship in the year 81. Convinced that Rome would never enjoy peace so long as the Sen-ate and the Plebeian Assembly clashed over the management of the empire, Sulla had enacted two radical reforms. First, he stripped tribunes of the right to propose legislation to the assembly; the only bills that could be voted on had to be proposed by the Senate. Sec-ond, Sulla debarred those elected to the tribunate from further po-litical office, a clear deterrent to anyone of talent and ambition.

Citizens chafed at the loss of their centuries-old right to pass laws through their tribunes, and the tribunes themselves, eager to extri-cate themselves from their dead end of an office, saw a great reward in agitating for a repeal of Sulla's measures. Already in 78, the year of Sulla's death, they raised the issue, without success. Two years later, another tribune, Sicinius, tried again, also without success. Sicinius was able on at least one occasion to demand that the two consuls appear on the Rostra to defend some action or other. One of the consuls, Octavius, purportedly was suffering from gout at the time, and he sullenly sat in silence, wrapped in bandages. The other, Curio, began giving one of his typically florid harangues, in which he swayed from side to side. "Octavius," Sicinius quipped, "you will never be able to repay your colleague. If he had not flung himself around in his usual way, the flies would have eaten you alive today."[4]

Sicinius's jokes made him a star in the Forum, but citizens wanted their tribunes not just to jest but to legislate, especially as the Senate looked less and less capable of handling the major problems Rome was facing. Most troublesome to the people were ongoing shortages of grain and associated price spikes, brought on by the pirates' interruption of maritime commerce. It became clear that unrest was reaching a fever pitch when a mob of angry Romans physically attacked the two consuls of 75 BC and then tried to tear down one of the consuls' houses. In a clear concession to the masses, later that year the Senate passed a law restoring to tribunes the right to stand for higher office.

Another frustration was a seemingly endless rebellion in Spain, led by a tough old officer of Marius's, a new man named Sertorius.[5] Back in 80 BC, Sertorius had set up a small breakaway state in the Iberian Peninsula that offered refuge to exiles of Sulla, including the proscribed. When the rebellion that was launched in Italy after Sulla's death in 78 failed, more prominent Romans joined the movement. For years, Sertorius eluded the Senate's armies. The man seemed indestructible. When he lost an eye in battle, far from letting that slow him down, he took pride; it proved his valor better than any medal, crown, or ancestor's funeral mask.

These popular frustrations made further reform an inevitability. With the outbreak of the Spartacus revolt in 73 and the humiliating defeat of both of the next year's consuls, the Senate looked weaker than ever. Just as soon as Spartacus and Sertorius could be defeated, the Senate would have to act to save themselves from an increasingly angry populace. For now, it would have to quell these conflicts, and quickly.

In desperation, the Senate turned the war against the slaves over to Marcus Licinius Crassus, who as a young officer under Sulla had acquired a reputation for brutal efficiency.[6] After recruiting a massive army, Crassus overwhelmed Spartacus in battle and then relentlessly hunted down the survivors. Altogether, six thousand slaves were captured and crucified along the Appian Way from Capua to Rome. Meanwhile, an additional five thousand fugitives were caught by Pompey, who had just returned from Spain, where he had finally defeated the rebellion of Sertorius—after disgruntled officers of the one-eyed general had stabbed him to death at a banquet.

Though Pompey and Crassus had long been rivals, the two now demanded that the Senate recognize them with triumphal honors and also permit them to stand for the consulship of 70. Pompey, who had held no magistracy and was not even a member of the Senate, technically was ineligible. But in the face of overwhelming popular support, not to mention the two victors' armies lurking on the outskirts of the city, the Senate capitulated. Pompey and Crassus were duly elected consuls, and once in office the following year, they fully restored the tribunate.

Recognizing where power now lay, Pompey added fifteen extra days of entertainment for the people before the regularly scheduled Roman Games of September. Meanwhile Crassus, not to be outdone, held a great sacrifice in honor of Hercules, feasted citizens at ten thousand tables set up throughout the city, and distributed three months' worth of grain. It was a festive time. With the defeat of Sertorius, civil war was finally extinguished throughout the Roman world, and, in a welcome change from Sulla's ruthlessness, there were no reprisals against the surviving followers of Sertorius. A tribune even passed legislation that invited back to Rome the men who had participated in the consul Lepidus's revolt following the death of Sulla.

Adding to the sense of a fresh start, for the first time in over fifteen years a full census was held. The two men elected as censors were both friends of Pompey, and they pitched in with the cleanup of senatorial government. To popular applause, they expelled sixty-four members of the Senate for misconduct. The censors also completed a thorough registration of voters. Since the last census, which took place in 85 BC, the number of adult male citizens had nearly doubled, from 463,000 to 910,000, a staggering number. Perhaps only a third of them lived close enough to Rome to be able to come into the city with much frequency, but for special events, such as the annual consular elections, citizens who resided farther away, even as far north as the Po Valley, participated, especially those of means.[7] The Forum remained the main scene of politics, but leaders who found ways to reach citizens far beyond it were rewarded.

The end of senatorial dominance, the restoration of the tribunes' power, and the expansion of the electorate were all welcome changes as far as Caesar was concerned. To a modest extent, he had even helped usher them in. After being elected to his military tribunate, he had lent his support for the final push to reestablish the tribunes' legislative initiative. In 70 BC, he spoke on behalf of the tribunician bill that restored Lepidus's supporters, among whom was Caesar's own brother-in-law, Lucius Cornelius Cinna. The speech provided him a chance to look back critically at Sulla's dictatorship, breaking the silence he had been carefully keeping.[8]

With the restoration of the tribunate, popular demands were answered, but then the more traditional tension between the Senate and the Plebeian Assembly resumed. Two types of politician in particular struggled against one another. On one side was a relatively small but powerful group of leaders determined for the Senate to keep its grip on affairs, especially foreign policy and finance, as much as possible. Because the Senate was guided by the consuls and other senior ex-magistrates, in practice this meant the dominance of the noble families. That authority should be restricted to a narrow few did not bother this group—indeed, just the opposite. They felt they could make sensible decisions on behalf of the public interest and spare Rome the controversies that had led to civil war. Their enemies may have called them a "clique" (*factio*), but the loftiness of their vision was shown by the names they sometimes called themselves, including *optimates*, "the best men," and *boni*, "the good men."

Ranged against them were politicians who looked to the Plebeian Assembly as a major source of power. Even though they had a Latin name, *populares*, meaning "men of the people," this was a far less coherent group than the *optimates*.[9]

Some *populares* were new men in the tradition of Marius who relished the chance to attack the corrupt nobility. Others were descended from old and distinguished families but maintained, out of conviction or political calculation, that the public welfare was better upheld by legislation that might reward citizens with land in newly created colonies or make grain available at a fixed price in the volatile city of Rome. While *optimates* sought to dominate Rome by controlling the Senate, *populares* might stitch together broader, sometimes unstable, coalitions of supporters who felt ignored by the senatorial nobility. They appealed to city dwellers in Rome who could most easily appear in the Forum to lend support. They also cultivated the small-scale farmers of rural Italy, who only occasionally came to Rome to vote. They sometimes even reached out to groups of individuals who lacked Roman citizenship but sought it.

Seemingly with no hesitation, Caesar followed—as Cicero would later put it—"the popular way."[10] His family's relationship to Marius and his harsh experience under Sulla had always made it likely that he would. The *optimates* were dominated by old associates of the dictator—senators such as Quintus Lutatius Catulus, such a strong

Sulla supporter that Sulla himself had called him the best of his followers. He maintained his loyalty after Sulla's death by suppressing the subsequent uprising and then leading the opposition to the restoration of the tribunate.[11] After that battle was lost, the goal of the *optimates* was to uphold Senate authority and curtail popular champions.

Privileged as Caesar in many ways was, he harbored sympathy for the out-groups the new man Marius had championed, having faced struggles of his own and after seeing friends and relatives like his brother-in-law Cinna suffer. But the popular route in politics appealed to Caesar for a deeper reason. It was a strong belief of the *optimates* that no one should become too powerful, and to the extent that there was a first man, he should be a senior member of the Senate, an ex-consul respected by his peers. Recent years had thrown up individuals whose achievements were so impressive they could not be honored by such traditional means. Sulla himself had been awarded the new name Felix (meaning "Blessed") to underscore a greatness that seemed to be the gift of the gods. Even more remarkable were the honors of Pompey—his first triumph at the age of twenty-four, the consulship without any prior magistracy, and his own special name, Magnus (meaning "the Great"), as if he were Alexander. If there had been any doubt before, by 70 BC it was clear that Pompey was the first man of Rome. This was greatly frustrating to *optimates*, who feared that the extraordinary power in Pompey's hands threatened republican government. Others, though, were less bothered by the position Pompey had achieved than desirous of obtaining it themselves. This was especially true of Crassus, who felt Pompey had stolen the glory of ending the Spartacan War. Increasingly, it was true of Caesar as well.

The first sign of Caesar's audacity came at the funeral for his aunt Julia, held shortly before his departure for Spain. In the Forum, before a large crowd, Caesar produced the mask of Marius, in violation of

the ban of Sulla. Citizens were delighted to have their old hero recognized, whom they remembered with far more fondness than Sulla, the
people's enslaver.[12] The display won Caesar a great deal of popularity.

By a sad coincidence, Caesar's beloved wife, Cornelia, died
around the same time as his aunt. This was a blow, but it prompted
Caesar to win more favor by appealing to the people with another
spectacle. Though it was untypical, perhaps even unprecedented, to
honor a younger woman with an elaborate funeral in the Forum,
Caesar did so for his wife. Romans were touched by the feeling he
showed in his eulogy, which must have recalled the hard times the
couple had known under Sulla. Almost certainly, Caesar also took
the chance to display the mask of Cornelia's father, Cinna, just as he
had Marius's. Through the funerals, he was suggesting that he was
the heir of both men and would uphold their legacy.[13]

Not long after these events came the next bold appeal as Caesar
reached out to those who lacked voting rights. When citizenship
had been extended in response to the great Italian rebellion that
broke out in 91 BC, those north of the River Po were left out. The
Gauls living there had been a formidable enemy of Rome in earlier
centuries, and prejudice against them lingered. Irritated at their ex-
clusion, the Transpadanes, as they were known (the name referring
to those "across the Po"), were now agitating for change, perhaps
even contemplating the threat of armed revolt. On his way back
from his quaestorship in Spain, Caesar stopped in northern Italy
and expressed support for their cause.[14] Nothing came of Caesar's
outreach. Citizenship bills were hard to get through the assembly,
and the consuls of 68 ensured that legions recruited for wars in the
east were kept in Italy to tamp down any violence if it did flare up.
But Caesar laid the foundation for a relationship with the leading
men of this wealthy region that would prove valuable in later years.

Back in Rome, Caesar cultivated citizens much as he had before.
He greeted them in the Forum, helped them with their problems,
hosted generous receptions at his house. The residence—perhaps
inherited from his father—was a fairly modest one. It was located

in a neighborhood known as the Subura, an area with many work-shops, taverns, and tenements as well as residential houses.[15] With his excellent sense of taste, Caesar at least made sure that it was well appointed. People talked about his lavish spending, and also his love life. He had taken a new wife, Pompeia, the granddaughter of Sulla. This might seem surprising, but perhaps the union was meant to signal that Caesar was still happy to work with old Sullans, as he had before entering political office. Very likely Pompeia had a good dowry as well. At least according to rumor, Caesar also started carrying on affairs with other noble women.[16]

Soon he plunged into a legislative battle that would mark a de-cisive defeat of the *optimates* and their goal of senatorial author-ity. The problem of piracy—known so well to Caesar—had reached scandalous new heights. Fleets were ravaging the coasts of Italy and even sailed into Rome's main harbor at Ostia to burn ships and warehouses there, jeopardizing the grain supply. Two praetors were kidnapped and carried off in their purple-edged togas with their attendants, a terrible blow to Roman pride. The people were fed up with the Senate's piecemeal solutions, and a tribune presented legislation to the Plebeian Assembly to establish an extraordinary Mediterranean-wide command for the great soldier and organizer Pompey to solve the problem once and for all. Quintus Catulus, leader of the *optimates*, helped swing the Senate against the bill. Fearlessly Caesar broke ranks and went to the Rostra to support the law, which, despite a passionate denunciation by Catulus, passed.[17]

Pompey enjoyed a stunningly quick success against the pirates, and when similar legislation was put forward the following year to turn over the war against Mithridates to him, Caesar supported that too. Again Catulus tried in vain to block the proposal, con-vinced that such a concentration of power endangered republican government. "Let there be no innovation contrary to the precedents and practice of our ancestors" was his line.[18]

Supporting Pompey helped Caesar to build his own following, but in Pompey's absence Crassus provided something else Caesar increasingly needed: financial support. During the Sullan proscriptions Crassus had amassed a portfolio of real estate and then expanded it by purchasing distressed properties throughout Rome. Allegedly he would even show up in the midst of the fires that frequently broke out in the city and snap up buildings at a low cost from their panicked owners, only to redevelop them with teams of hundreds of specially trained slaves. Politically, he operated much the same way, looking for opportunities he could exploit to enhance his own power. No friend of the *optimates*, who distrusted his endless intriguing, he won the backing of the wealthy businessmen who fulfilled lucrative government contracts to supply the army, collect taxes, and more. He also tried to cultivate ordinary Romans, opening his house to everyone and inviting them in for good—though certainly not expensive—meals. Above all, he lent out the money he raised through his real estate ventures to indebted politicians and in return demanded their support, on key Senate votes for instance.[19]

As Caesar spent, Crassus helped keep the loans coming. The two were not true soulmates—the miserly Crassus snorted at Caesar's expensive tastes—but they could work together on the sorts of audacious projects that appealed to both of them. As censor in 65, Crassus tried to register all the Transpadanes as citizens.[20] Even more boldly, he embarked on a plan to annex Egypt, with support from Caesar, who hoped to gain a military command there.[21] This Egyptian plan, while of course redounding to the two men's own benefit, had precedents in earlier annexations that had been carried out to enrich the treasury and fund welfare programs for citizens. Neither effort succeeded, thanks to skillful opposition by Crassus's colleague in the censorship, the *optimates'* leader Quintus Catulus.

In the same year, 65 BC, Caesar served in the office of aedile. No magistracy was legally required between the quaestorship and the praetorship, which Caesar would be eligible to hold in 62. But since there were only eight praetors, as opposed to twenty quaestors, competition for the higher office was fierce; to keep himself in the public eye, a politician was well advised to run for the aedileship or, after the reform of 75, the tribunate. Only four aediles were elected annually, and it was an attractive post because the main responsibility was to oversee the city of Rome's streets, markets, and water distribution, as well as the grain supply and many of the public games. Held in honor of the gods and goddesses, the games featured theatrical shows, chariot racing, and staged animal hunts witnessed by thousands—a golden opportunity for publicity.

Citizens expected holders of the office of aedile to draw on their own funds to make the games memorable. The hope was for a sensation. Aediles might import exotic animals—elephants, leopards, crocodiles. They built temporary theaters of the greatest lavishness, with gorgeous painted scenery, fine marble columns, even stages that could revolve. There were elaborate props and costumes. Separate displays were often held of rare artistic masterpieces, borrowed—or stolen—from Greek cities and kingdoms.[22]

Caesar made sure his aedileship could not be outdone. His theatrical shows and beast hunts were sumptuously produced. He set up exhibitions of the stage equipment in the Forum, in its surrounding basilicas, and on the Capitoline Hill. Most impressively, he added personally sponsored gladiatorial games. These were only allowed in honor of the dead, and so Caesar claimed that his show was given in memory of his father, who had died twenty years before. Spectators gasped when they saw that all the appointments for the arena were made of silver, even the gladiators' equipment.[23]

Caesar's vast outlays, while delightful to ordinary Romans, outraged fellow politicians. In a most unrepublican way, he seemed to reap all the credit for the games, which in actuality were coorganized with his aedilician colleague, Marcus Calpurnius Bibulus. Bibulus complained that his was the fate of Pollux, the twin brother of Castor. There was a temple erected in the Forum in honor of the two deities, but it went by the name of Castor alone, "and so my generosity and Caesar's is called Caesar's alone," Bibulus grumbled.[24] But many beyond Bibulus were alarmed, especially at the hundreds of gladiators Caesar was bringing into the city for his private show.

The Senate imposed new regulations, forcing Caesar to cut back. Caesar was doubtless annoyed by this interference, as he certainly was over the *optimates'* foiling of his plan for an Egyptian command. Eager to dent their prestige, he planned one final coup de théâtre for his aedileship. In secret he rebuilt the large, gilded statue groups that commemorated Marius's victories over Jugurtha and the Germans, and then one night he had them transported to the Capitoline Hill, where they had stood before Sulla tore them down. A crowd swiftly gathered the next morning and soon took over the whole area, cheering for Caesar. Marius, the guardian of the empire, had been restored to his proper place in the city.

The Senate met to decide how to respond to Caesar's audacity. Quintus Catulus stood up and denounced Caesar with a remark remembered afterward: "You are no longer laying siege to the Republic with tunnels, Caesar, but now use battering rams."[25] When called on to respond, Caesar insisted that he had no such plans. A majority of the Senate took his side. The glittering trophies would stay up, a tribute to Marius's victories and also to Caesar's own ascent as a politician who commanded wide support in the city of Rome and across Italy—and who could defeat the *optimates* on their own turf, the Senate.

If there was a single defining quality of Caesar's early years in political office it was lavishness. He spent heavily to entertain the people at shows and in his own house. Personal extravagance and ambitious political programs went together. Cato, by contrast, was to brand his politics in Rome very differently—by deliberately avoiding lavishness altogether. He sought to restore life in the Republic as it once had been, or was imagined to have been—less dazzling, but also less corrupt. Caesar tricked his gladiators out in silver. Cato, when he was helping a friend organize games, insisted they give out radishes and cucumbers instead of the usual expensive prizes.[26]

It was in the year of Caesar's aedileship that Cato returned to the city from his travels in the east, the philosopher Athenodorus in tow. Caesar's junior by five years, Cato was just at the age where he could run for the quaestorship and start to make his mark. His conduct over the last few years had given hints about where he was headed. Cato had no interest in charming citizens with sleek grooming and smiles. Riding a wave of popularity to become a near god, as Pompey had, was a revolting thought for him. The sort of hero he wanted to be was like those you could see in ancient statues around the city: austere, unkempt even, willing to make any sacrifice for the Republic. In Cato's view, much of contemporary politics, whether it was tribunes throwing land at the people, or candidates for office putting on dinners and shows, was little more than bribery. A politician should build his reputation by rectitude alone.[27] Already in Asia Cato had made a point of refusing excessive hospitality and turning down the gifts of King Deiotarus.

Behavior like this, however traditional Cato claimed it was, struck Romans as remarkable—and was meant to. Whereas Caesar could travel the familiar path to popularity with little difficulty, Cato forged his own arduous road. Hardly eager to see Rome governed out of the often rowdy assembly, he sympathized with the *optimates*' ideal of rule by the noble few, but besides a nobility of birth he wanted one of virtue that would inspire all Romans to act righteously.

In his canvassing for the quaestorship he began crafting one distinctive role for himself: guardian of the public money. Before even announcing his candidacy, he carried out a thorough study of the quaestorian office, pestering those who had expertise in the area with questions, just as he had his tutor Sarpedon in childhood. The other young men who ran for and held the office were content to let the permanent civil servants, who worked in the treasury and who traveled with magistrates to the provinces, handle the complex task of keeping the official accounts.[28]

Cato's study paid off when, after securing electoral victory, he was assigned one of the urban positions. For a glorious year he would have oversight of the treasury itself, headquartered in the ancient Temple of Saturn that loomed over the Forum. Built on a spur of the Capitoline Hill, the temple rested on a lofty podium within which ran a warren of rooms where bullion was stored along with state documents. The latter included not just financial records but also copies of all the assembly's laws and the Senate's decrees—such a mass of material that almost certainly some of it was kept in a nearby archive that held additional office space.

On his first day of office Cato marched to the treasury ready for battle. He demanded that the scribes show him their accounts and immediately began pointing out mistakes. Some of the errors were made through ignorance, but others, he insisted, through deliberate wrongdoing. Through the power the scribes wielded over the treasury and its records, they did favors for the senators, in exchange for which the senators gave the scribes a free hand to pursue their own interests—waiving a debt for a friend, for instance. Accustomed to cozy relationships with the magistrates, the scribes were outraged by Cato's confrontational tactics.

Soon it was open war. Cato dismissed one scribe for misconduct in the settling of an inheritance and was on the point of dismissing another for fraud. The second scribe, though, refused to go and enlisted the help of no less a man than Catulus, the censor, to appeal his firing. A trial was held, during the course of which evidence piled up against the accused. Catulus insisted on pleading for mercy anyway. Cato, refusing to back down, fearlessly pointed out to the far more senior magistrate where a censor's duty lay. In the end, Catulus sent for Cato's fellow quaestor, who had been too ill to attend the hearing but was now brought on a litter to cast a deciding vote for acquittal. Even after he was seemingly outwitted, Cato had one final move: he would cease to ask the scribe to do anything and cut the scribe's salary to zero. With that masterstroke Cato solidified his control, and the scribes let him manage the treasury as he saw fit.

Now fully under Cato's control, the treasury's reputation for efficiency and fairness soared. Cato found many debts of long standing owed either by or to the treasury and demanded they be collected or paid out at once. He also discovered forged documents, including even Senate decrees. It was a familiar practice in Rome to get the Senate to pass a decree exempting specific individuals from a law, and evidently the custom led to citizens filing spurious grants on their own behalf. These were rooted out. On one occasion, when Cato was doubtful of a decree that many insisted was valid, he required the consuls to come and testify on oath to its authenticity.

Cato's victory over the scribes not only gave him power in the treasury; it also raised his profile in Rome. Citizens were impressed by his constant and tireless efforts. Each day he was the first to arrive at the treasury and the last to leave. Fearful of politicians trying to sneak in a remission of taxes and debts or commit some other special favor for their friends and supporters, he made sure to be present for all meetings of the assembly and the Senate. Although Cato was never likely to support crowd-pleasing schemes like Pompey's extraordinary command against the pirates or Crassus's annexation of Egypt, as the foe of senatorial corruption he gained in popularity.

And as irritating as Cato could be to colleagues, they started to find uses for him too. When pressed by friends for special favors, politicians now had the perfect excuse: "It's not possible; Cato won't allow it." Though he had refused to defer to Catulus, the *optimates* saw that Cato's reverence for the traditional ways of the Republic would make him a valuable ally in their ongoing efforts to thwart those whose power and ambitions they deemed a threat, Pompey above all.

As was so often the case in Roman politics, a marriage proved helpful in bringing the new allies together. The background for it was one of the great political dramas of those years, a struggle that helped prepare the way for the feud between Cato and Caesar.

Back in 74 BC, when hostilities between Rome and Mithridates resumed, command of the war had been given by the Senate to one of the consuls of that year, Lucius Licinius Lucullus. A highly trusted officer of Sulla's who became the executor of Sulla's estate, Lucullus was committed to strong, but also just, senatorial government. He took haughtiness to an extreme. Once when he was dining alone and a modest one-course meal was brought to him, he angrily summoned his cook. After the slave explained that, seeing as there were no guests, he thought Master would not want anything too elaborate, Lucullus replied, "What are you talking about? Don't you know that today Lucullus dines with Lucullus?"[29]

A competent general, Lucullus enjoyed a series of victories in the east, and by 70 the war seemed all but over. Mithridates had fled his kingdom, which would be turned into a Roman province, and sought refuge with his son-in-law, the king of Armenia. Lucullus pursued him there and in 69 successfully took the wealthy Armenian capital, but without capturing Mithridates.

In Rome, meanwhile, newly emboldened popular politicians started to raise suspicions that Lucullus was prolonging the war to fill his own coffers. One tribune even exhibited a picture of a luxurious villa Lucullus was building on the Bay of Naples to suggest where the money was going. Adding to Lucullus's troubles, his own troops mutinied after he took them into the difficult Armenian highlands. The chief instigator of the rebellion was a brash young noble on Lucullus's staff, his own brother-in-law Publius Clodius. Clodius's motive appears to have been resentment at what he considered Lucullus's arrogant treatment of him, but the trouble the general experienced with his army seemed to confirm the charges being made back in Rome.[30]

The Plebeian Assembly removed command of the Armenian war from Lucullus and awarded it to Pompey, who was well positioned to take over following his stunningly swift defeat of the pirates in

67. Pompey would be sure to claim all the credit for the inevitable final victory over Mithridates. Many senators, certainly the leading *optimates*, were horrified: unscrupulous tribunes and mutinous soldiers should not be setting the Republic's foreign policy. This was a matter for the steady and seasoned few, not large and fickle mobs. But there was little the Senate could do, other than vote Lucullus a triumph to impress on citizens all that he had achieved. As for Lucullus himself, he at least could have revenge on Clodius. Upon returning to Rome, Lucullus announced that he was divorcing his wife, Clodia, claiming to have discovered that she had been sleeping with another man—her own brother, Clodius.[31]

The search for a new wife was also a way for Lucullus to seek out political support. While the Senate had voted the general a triumph, additional legislation was required from the assembly to celebrate it, and here Lucullus ran into trouble. The familiar charges of needlessly prolonging the war and diverting its profits to himself were dragged back out, and the assembly refused to authorize the general's right to march into the city with his army.[32] Friends of Pompey, or those seeking to win Pompey's favor, saw opportunity in blocking Lucullus.

For his new wife, Lucullus selected the daughter of Cato's beloved half brother, Caepio. Caepio, of course, was dead, and it was Cato whose consent would be required for the match to go forward—just as it was Cato whom Lucullus was really after.[33] Though the exact date of the marriage cannot be recovered from remaining evidence, it is clear that the old general had spotted a rising star in Cato, who not only would do combat with troublesome tribunes but was willing to take on what Lucullus and other *optimates* really fretted over, the power of Pompey.

The controversy over Lucullus's triumph was merely part of a larger confrontation shaping up among citizens and their leaders over how to recognize Pompey's achievements in the east and how to reintegrate him into domestic politics upon his return. Some wanted to embrace Pompey and use him; others, such as Cato and Lucullus, yearned to shun him and weaken him.

Before Cato's term of quaestor finished, he took one more bold action. Over the preceding few years, a number of Sulla's harsh actions as dictator had come under new scrutiny. Caesar had challenged the ban on the display of Marius's image, for instance. Now Cato insisted that those who had collected the reward of around 50,000 sesterces for killing one of the proscribed should surrender that money back to the treasury. These executioners were widely hated, and Romans were thrilled to see Cato, after combing through the treasury records, call them in one by one and make them return their bloodstained profits.[34]

After this, pressure grew for executioners to be put on trial for murder. Perhaps because of the anticipated volume of cases, an extra court was established. And as was typical in such situations, an ex-aedile was appointed to preside over it: none other than Caesar. Installed on his tribunal in the Forum, he made it clear that he would indeed hear cases against those who had received money from the treasury for bringing in the heads of Roman citizens, even though they had been exempted by Sulla's laws. Caesar secured at least a couple of high-profile convictions. One to fall was a former officer of Sulla's who was said to have amassed the vast fortune of over 10 million sesterces. Like the confiscations of the blood money, these condemnations were immensely popular. Finally, Sulla's tyranny seemed to be extinguished.[35]

Of course, the trials would have seemed unfair to the accused. But nobody had forced them to stalk fellow Romans. Ensuring that even a few men paid a penalty for what they did might prevent a similar bloodbath from happening again. On this not only could Caesar and Cato agree; it was the two of them more than anyone else who made the trials and convictions possible. Though it is unclear just how directly they collaborated, they were at least able to cooperate this one time, just before the rift between them would open. A shared disgust for what had happened in their childhoods briefly brought them together.

Each could see many faults in the senatorial nobility, but they responded differently. Caesar wanted to empower the people, Cato to reform senatorial government. In Cato's eyes, Caesar was pandering to the people, while in Caesar's, Cato was blind to the difficulties ordinary Romans faced.

As Cato's stature grew, it was inevitable that he would come into conflict with Caesar. Cato could never resist a confrontation with anyone he thought was acting unjustly—whether it was Catulus defending the corrupt official, King Deiotarus with his piles of gifts, or the bullies at the childhood birthday party all those years before. On the last day of his quaestorship, he had just been escorted home by a throng of grateful citizens when he heard of mischief back at the treasury. Another quaestor, who happened to be an old friend of Cato's, was being pressured by a group of influential men to register an unauthorized remission of moneys owed. Cato returned at once, and when he found that the remission had been registered, he asked for the tablets and erased the entry. The compromised quaestor stood by and said nothing, tacitly acknowledging that he had erred.[36]

When Cato rose to challenge Caesar, the response would not be so placid.

CHAPTER 4

THE CONSPIRACY OF CATILINE

As Cato finished his quaestorship and Caesar stepped down from presidency of the murder court at the end of 64 BC, the most burning issue in politics was the impending return of Pompey. Pompey's recent victories over the pirates and then Mithridates—really, his whole career—lay right at the heart of the dispute over where power should reside in the Republic. The Pompey problem was starting to split Cato and Caesar apart. Then an unexpected development in the year 63 made matters far worse: Catiline's conspiracy to seize control of the Republic.

Born, like Caesar, into a distinguished patrician family whose fortunes had decayed, Lucius Sergius Catilina (known in English as "Catiline") acutely felt a lack of status and struggled his whole life to regain it. Around twenty-five years old when Sulla marched into Rome the victor of civil war, Catiline was among those who flocked to the dictator, and he proved particularly unscrupulous. At the time of the proscriptions, he killed at least several men and bought up confiscated land. His subsequent life seems to have been equally unsavory, even if his enemies almost certainly exaggerated his enormities. In 73, he was suspected of sleeping with a Vestal Virgin, a serious charge. He was saved from punishment when she was acquitted in a trial, but his bad behavior continued several years later when, while governing Africa, he pillaged the province so extensively that provincials came to Rome to complain while he was still in office. When put on trial after his return to the city, he once again managed an acquittal—though it was said that this was the result of bribery and the intercession of powerful friends in the nobility. He had to delay a planned run for the consulship to 64 and, despite yet more bribery, was defeated. To add to his humiliation, one of the candidates he lost to was Marcus Tullius Cicero, a new man, the first member of his family to hold political office. "A squatter in Rome" was how Catiline tauntingly referred to Cicero, who came from a small town southeast of Rome.[1]

Trying to overcome his sense of inferiority, Catiline had always lived profligately. He enjoyed lavish parties at which senators and their wives drank, danced, and giddily plotted with him about rising to the top in Rome. Catiline preyed especially on a group of young men, allegedly making available to them the most beautiful prostitutes he could find. Some of the boys, it was also suspected, wanted to sleep with Catiline himself, a handsome and powerfully built man. Catiline masked his anxieties with bluff and bravado, and his grandiose talk excited these bored youths. With carefully groomed hair and loose-hanging clothes that shocked their elders, the boys accompanied Catiline around Rome as a form of protest.[2]

More and more, talk, and perhaps the occasional sexual favor, was all Catiline had left to offer. His extravagant lifestyle, along with all he had spent on bribes, had left him perilously close to bankruptcy. The consular election of 63, Catiline saw, was his last chance. A victory would allow him to finally attain the recognition he felt that he and his family were owed. Moreover, he would gain immunity during his term of office from the legal troubles that always seemed to hound him, and he could afterward go on to another lucrative provincial governorship. A defeat, on the other hand, could spell ruin. If his credit ran out, he risked loss of his Palatine house, expulsion from the Senate, and perhaps even exile.

The stakes were higher for Catiline in 63 than they had been during his failed campaign the year before, and the contest harder too. In 64, Catiline had enjoyed considerable support. One of his backers was Crassus, who drew on his immense fortune to help fund Catiline's campaign—in the expectation of help with various schemes from Catiline if elected, including perhaps another attempt on Egypt. Along with Crassus came Caesar, who could exploit his great popularity to help deliver votes to Catiline. But even their intercession hadn't been enough to swing the election.

Now, as the make-or-break election of the summer of 63 drew near, the ever more desperate Catiline looked increasingly like a bad investment. A wine-soaked party or two might attract young men looking for excitement but was scarcely going to impress this hardheaded pair. Practically the only financial backer Catiline had left, it seems, was his wife, Orestilla, whose reputation was almost as dubious as Catiline's. There was little to praise in Orestilla, it was acidly remarked, except her beauty.[3]

Yet even if Catiline could have raised substantial funds, he faced other problems. Since the consular campaign of 64, Cicero had grown increasingly convinced that Catiline, if elected, would threaten the interests of the wealthy Romans that made up Cicero's base. Those with spare capital often lent out money at high rates of interest—a standard rate was 12 percent per annum—and they stood to lose much if Catiline gave in to a growing demand for a general cancellation of debts or some other form of relief. Cicero would use all his power and influence to stop Catiline. Furthermore, the Senate, concerned about the growing use of bribery, successfully demanded passage of new legislation before the election that increased the penalty for those convicted of electoral misconduct to ten years of exile.[4]

So it was that even if Catiline could eke out an election victory and save himself from his financial woes by the perquisites of office, he stood at risk of being prosecuted and then banished from Rome during the several months before he entered office, in order to free up a spot for a defeated candidate more favored by the wealthy.

Around the time the bribery law passed, Cato started speaking out in the Senate. After joining the body a couple of years before, he had always attended the Senate's meetings, which took place either in the custom-built Senate house at the edge of the Forum or in one of the city's larger temples. Cato was the first to arrive and the last to leave, though often, while the others slowly assembled, he would sit quietly on his bench and amuse himself with a book of Greek philosophy that he stowed in his toga. Once a meeting was under-way it had Cato's full attention; he thought he should be as attentive to public business as a bee to its honey.

Like other young senators, even those from the noblest families, he at first said little or nothing in debates. Senate rules dictated that the presiding magistrate—usually a consul—call on incom-ing and former magistrates to speak in order of rank, starting with the consuls-elect and then moving down. (Current occupants of of-fice could speak at any time.) Of the several hundred senators who might be present at a meeting, most did not say much. They indi-cated their views by nods, applause, cheers, catcalls, hisses. They also might stand up and walk toward a senator they agreed with or leave the bench of one whose views they disliked.[5]

In the summer of 63 BC, Cato was elected tribune of the plebs for the following year, in a race that was held prior to the consular election. He had not been planning to run. During the usual recess from public affairs in late spring, he set out with his books and his philosophers to enjoy a retreat at a property he owned in southern Italy. On the way there he ran into a huge train of animals car-rying baggage. Metellus Nepos, a brother-in-law of Pompey who had been serving as an officer in Pompey's eastern wars, was un-expectedly back in Italy and planned to run for one of the ten po-sitions of tribune. With his dingy entourage, Cato seems to have gone unnoticed by Nepos, but Nepos could not be missed by Cato. Cato turned around, went back to Rome, and declared his own candidacy. "Don't you know that Metellus is already frightening enough on his own because of his lunatic behavior," Cato reportedly asked his friends, "and now that he has come at Pompey's bidding he will strike the Republic like a bolt of lightning and wreak havoc on everything?"[6] As tribune, Cato could use his veto to block the laws that Nepos was sure to pass in 62 on behalf of Pompey.

As tribune-elect, Cato exercised his new prerogative to speak. Since it was clear by then that Pompey himself would soon be back in Rome to celebrate a triumph, certain senators, eager to ingratiate themselves with the victorious general, began discussing honors for him. Two of the tribunes proposed that Pompey should be allowed to wear triumphal robes at public games for the rest of his life, and Caesar warmly endorsed the motion. Cato spoke against it.[7] In his view, Pompey's whole career had undermined the republican princi-ple that no one man should be too powerful. Cato knew that speak-ing against the proposal would win him favor from the influential *optimates* who hated and feared Pompey. The speech was also meant to show everyone that Cato, even at a young age, was not afraid to challenge Pompey. It did not carry the day, but the challenge repre-sented a courageous display all the same.

Soon Cato began clashing with Catiline. As appalled as Cicero at the thought of the reckless patrician—or anyone else, for that matter—buying his way into the consulship, Cato gave a speech de-nouncing citizens for accepting bribes. As Cato saw it, bribes, which included not just cash payouts but free meals, tickets for shows, and other gifts, might sway the people from voting for the candidate who would best serve their interests. In his speech, Cato promised to press charges, as soon as the election was over, against any candi-date who had distributed money. Unusually for Cato, though, there was an exception: he would not prosecute the husband of his older half sister Servilia, Decimus Junius Silanus. Silanus, who had already lost one race for the consulship, was struggling to find support among the electorate, and Cato's exemption was an all but outright admission that bribery was required to lift Silanus to the top of the polls.[8]

It was natural for Servilia, Silanus, and Cato to work together, but the three shared an uneasy secret: Servilia was in the midst of a passionate love affair with Caesar. Although Caesar slept with other men's wives and was himself married to Pompeia, he had developed an unusually strong attraction toward Servilia. Servilia, not otherwise known to have been promiscuous, fully reciprocated his interest.[9] There was more than just physical desire between them. They respected each other's intelligence, understood each other's determination. Servilia's family on her father's side, the Servilii Caepiones, were patrician and had suffered many reverses in recent decades. Her first husband, Brutus, was killed in the revolt that flared up after Sulla's death. Since then, she had been amassing wealth for herself, raising her fatherless son for a great political career, and trying to restore the luster of the Servilii Caepiones. With Caesar she could share her hopes and worries, and he with her.

Silanus, within his rights to divorce his errant wife, chose to stay married. Extramarital affairs were sometimes tolerated in senatorial circles. Servilia was discrete, and, what is more, she could help deliver Caesar's support to Silanus in his canvassing.[10] Caesar himself was running for the office of praetor in 63, and the contest put him in touch with voters. This was just the sort of arrangement to disgust Cato. When Cato's own wife came under suspicion of infidelity—probably a couple of years after 63—he divorced her, despite the two children she had given him, a daughter and a son.[11] But there was nothing he could do about his sister and Caesar, at least not until Silanus secured a victory and Catiline was defeated.

At a Senate meeting shortly before the election, Cato directly threatened Catiline with prosecution. Catiline replied with a menacing pronouncement. If his enemies tried to destroy him, he said, he would put out the fire not with water, but with general destruction.[12] The rickety and densely packed tenements most Romans lived in made the city a firetrap, and it was common practice to stop a conflagration by destroying whole blocks of buildings. Catiline was saying that he would protect himself, whatever damage it did to him—and Rome. Cicero and his friends groaned loudly.

Catiline had by now adopted a new strategy to win. He even more openly sought the support of those in debt. Widespread indebtedness was a chronic problem in Rome but particularly acute in 63 because, with peaceful conditions returning to the Roman east, moneylenders were calling in loans they had placed in Italy so they could reinvest their capital at a higher rate of interest abroad. Bankruptcy, and the terrible stigma it brought in Rome, awaited not just Catiline but thousands more. Who was a better champion for victimized Romans, Catiline asked, than a man who was himself a victim of the corrupt political establishment and its banker friends?[13]

Many flocked to Catiline's call for a remission of debts— including fellow nobles, some hopelessly in debt, and others nursing grievances they hoped Catiline's revolution would address. Among them was a former consul and patrician named Lentulus, who had been kicked out of the Senate years before and was now having to serve in the lower office of praetor a second time to regain membership. He burned with resentment at the comedown—and took solace in repeating a prophecy he had heard that three Cornelii were fated to rule at Rome. Cinna and Sulla had come before him; he, Cornelius Lentulus, would be the third.

But beyond fools like Lentulus and the handsome young men with their well-pomaded hair, Catiline did attract the truly desperate. The urban poor, always struggling to make rent on those unstable apartments, found solidarity with the patrician. So too did the farmers of Italy, saddled with high mortgages on their lands. Though he no longer supported Catiline, Caesar must have felt sympathy for the appeals Catiline made to these groups. Catiline was a deeply flawed champion, but the cause he espoused had justice.

The most powerful partners Catiline found were an army of especially downcast men from the rich lands of Tuscany. The civil war of the 80s BC had turned that picturesque landscape into a scene of misery and terror. Farms were destroyed in fighting, and colonists sent by Sulla clashed bitterly with dispossessed supporters of Marius for years afterward. One old officer of Sulla's named Manlius, who had settled in Fiesole, in the hills just outside Florence, was the local version of Catiline. Massively in debt, he stirred up the depressed populace with talk of revolution. The band of men he assembled, which included other Sullan veterans, came to Rome for the consular elections of 63 to vote for Catiline—and, perhaps, to intimidate their opposition.

More and more, Catiline's following was looking like an army. Washed-up aristocrats and bored young men were its officers, peasants and the poor its far more convincing foot soldiers. Such supporters might help Catiline win the consulship, but if he lost, as looked increasingly likely, he could still use them to gain power by force. At a meeting at his house shortly before the election, according to Cicero, Catiline gave a fiery speech saying that the poor should look to the rich no longer and should trust one of their own, a man in great debt himself; he would be the leader and standard-bearer of all unfortunate men.[14] The military metaphor was not an empty one.

After learning of Catiline's speech, Cicero persuaded the Senate to postpone the elections, and he called on Catiline to explain himself. Catiline made little effort to deny the consul's report of what had transpired and instead issued another of his cryptic threats. "There are two bodies in the Republic," he taunted, "one feeble with a weak head, the other strong, but headless."[15] He meant to become the head of that strong body. Cicero was horrified, but he failed to persuade his fellow senators there was enough evidence to take action against Catiline.

Election day finally came. For the consular race, voting took place on a large floodplain of the Tiber River located just outside the old city walls; it was called the Field of Mars since military exercises were also conducted there. As the sun rose, citizens started streaming in by the thousands. The candidates appeared a little later, dressed in specially whitened togas and accompanied by retinues of supporters. They took the opportunity to shake voters' hands a final time. When it was time to ballot, the presiding magistrate—Cicero, in 63—climbed onto a high platform to give a brief prayer and issue instructions. Convinced that Catiline meant to kill him, Cicero surrounded himself with a bodyguard of burly young men he had summoned to Rome from a town in the rugged inland of Italy. He had also put on a well-polished breastplate and made sure to let his tunic slip so voters would catch a glimpse of the plate and think they were in peril from Catiline.[16]

Actual voting took place in an unroofed wooden structure called the Sheepfold (to the practical-minded Romans, that was what the building most resembled). Ropes were stretched down its length to divide it into aisles, which voters walked along in single file. They were handed wooden ballots covered with wax, which they marked with the names of their two choices and then dropped in urns. Counting such ballots was time consuming, and voters and candidates alike often had to wait hours for the results.

It fell to Cicero to announce the winners. Silanus earned one place, and the other went to Lucius Murena. Both had engaged in bribery, which paid off. Catiline, for the second time in as many years, had lost. His immediate response is not recorded. But it was clear that his only option left was to set his conspiracy fully in motion.

True to his oath, Cato soon initiated a prosecution against Murena, who was acquitted, thanks in part to a skillful defense by Cicero. A copy of Cicero's defense survives, and it reveals some of

Cato's arguments. Not only did he accuse Murena of election fraud; he also called him something almost worse than a briber. Murena, Cato said, was a dancer.[17]

Silanus, of course was spared a trial. Despite Servilia's infidelity, she had helped to deliver him his consulship. And at the subsequent praetorian election, Caesar was, to no one's surprise, elected praetor. Catiline, meanwhile, grappled with plans to seize the consulship and take over Rome, as if it were the days of Marius and Sulla again.

For all the troubles that his former ally Catiline was experiencing, Caesar was having a splendid year. His affair with Servilia was exciting. He had won the praetorship. And there was something far more impressive than that.

The pontifex maximus, Rome's chief priest, had recently died, triggering a special election to fill the post, among the very highest honors for which senators competed. The office, held for life, usually went to a former consul with high distinction and great influence in the Senate. In 63 BC two such candidates came forward: Publius Servilius Isauricus, the consul of 79, and Quintus Lutatius Catulus, the consul of 78.[18]

It was a glittering prize, and the idea of beating his enemy Catulus—the strongest candidate—made it all the more alluring to Caesar. To the delight of his supporters, he put his name forward as a candidate. But defeating such distinguished opponents was no easy task, even for one with Caesar's popularity. To help his chances, he resorted to bribes, doubtless supplied chiefly by Crassus (who, not a current member of the pontifical college, was ineligible to run himself). And that was not all. As dictator, Sulla had restored an earlier practice of letting the priestly colleges themselves select new members when any vacancy opened; only the pontifex maximus was elected by the people. To build support for his candidacy in 63, Caesar worked with one of the tribunes to pass legislation that brought back elections for all the priesthoods, an immensely popular measure.[19]

As he saw his chances slip away from him, Catulus, growing desperate, offered to pay Caesar to withdraw from the race. Caesar coolly replied that he would only borrow more and fight to the end.

On election day, the usually steady Aurelia was in tears as she saw Caesar off from the house they still apparently shared. He gave her a kiss and said, "Mother, today you will see your son either pontifex maximus or an exile."[20] As it had so often over the preceding few years, Caesar's great risk would pay off. When the votes were counted up, Caesar emerged the triumphant winner. He had outpolled his rivals even in their own voting districts.

The election was an extraordinary boost for Caesar's prestige. He got to move into the official residence of the pontifex maximus in the heart of Rome and leave behind his house in the unfashionable Subura neighborhood. He would preside at meetings and banquets of the pontifical college. The election also further embittered Catulus against Caesar, a fact that potentially created a larger problem for Caesar—and Crassus—as Catiline moved forward with his plans. As one-time supporters of Catiline who also championed popular causes, Caesar and Crassus were vulnerable to accusations of complicity in the growing unrest. Given even half a chance, Catulus and his friends would be sure to strike.

Reluctant as they were to support Cicero and his conservative base, Caesar and Crassus still needed to distance themselves from Catiline's plot. Caesar did so by quietly passing along to Cicero some information he had received about the conspiracy.[21] Crassus, who wanted more protection, acted with greater flair. One evening in October he went with two other senators to Cicero's house at midnight and woke the consul. Shortly after dinner earlier that night, Crassus explained, his doorkeeper had handed him and his guests some letters brought by a stranger. Unsigned, they were addressed to various people, with one for Crassus. Crassus read this letter only, which warned him that Catiline was planning many murders and Crassus should flee for safety. The other letters Crassus turned over to Cicero unopened.[22]

The letters gave Cicero something he wanted: hard evidence he could hand over to the Senate to force the senators to take action. Of course, the letters were anonymous, and it is a good guess they were forged by Crassus to protect himself from a charge of conspiracy and win Cicero's support. The truth mattered little as far as Cicero was concerned.

At dawn the next day Cicero summoned the Senate and presented the unopened letters to their addressees to be read aloud. All told of the same plot described in the letter to Crassus. A senator then furnished a report that soldiers were mustering in Tuscany, with a particularly large force under Manlius. Alarmed by the news but reassured that Crassus was not backing Catiline, the Senate passed an emergency decree that granted Cicero extraordinary military powers. Troops were mustered, gladiators removed from Rome as a precaution, and watches posted throughout the city. About Catiline himself, who remained in Rome, the senators still said nothing. They had no firm evidence that he had done anything wrong, and many did not want to believe the new man Cicero's claim that a patrician was so embittered that he would bring war on his country.

But Catiline was notorious for needing no sleep, and he worked late every night furthering his plans. About a week after the Senate meeting, on October 27, Manlius raised the standard of revolt in Fiesole. In Rome, Catiline held a secret meeting for the officers of the conspiracy. Revolts were to spring up across Italy, Catiline promised, and he was eager now to join Manlius, just as soon as Cicero, "the one who really interferes with my plans," was removed.[23] Two of the conspirators volunteered to pay a visit to the consul at home first thing the next morning and slit his throat. Tipped off by one of his spies, Cicero blocked the entry to his house and was saved.

The next day in the Senate, Cicero gave a passionate speech against Catiline to his face. Senators were aghast, and all the benches around Catiline soon emptied out. Outraged, Catiline stood up and told his colleagues not to believe a word that the "squatter" Cicero had said.[24] But by that evening, Catiline decided it was time for him to go north and take command of the forces Manlius was assembling. A few of the conspiracy's other leaders would remain in Rome to kill Cicero and prepare for Catiline's triumphant return.

With his arrival in Manlius's camp, Catiline's guilt was incontrovertible, and he was declared a public enemy. But Cicero still needed to secure hard evidence against those who had stayed behind and were plotting to torch Rome. An opportunity came when Lentulus, still nursing his dream of being the third Cornelius to rule Rome, made a blunder. Ambassadors representing the Gallic tribe of the Allobroges had come to Rome seeking relief from their debts, and when Cicero and the Senate refused to help, Lentulus approached the envoys with an invitation to join the conspiracy. The envoys were tempted but in the end shrewdly reported everything to Cicero. He instructed them to ask Lentulus and the other leaders for written pledges of support, and the conspirators fell into Cicero's trap.

Armed with the signed letters, early in the morning of December 3 Cicero ordered Lentulus and four others to be brought to him. He summoned the Senate to meet in the Temple of Concord. An imposing building that overlooked the northwestern corner of the Forum, the temple had been erected centuries earlier to mark the end of a period of civil strife. The resonance must have been pleasing to Cicero, but the temple's appearance that morning suggested anything but peace. On its front staircase, and amid the tall columns of its lofty podium, Cicero had stationed armed guards. Throughout the meeting, guards stood watch at the open door leading to the temple's inner chamber, in case there was trouble.

At the meeting, in addition to unsealing and reading the letters, Cicero summoned the Gauls to testify. They told of how they had been asked to send cavalry to Italy as soon as possible. They also revealed Lentulus's endless rantings about the three Cornelii who would rule Rome. And then there was the cache of swords and daggers found that morning at one of the conspirators' houses. The evidence of conspiracy was overwhelming.[25]

At the end of the meeting, all the senators voted a motion of thanks to Cicero. They also issued orders to arrest several more men implicated in the plot. Those already detained would for the time being be held separately in custody at the houses of Crassus, Caesar, and several other prominent senators.[26]

Crassus and Caesar had no choice but to agree. Cicero's strategy was to create a united front against the conspirators, and he and the Senate likely chose Crassus and Caesar to make them show they had rejected their old friends. Almost certainly they had, as Crassus's turning over of the letters had revealed. As Rome's wealthiest man, who owned tenements throughout the city and held an extensive portfolio of loans, Crassus did not relish the prospect of violent revolution or even moderate debt relief. Nor did he want to see his old rival Pompey summoned back from the war that was just ending in the east and given a powerful command in Italy against the Catilinarians. Caesar was more sympathetic to Pompey, but he had to worry that his enemies among the *optimates*, Catulus especially, might see an opportunity to sweep him away along with the conspirators already in custody.

On December 4 an informer was brought before the Senate, a man allegedly arrested on his way to Catiline. In exchange for a pardon, he was invited by Cicero to tell what he knew. Mostly he repeated what had been heard the day before about the intended fires, the murder of politicians in Rome, and the march of the rebels. But there was one sensational addition: the informer claimed that he had been sent by Crassus to Catiline with a message to speed up his arrival in Rome. While some senators were willing to entertain the charge, many were not; quite a few senators were under obligation to Crassus or hoped to have his help in the future and dared not risk offending him. The Senate rejected the accusation, and the informer was kept under guard until he revealed at whose instigation he had lied. He never ended up confessing, but the incident left Crassus rattled.[27]

Meanwhile, Catulus made his move. Like Catiline, Caesar was well known for his debts and almost seemed to flaunt them as if they were battlefield victories. As Caesar saw it, to borrow heavily was practically a sign of manliness. It showed confidence that you were clever and strong enough to make it all back. It should be easy, then, Catulus thought, to implicate Caesar in the conspiracy, and he went to Cicero with an accusation to that effect. But the aggrieved ex-consul could get nowhere with Cicero, who was keen to maintain the impression that all the most important senators supported him. So Catulus took matters into his own hands and spread falsehoods about Caesar he claimed to have heard from the Gallic envoys. He was helped by another of the *optimates*, the former consul Gaius Piso. Piso had recently been unsuccessfully prosecuted by Caesar for unjustly executing a Transpadane and other abuses as a provincial governor in northern Italy.[28] Catulus's and Piso's stories might not have impressed Cicero, but they did excite the bands of young men the consul had assembled as his police force. The armed youths relished the prospect of bullying, perhaps even bloodying up, a senator.

Cicero again surrounded the Temple of Concord with his armed gangs on the morning of December 5, when he summoned the Senate to debate what should be done with the five conspirators held in custody. Crassus and Caesar knew the safest course for them was to continue to support Cicero, who was sure to advocate executing the prisoners. But yielding too much to Cicero and his allies was a disagreeable prospect for politicians whose brand was championing the people. Crassus decided simply not to attend the meeting. For Caesar, that looked like weakness.

Cicero opened the debate with a brief statement and then began calling on senators in the standard order, by rank. As consul-elect,

Silanus was recognized first. He proposed that the five prisoners deserved "the extreme penalty." Everyone understood this to be execution, even though the Senate normally would never vote on such a matter. Roman law was clear that a citizen could only be put to death after a trial held before the people or in a court sanctioned by the people. The guarantee of a trial was one of the most sacred rights of a citizen, held dear by ordinary Romans fearful of magistrates abusing their power. In Cicero's view, however, an enemy of the state had ceased to be a citizen and lost all rights.[29] The other consul-elect, Murena, supported Silanus's proposal. Cicero then called one by one on the ex-consuls, fourteen of whom were present. They too supported execution.

It was now the turn of the praetors-elect, and Cicero called on Caesar. As Cicero must have appreciated, Caesar was in a bind. Caesar could go along with the others and satisfy the prevailing sentiment in the Senate. But to do so meant consenting to the execution of citizens, something that Caesar, scarred by the terror he had witnessed in his teenage years, found abhorrent. Only the year before, he had presided over the court that convicted men who had taken the lives of fellow citizens without a trial during the Sullan proscriptions.[30] While the conspirators were now widely feared by the people of Rome thanks to Cicero's reports of their plans to torch the city, Caesar knew the execution would set a precedent that could be abused later.

Caesar stood up and began speaking in his calm and clear style. No torture, he said (at least in Sallust's version of the speech), was too harsh a penalty for the crimes the conspirators had planned.[31] But senators needed to think through the consequences of their actions. At present nobody was likely to criticize the execution of traitors. But what if the punishment was extended in future years to those who did not deserve it? The precedent would have been set.

The Senate, and Cicero in particular, was running a risk. However unlikely it might seem now, there was a good chance that the people would come to regret the loss of their champion Catiline and could take revenge on those who supported or carried out executions of his followers.

Death, Caesar told the Senators, had been fixed by the gods not as a punishment, but as a natural end or a release from pain and suffering. Brave men even looked forward to it. A better penalty for the traitors would be to lock them in chains for the rest of their natural lives. Each should be sent to a different town of Italy and kept under guard. And, Caesar continued, the Senate should stipulate that no one was ever to bring up the conspirators' case again in either the Senate or the assembly. They should have no hope, and to ensure that their lives were as miserable as possible, all their property should be confiscated.

It was a brilliant speech. With his proposal of life imprisonment—not a familiar punishment in Rome—he had shown severity to the conspirators. He had also stood up for the rights of the people. Whatever he said about not revisiting the matter, he probably figured that the conspirators could always be tried later.

Caesar seemed to have found an almost perfect way of dealing with the situation, and the mood of the Senate shifted. Those who spoke after him endorsed his proposal or at least recommended holding off on execution. In an embarrassment for Cicero, even Cicero's younger brother Quintus—like Caesar, a praetor-elect—took this view. Caesar, it appeared, had not just survived the moment. He had triumphed. As senator after senator came around to his position, he must have thought that he, not Cicero or Catulus, was the real master of the Senate. With his recent election as pontifex maximus, it might have seemed he was even on his way to becoming the first man of Rome.

Cicero was dismayed at the turn the debate had taken and gave a speech urging reconsideration. He reviewed Silanus's and Caesar's proposals, dealing with both politely, and then insisted that Silanus's was the more lenient. "What cruelty can there be," Cicero asked, "in punishing the enormity of such a crime?" Cicero was not being vindictive but compassionate. "I picture this city, the light of the world and the citadel of all nations, suddenly falling into ruin through one conflagration."[32] He asked the senators to state their views once more, beginning with the incoming consuls.

The speech did nothing to shift the strong inclination toward Caesar's view. In another great embarrassment to Cicero, Silanus retracted his original proposal, offering the feeble excuse that when he had spoken of "the extreme penalty" he had meant life imprisonment. Those who followed also supported Caesar's position, except for Catulus, who again spoke out for execution—to no effect.

Finally it was the turn of the incoming tribunes, and Cicero recognized Cato. As always, Cato's mind was already made up. The senators, including his brother-in-law Silanus, had shown deplorable weakness. They had not faced up to the danger Rome was in. Citizens of the highest rank were plotting against the country, and more might join them if decisive action was not taken. And as for Caesar's speech and the wide assent it commanded: that was an outrage. Catulus, Cato thought, had been right about Caesar's involvement in the conspiracy. Why else was Caesar trying to let the conspirators off? Silanus and Caesar and their triangle with Servilia: they all repulsed Cato.

Cato stood up and began speaking with an anger and passion that gripped the Senate. He criticized Silanus for his backsliding. He turned on Caesar and lashed out even more bitterly. Caesar's proposal might look appealing, Cato fumed, but it was really intended to undermine the city and intimidate the Senate. Caesar was the one who should be afraid. He had escaped punishment, even suspicions, for his past intrigues. He was not going to get away with saving his old friends now.[33]

By a strange coincidence, as Cato delivered his attack, a messenger came into the meeting and handed Caesar a small writing tablet. Cato gambled on a chance to incriminate his rival. Look, he said, even now Caesar was getting a message from the enemy.

Senators started shouting, and Cato demanded that Caesar read the note aloud. Either it would incriminate Caesar, or, if Caesar refused, he would look guilty. Caesar passed the note to Cato. As Cato read it in silence, his face started to twist with rage. It was not instructions from a fellow conspirator, but a love letter from Servilia to Caesar. "Take it, you drunk!" Cato cried out in fury, as he flung the tablet back at Caesar.[34]

To his credit, Cato regained his composure and started building to a powerful climax. If the senators wanted to save the Republic, he said, they needed to act. This was not a debate about taxes or provincial administration. The senators' freedom, their very lives, were in danger. The enemy was inside the walls, even in the very heart of Rome. They had openly confessed in the Senate that they had been planning murder, arson, and other outrages. The great Romans of the past wouldn't have hesitated over what to do. They killed their own sons if they caught them plotting against the Republic. The only possible course of action was a sentence of death.[35]

As Cato concluded, the senators burst into applause and started thronging around him. His tough words coursed through them, aroused them, stirred their emotions. Cato hadn't just denounced the conspirators. He had taken on his brother-in-law and all those weak former consuls. He had attacked Caesar too. Perhaps Cato couldn't prove Caesar's involvement, but that he had even mentioned it showed he had guts. Cato was right. The senators had lost their nerve. Their ancestors wouldn't even recognize them.

Recognizing that the mood of the Senate had changed decisively, Cicero put Cato's motion to a vote, and it passed overwhelmingly. Those in favor of a motion moved to the side of the chamber where its proposer stood. Caesar was left practically alone.[36]

To see his proposal defeated was humiliating for Caesar. And the personal attack from Cato was even more mortifying. Caesar's victory had turned into a rout; his string of successes that year was over. As he started to make his way out of the Senate, Cicero's armed guards, standing just outside the chamber door, drew their swords and threatened him.[37] The rumors Catulus had been spreading, along with Cato's tirade on Caesar's treachery, had incited them. Cicero, grimly focused on carrying out the executions, immediately signaled to the young men to stand down. Still, Caesar and his supporters saw that his opponents truly wanted to destroy him, and these opponents now included Cato. The danger Caesar had experienced as a teenager had returned. He would have to use all his strength to defend himself.

For Cato, the Senate meeting of December 5 was a turning point. Though only a tribune-elect and in his young thirties, he instantly replaced the aging Catulus as the natural leader of the small but powerful group of senators who were determined to uphold the Senate's authority and to thwart popular champions in the mold of Caesar. Cato's admirers forever afterward rhapsodized about how he had won the debate. The speech he gave was the only one of his published—not by Cato himself, who never published his speeches, but by Cicero, who had taken the unusual step of employing a team of shorthand writers to record the proceedings of the Senate.[38]

Paradoxically, the Catilinarian conspiracy ended up mattering most not because of what happened to Catiline or Cicero, but because of the consequences for Cato and Caesar. This was the moment Cato turned on Caesar. Cato no doubt had long hated Caesar's populist politics and his ongoing support of Pompey. With the bribes dished out to become pontifex maximus, Caesar had appealed to voters' basest instincts, Cato felt. Caesar was corrupt, constantly scheming for his own gain in public life, and in private devoted to nothing but pleasure. The affair with Servilia rankled. But with Caesar's plea to spare the conspirators on December 5, Cato's suspicions hardened into a deeper fear and hatred. The incident with the writing tablet might almost seem comical, and it was probably friends of Caesar's who liked to repeat the tale in later years to diminish Cato, but it only added to Cato's feeling that Caesar was wrapped up in his own gratification.

As for Caesar, he was appalled by Cato's rage-filled attack, and by how Cato carried the Senate with him. Caesar had expected Quintus Catulus's effort at revenge, and Catulus he could and would deal with. In Cato, he had a far more determined and dangerous enemy.

The deadly rivalry had begun.

CHAPTER 5

SHOWDOWN IN THE FORUM

A S SOON AS THE SENATE ADJOURNED, CICERO HAD THE FIVE
conspirators taken to the prison next to the Temple of Concord and strangled with a noose by the public executioners. He then returned to the Forum. Crowds had waited all day in suspense to learn the fate of the guilty men. With night falling, there was no time for a speech, and so Cicero solemnly uttered a single word: *Vixere*—"They have lived." It was a euphemism for "They're dead." Members of the crowd cheered and clapped. As jubilant masses escorted Cicero home through the torch-lined streets, some even hailed him as their savior.[1]

But as fears of the city going up in flames subsided over the ensuing days, Romans began to reckon with the bitter reality that Cicero and the Senate had still done nothing to alleviate their debts and hunger. And when the new tribunes entered office, one of them, Metellus Nepos, started holding public meetings in the Forum at which he drubbed Cicero for executing citizens without a trial. Caesar, still angry over the accusations made against him in the Senate, joined Nepos in the attacks, and soon the crowds were singing their praises, not Cicero's.[2]

Under normal circumstances Cicero should have been able to defend himself. Whereas tribunes started their year of office on December 10, most of the other magistrates, including the consuls, were replaced on New Year's Day. So Cicero still enjoyed the right to summon meetings. The problem was that Nepos and another tribune had moved their official benches to the top of the Rostra and were denying Cicero access. When the tribunate had first been established centuries earlier as a safeguard against the senators, the plebeians swore an oath that made the tribunes sacrosanct. If anybody, even a consul, laid a finger on them, he would be cursed. From this inviolability flowed the tribunes' power of intercession, the ability to stop almost any official action that was already underway, such as the enactment of a law or the speech of another magistrate. In political battle, this was a potentially awesome weapon, and tribunes were expected to justify their use of it. Nepos did just that when he declared that anyone who had punished others without a hearing had lost the right to speak.[3]

Dramas like this, playing out before the eyes of the people in the Forum, were increasingly frequent in Cato and Caesar's day. Roman politics was by nature a "theater of power," with magistrates the leading actors.[4] Even some of the most routine actions of the magistrates were highly choreographed. When consuls and praetors walked through the city, for example, they were accompanied by attendants who carried on their shoulders bundles of rods strapped together with red bands, known as the fasces. The attendants, known as lictors, processed in a single line ahead of the magistrate and removed anybody who stood in the way. They accompanied the magistrate to the baths, the theater, even private houses, where they would knock on the doors with the fasces. Whenever the magistrates appeared before popular assemblies and meetings, the lictors were supposed to lower their fasces out of respect for the people.

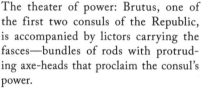

The theater of power: Brutus, one of the first two consuls of the Republic, is accompanied by lictors carrying the fasces—bundles of rods with protruding axe-heads that proclaim the consul's power.
Credit: Courtesy of the American Numismatic Society

Atop the Rostra—the curved speakers' platform, decorated with the rams of ships—sits the bench of the tribunes, from which they heard appeals from citizens and legislated.
Credit: Courtesy of the American Numismatic Society

As magistrates grew more willing to clash with each other, politicians seized opportunities to further heighten the spectacle. As the final weeks of December 63 showed, on the Rostra itself they sometimes almost literally tried to upstage one another. On the last day of the year, Nepos refused to let Cicero deliver the farewell address normally given by outgoing consuls and allowed him only to swear the traditional oath that he had obeyed the laws during his year of office. Nepos probably hoped to use that oath against Cicero later, but Cicero, whose rise in politics owed much to his instinct for showmanship, outwitted the tribune. The consul stepped onto the Rostra and, after obtaining silence, swore not the usual formula but one of his own making. The city of Rome and the Republic, he cried out loudly, had been saved by him alone.[5]

By coincidence, Cato started his tribunate in December of 63, and Caesar his praetorship just a few weeks later. Both would have starring roles in politics at the same time—and new opportunities to clash. The argument over the execution of the conspirators was really just the next installment of that much bigger drama: the

return of Pompey after his defeat of Mithridates and other spectacular victories in the east. The suffering people looked to Pompey as
a rescuer from their miseries, and popular politicians such as Caesar
latched onto measures on Pompey's behalf as a way to enhance their
own power. Cato and the *optimates*, on the other hand, felt nothing
but dread about the general's return with his army. What demands
would Pompey make? Would he become another Sulla?

The tribune Metellus Nepos was among those who saw opportunity in flaunting support for the returning general. A member of
the great noble house of the Caecilii Metelli, he, along with other
members of his generation of the family, had for years been attached
to Pompey.[6] Both Nepos and his slightly older brother, Celer, had
served on Pompey's military staff in the east. Even more important, their half sister Mucia had married Pompey after the death
of his previous wife, Sulla's stepdaughter. In her husband's long
absence, Mucia served as his surrogate in Rome and in that role
worked closely with Cicero. In 63, Cicero pleaded with her to get
her brother to give up his attacks—to no avail.[7]

Challenging Cicero's execution of citizens allowed Nepos to tap
into long-standing popular concerns over the abuses of the magistrates and the Senate. It also prepared the way for what the tribune really hoped to accomplish: legislation summoning Pompey
back with his army to stamp out the last embers of Catiline's rebellion and reestablish order. From a military perspective, there was
no need for any such order. The Senate had adequate generals in
the field, including Nepos's brother Celer. The point of the law was
rather to inflate Pompey's already high reputation and to dent senatorial authority.

Given that the measure was a clear people-pleaser, Caesar backed
it and became an unofficial sponsor alongside Nepos. For Cato, the
bill raised the Sullan specter of armies in the city and tyrannical
rule. Nepos had to be stopped, and the tribunate gave Cato tools to

do so. He could use his magisterial power to stage shows of support for Cicero. Already the Senate had heaped honors on the consul, including a thanksgiving to the gods for Cicero's role in saving Rome. Catulus had gone further and said that Cicero should be known as the father of his country, a title previously only given to Rome's founder Romulus, and then later to Camillus, who rebuilt Rome after its sack by the Gauls in the fourth century BC. Cato summoned a meeting in the Forum and had those assembled acclaim Cicero the same way. Cato would have lined up supporters of Cicero in advance to ensure that the consul received the thunderous applause he needed.[8]

There was more. As Cato himself put it, the tribunate was "a great power and office."[9] It was like strong medicine; it should be used only when urgently needed—when the health, even the very life, of the Republic was at risk. Normally, for the *optimates*, the tribunate was best employed to block popular politicians from jacking up their own power, or—what was even worse—that of extraordinary commanders such as Pompey. After all, Cato himself had only decided to run for the office to put a check on Nepos. When the time came, he could, if necessary, use his veto to slow down or block Nepos's law altogether.

But the tribunate could also be used to seize the initiative from opponents. Recognizing that the people of Rome were still suffering from the economic turmoil that had given rise to the Catilinarian conspiracy—misery that Nepos and Caesar could exploit—Cato went to the Senate and implored the senators to authorize new legislation to extend an existing program of subsidized grain distribution in the city.[10]

This was a highly popular measure. The people's hero Gaius Gracchus, back in the second century BC, had first passed legislation that made grain available at a low and fixed price, ending one of the great uncertainties of life in the city. Sulla had abolished, or at least curtailed, the subsidy, but it was restored by consuls in the later 70s for perhaps 40,000 citizens. Cato now persuaded the

Senate to hike spending. The total number of recipients would rise to about 150,000, maybe more.

The action not only would tamp down current protests but also would steal one of the popular politicians' most attractive causes from them. What made the bold proposal acceptable to senators was that that the Senate collectively would get credit for the measure—rather than Cato himself. Cato also drew upon the reputation that he had secured as watchdog of the public money. After laying down his quaestorship a couple of years earlier, he had sent his own slaves to the treasury every day to record all transactions, and he also paid to have a copy made of all the accounts going back to Sulla, ledgers he always kept on hand.[11] It was now clear what power this gave Cato: if he said the state could afford the additional payments, it had to be true.

For his entry into office on New Year's Day of 62 BC, Caesar took advantage of his new magisterial powers to offer a spectacle of his own. Just over twenty years before, the great Temple of Jupiter on the Capitoline Hill had burned down. Dedicated in the very first year of the Republic, and by far the largest of the city's temples, it had symbolized Rome's dominance. Rebuilding it was an urgent task. Sulla began the massive job, and upon his death it passed to his political heir, Catulus. As revenge for Catulus's efforts to implicate him in the Catilinarian conspiracy, Caesar summoned a public meeting in the Forum and began denouncing Catulus for his failure to complete the restoration of the temple. The reason for the delay, Caesar said, was plain: Catulus was embezzling the funds designated for the project. Catulus should turn over a full set of accounts to the people immediately. And not only that: Caesar announced that he would be sponsoring legislation to transfer completion of the work from Catulus to Pompey. Catulus's name would be chiseled off the rebuilt temple, and Pompey would get to inscribe his instead.[12]

This was a clever provocation. The embezzlement charge was clearly outrageous, and Caesar must have winked his bright eye as he turned Cato's pose as the defender of the public money against the champion of the *optimates*. Few could doubt, however, that were Pompey entrusted to finish the job, he would achieve quick results—and then be all too happy to emblazon his name across the temple pediment, surely in gold letters. As word of the meeting spread, Catulus and his senatorial supporters, who were up on the Capitoline Hill watching the new consuls be inaugurated, rushed down into the Forum and began protesting. Caesar refused to let Catulus onto the Rostra and only allowed the former consul to speak at ground level—a tremendous humiliation that mirrored the silencing of Cicero in the weeks before.

Meanwhile, the even bigger battle over Nepos's proposal to summon Pompey back with his armies was coming to a head. The mandatory review period for proposed legislation would shortly end, and Nepos could go to the Plebeian Assembly.

Nepos and Caesar needed to act fast. Already by January 1, it was hard to see Catiline as posing much of a threat: the execution of the conspirators, however controversial, had led to mass desertions from Catiline's army. Caught in northern Italy between the forces of Metellus Celer and of Cicero's consular colleague Antonius, Catiline would likely be defeated very soon. Still, Nepos and Caesar were determined to move forward and win credit from Pompey's base of supporters.

At a meeting of the Senate, Cato managed to refrain from his usual harsh attacks and politely pleaded with Nepos to drop his plan. The Caecilii Metelli, Cato pointed out, had always been "good men"— which was to say, not popular politicians. But despite Cato's moderate tone, Nepos refused to budge. With the arrogance typical of members of his family, he launched into a threatening speech full of violent language. He would get his way, he said, even if the Senate opposed him.

Cato's face hardened back into its usual scowl. After delivering a good tongue-lashing to Nepos, he ended with his own ultimatum: "As long as I live, Pompey will not enter the city in arms."[13]

With neither tribune willing to find a compromise, there was nothing more the Senate could do. The struggle would move to the Plebeian Assembly. That meant more theater, but as Cato's heated response seemed to hint, it might also mean violence.

In the face of a tribune's persistent use of a veto against a law with substantial support, popular politicians had worked out two ways of responding: either put forward a bill that deposed the uncooperative tribune, on the grounds that he was thwarting the people's wishes, or use physical force to intimidate or coerce the obstructer. With Catiline likely to be defeated any day, Nepos did not have much time to enact a law to depose Cato. Restraining him was the better option.

Cato appeared to prepare for the assembly meeting as if it would be like any other, even as his family and allies grasped the possibility of danger. According to the memoirs later written by Munatius, panic descended on Cato's house. The night before the assembly was to meet, his friends sat up worried and could eat nothing. Servilia and the other women wept, as high-ranking Romans of both sexes not uncommonly did when they wanted to show they were upset. Cato himself, however, took supper and spoke confidently. He slept so soundly that he had to be wakened the next morning by one of his fellow tribunes, Minucius Thermus.[14]

As Cato and Thermus walked down to the Forum, accompanied by just a few persons, they received warnings: Nepos and Caesar had filled the public meeting that preceded voting with their supporters, some of them armed. Meetings directly before voting typically took place in the more spacious eastern end of the Forum, where the great Temple of Castor stood. The building rested on a high podium, the front part of which, protected by rails, functioned as a speaker's platform—a sort of second Rostra. It rose from about eight feet to fourteen feet above the sloping ground and was accessed through staircases on the sides.[15] That morning, as Cato entered the Forum, the temple was surrounded by armed men, the staircases were guarded by gladiators, and sitting high on the platform next to Nepos was Caesar. When the actual casting of ballots began, Caesar, as a patrician, would have to leave, but until that point he could participate.

Those occupying the steps made way for the sacrosanct tribunes Cato and Thermus, but they let nobody else through. Cato was able to drag Munatius up by holding his hand. Cato then walked to the middle of the platform and plopped himself down between Caesar and Nepos, thereby cutting off their ability to speak to each other. Cato's supporters in the crowd cheered.

When the clerk began to read the law, the last step before voting, Cato interposed his veto and told him to stop. Nepos grabbed the document and began to read it himself. Cato snatched it away. Nepos, prepared for this possibility, had learned the bill by heart and began to recite it. Thermus clapped a hand over Nepos's mouth.

Nepos gave the order for his armed men to come running up and shout. Sticks and stones started flying, much of the crowd dispersed, but Cato stood unflinching on the platform. Had he remained much longer, he might have been hurt, but the consul Murena stepped forward and, holding his voluminous purple-edged toga in front of him as if it were a shield, ordered those throwing rocks to stop. Murena then wrapped his strong soldier's arms around Cato and hustled him inside the temple.

Nepos's opponents fled, and as the area in front of the Temple of Castor emptied, he thought he had won. He ordered the armed men to leave and resumed enacting the law in an orderly fashion. But then another crowd of people rushed into the Forum, at least some of whom appear to have been armed, since now Nepos's voters ran. Finally Cato himself returned to the podium. As he spoke, he somehow managed to reestablish order. He then broke up the meeting. It was almost like Neptune calming the waters after a storm.[16]

Who guided the mob against Nepos is unclear, but it could not have been Cato. Cato always opposed the illegal use of physical force in political settings. Crucially, he could only be seen as a victim of violence, and this likely was his plan all along. While some, perhaps many, citizens would have complained that his persistent veto was a frustration of their will, there was something impressive about Cato standing high on the temple podium enduring abuse on behalf of his beliefs. Cato had displayed the much-prized Roman virtue of *constantia*—steadfastness—for which he was to become famous.[17]

The Senate convened that same day. No doubt there was revulsion over the violence Nepos had unleashed, but—again as Cato probably intended—the violence gave Nepos's opponents all they needed to defeat his proposal. The senators voted to put on mourning, which meant exchanging their pristine togas and tunics for filthy tunics alone. Defendants at trials often dressed like this, but when all the senators did so, the aim was to arouse fear and pity in the people as a whole.[18] The senators also passed their emergency decree and entrusted the consuls with special powers to protect the city. The consuls were to see to it that Nepos and Caesar be removed from their public duties.[19]

Immediately afterward, Nepos rushed back into the Forum and delivered a long and harsh attack against Cato. Rome would soon repent of its dishonorable treatment of Pompey, he added menacingly. Then, although as tribune he was not allowed to be absent from the city for a single night, he set out for Asia to complain to Pompey about what had happened.

With Nepos's hasty departure, the crisis abated. Powerful voices in the Senate spoke in favor of a punishment against Nepos, at least for the offense of having fled Rome. Surprisingly, Cato said he opposed any such measure, and he brought the Senate over to his side. There was a risk of turning Nepos into a popular martyr and giving Pompey a pretext to return with force—exactly what Cato wished to prevent.

And so just weeks after his triumph in the debate over the conspirators' punishment, Cato had notched another victory. He had goaded Nepos into using violence and then rolled the whole Senate and both consuls over him. Cato had kept his hands clean, eschewing force himself, and the attack he had endured won him some sympathy, on top of the support he had earned with his extension of the grain subsidy. Nepos, on the other hand, was exposed for what he really was, a petulant noble.

Yet Caesar still remained.[20] Despite the Senate's decree, he refused to stop presiding over legal hearings in the Forum. He would have kept sitting, as praetors normally did, on an ivory chair placed on a high wooden tribunal, with lictors present. This was a regular part of the theater of magisterial power, but in these circumstances it proclaimed Caesar's defiance. It helped him maintain his recognized position, his *dignitas*. All politicians in Rome were touchy about their *dignitas*. Whoever was declared winner in an election first, for instance, lorded it over those whose spots were secured only after more ballots were cast. But Caesar was especially sensitive. His *dignitas*, he said, was more important to him than his life. If highway robbers helped him uphold his *dignitas*, he once claimed, he would return the favor.[21]

Caesar was ready to tough it out on his tribunal until he learned of a threat to use violence against him. Who lay behind the threat goes unnamed in the only surviving source. Perhaps one or several of Caesar's political enemies, such as Catulus, hoped to implicate him in further disorder. A cannier politician than Nepos, Caesar shifted tactics. He dismissed his lictors, put aside the purple-edged toga that praetors wore, and retreated to his house. This was his own gesture of protest, like the Senate's mourning. Within a day, a large and furious crowd of his supporters gathered outside his residence and demanded that he reassert his standing.

Like Cato on the temple podium, Caesar now had the chance for his own spectacle: with great ostentation, he calmed the rowdy demonstrators. The Senate, which had been summoned to take action about the gathering, heard of the stand-down and sent representatives to bring Caesar to the Senate house, where he was praised for his restraint and told to resume his duties. In turn, Caesar dropped his plan to transfer the restoration of the Temple of Capitoline Jupiter from Catulus to Pompey.[22]

Caesar cannot have been happy at the loss of standing entailed by his defeat in the contest with Cato and the Senate, but as in the years following his brush with Sulla, he was flexible enough to defer to those who held power over him, at least for the time being. It was standard for the Senate to assign praetors, after their year of service in Rome, a second year of military command in one of the provinces. The Senate had not yet determined the assignments, and Caesar did not want to risk losing his.

Nobody is known to have sustained serious physical injury in the scuffle in the Forum or the demonstration outside Caesar's house. Still, even if the violence was ratcheted down quickly, it was a worrying development that Cato, Caesar, and their respective sides had fought physically. It could happen again. Although Cato had not raised a fist, he learned the moral power to be gained from withstanding a physical attack. He had less incentive than ever to compromise the next time a difficult question came up. At the same time, Caesar learned that if obstruction was to be dealt with effectively, you had to be far better prepared than Nepos had been. You had to shape public opinion more fully—and, if force was to be used, you had to use it overwhelmingly to achieve victory.

The fracas of early 62 BC was owed in part to underlying weaknesses in the governance structures of the Roman Republic—such as the potential for abusing the tribunician veto, the impotence of the Senate to resolve its members' squabbles, and, above all, the ongoing question of how much authority, if any, the Senate should have over the people of Rome. For government to function peacefully, politicians could not push rules to the limits, and they sometimes needed to back down. To an extent, Cato and Caesar did finally back down, unlike Nepos—but only after they had helped to escalate the quarrel in the first place. Without Cato's heated rhetoric in the Senate and his extreme views on the tribunician veto, and without Caesar's willingness to incite crowds, the showdown in the Forum might never have happened. It was a foretaste of the later struggles that would bring about a full civil war.

News soon reached Rome of Catiline's defeat. With his forces cut to about three thousand men, he had hoped to escape to Transalpine Gaul but was blocked by the much larger army of Metellus Celer. Catiline decided to provoke battle with the other senatorial army, under the command of Antonius. Catiline thought that Antonius might be more easily beaten, but Antonius ended up pleading a case of gout and turned over operations to a highly competent subordinate. The Catilinarian forces were mauled. When Catiline's body was found, it was said, he was still breathing slightly and had on his face the same fierce expression he had always worn in life.[23] His head was cut off by Antonius and sent to Rome as proof of death.

The Senate could now be done with the whole Catilinarian affair. The trials of those suspected of conspiring, beyond the five already executed, were held in the regular criminal court for political violence. Cicero did not initiate the prosecutions but furnished crucial testimony throughout. Evidence was also supplied by a conspirator who had been granted immunity, the equestrian Lucius Vettius. Among those Vettius fingered was Caesar. The informer claimed that he had a letter to Catiline written in Caesar's own hand, which he would show in trial.

Around the same time, Caesar was also denounced in the Senate by a senatorial colleague, Quintus Curius. Like Vettius, Curius had initially been an ally of Catiline. Then, together with his mistress, the noblewoman Fulvia, he secretly supplied Cicero with information. For his efforts, the Senate had voted him a cash reward. Curius's new charges convinced nobody: why hadn't he said anything earlier? Not a bright man, Curius might have hoped to exploit hatred and suspicion of Caesar—feelings only increased by the Nepos affair—and gain further remuneration.[24] Equally implausible were

Vettius's allegations. Quite possibly he had been suborned by enemies of Caesar.

Caesar responded forcefully. He compelled Cicero to testify under oath that Caesar had voluntarily supplied information about the conspiracy the previous year, and he persuaded the Senate to rescind Curius's reward. As for Vettius, Caesar used his disciplinary powers as praetor to mete out a more spectacular punishment. Caesar entered Vettius's house and removed some of the property from it, summoned Vettius to the Forum, where a rough crowd had been gathered in advance, and finally threw Vettius into prison. Also thrown into prison was the president of the violence court—for having allowed a charge to be registered against Caesar, a sitting praetor.[25]

By law and custom, a great deal of deference was given to Roman magistrates, especially praetors and consuls, with their lictors, fasces, and tribunals. This was in part why Caesar's supporters were so outraged at the Senate's attempt to block him from carrying out his duties. But with the Senate united against him at that point, and with his chief tribunician ally in flight, Caesar had had no choice but to yield. Now the flimsy charges of Curius and Vettius gave him a chance to punch back. As before in his career, he knew how to choose his moments.

Yet more remained to be done for Caesar to recover. He could try to acquit himself well for the rest of the praetorship, but the real opportunity would come the following year, when he would be sent to govern a province, his first independent command. Nothing lifted a politician's profile like military success. A rich haul of booty would also allow him to start tackling his ever-mounting debts. He could even dream of winning an impressive-enough victory to merit a triumph. To reenter Rome in the horse-drawn chariot of a *triumphator* would be the best revenge. Caesar would be laughing all the way to the Temple of Jupiter on the Capitoline.

It is quite possible that Cato had Caesar and his upcoming governorship in mind when he proposed the only bill, aside from the grain subsidy, he is known to have passed during his tribunate. This piece of legislation aimed to regulate the awarding of triumphs by penalizing false reports about casualties in battle and requiring commanders to testify on oath to the numbers they reported. Such statistics, which factored into the Senate's deliberations, had long been subject to manipulation. Greater accountability suited Cato's views on how the Republic should be managed, of course, and doubtless he intended the bill to do more than curtail Caesar's ambitions, even if that was an important consideration.[26]

Pompey remained Cato's most immediate concern. Although the rout of Nepos and Caesar was a victory, the question remained of what the still immensely powerful commander would do now that he was returning from the east. Rumors circulated that Pompey intended to come to Rome with his army, to extort a consulship for himself, and perhaps more. Crassus spotted an opportunity to discredit his rival and engaged in one of his typical stunts. He gathered his family and money and then "secretly" withdrew from Rome so as to arouse fear over Pompey's intentions. It was good theater. A dispatch sent by Pompey, full of reassurances of his peaceful intentions, did little to quell senators' suspicions.[27]

And so when Pompey sent a request to the Senate to postpone the consular elections of 62 so he could support one of his officers in person, Cato saw a chance to add to Pompey's troubles. The majority of senators were inclined to grant Pompey's request, but Cato persuaded them to reject it. Denying the request was in one sense a small snub, just like a sneer Cato had earlier made that the Mithridatic War had been fought against a bunch of women. The letters and messages Pompey sent proved more than enough to carry the officer to victory. The real point of Cato's intervention was to suggest, once more, that Pompey was hoping to make it to Rome in time to sneak himself into another consulship, at the front of his army.[28]

With Cato as their leader, the champions of senatorial government were operating with a new energy. They basked in victories they had not known since the 70s. A strong Senate could stamp out revolutionary plans for debt cancellation, could thwart a tribune who tried to push through legislation against their wishes, could even trim the expectations of the over-powerful Pompey. Thanks to Cato, *optimates* could hope for more successes still.

After Pompey landed in Italy at the end of 62, he assembled his soldiers, expressed his gratitude and affection for them, and told them to return to their homes until it was time to celebrate his triumph in Rome.[29] For many, the sight of Pompey journeying to Rome with just a few men, unarmed, as if he were returning from an ordinary trip abroad, seemed a miracle. And along with it came an even greater surprise. Divorcing Mucia, Pompey sought a new marriage alliance, this time with Cato. It was an acknowledgment of Cato's power. It also gave the first hint of a realignment of the leading personalities who would ultimately go to war with one another.

CHAPTER 6

DIVORCES AND MARRIAGES

As MUCH AS CAESAR HOPED TO FINISH HIS PRAETORSHIP WITH-
out further trouble and move on to an overseas command,
fortune fancied otherwise. Toward the end of the year 62 BC, the
rumor of sacrilege within Caesar's household put him back on the
defensive and gave Cato an opening.

Among the most mysterious of the many deities worshiped
in Rome was one known as the "Good Goddess," or Bona Dea
in Latin. Every December a nighttime ceremony was held in her
honor at the house of a senior magistrate. The rites were led by the
magistrate's wife, with assistance from the Vestal Virgins and other
leading women of the city. Men were forbidden to participate and
therefore knew only a few details of the rituals: the house was decorated with flowers and vine branches, wine was brought in and
consumed, and there was music and dancing.[1]

In 62 it fell to Caesar's wife, Pompeia, to host the ceremony. The
couple had been married since Caesar's return from Spain in 68,

but as Caesar's affair with Servilia suggests, they appear not to have been close. When the handsome young Publius Clodius, a member of one of Rome's grandest patrician families, began to take an interest in Pompeia, she was receptive. Clodius, who always felt an itch for adventure, decided to disguise himself as a woman and enjoy a tryst with Pompeia at Caesar's house on the night of the ceremony, amid the wine, music, and incense.[2]

Dressed up as a lute girl, Clodius was admitted by a slave of Pompeia who was in on the secret. After the slave went off to fetch her mistress, a maid of Caesar's mother, Aurelia, appeared and invited Clodius to join the revelry. When Clodius started to speak, his voice gave him away. Aurelia's maid let out a loud shriek and ran off, crying, "I've caught a man!" Aurelia immediately put a stop to the ceremony, covered up all the sacred objects, and ordered the doors shut while she searched the house. Clodius, discovered hiding in a slave's bedroom, was driven out.

Unable to complete the rites, the women returned home and told their husbands what had happened. By the next morning, the news was already spreading throughout Rome. Clodius, the women said, had committed sacrilege and owed satisfaction not only to them but also to the gods and the city.

The incident was a great embarrassment for Caesar. Not only was his wife apparently unfaithful to him; her conduct might call into question the sanctity of his own priestly actions. Yet acknowledging it stood to make matters even worse. If Caesar sought retribution from Pompeia and Clodius, he risked giving further air to the scandal, lowering his standing even more. Between his many friends and relatives and his growing popularity among the people, Clodius was a dangerous enemy to acquire. And so Caesar resorted to the politician's classic fallback. He denied any knowledge of what had happened.

It proved impossible, however, to keep the matter out of the Senate, which had ultimate authority in everything to do with the gods. One especially strict senator raised the question of the impiety of the event, and then, as was traditional, the Senate referred it to the Vestals and the college of pontiffs, who pronounced that the occurrence was sacrilege. That was a judgment the senators could not ignore. They voted for the consuls to present a bill to the people that would establish an extraordinary court to formally try Clodius for profanation—the same charge a Vestal faced if she failed to preserve her chastity, the punishment for which was to be entombed alive.[3]

Caesar swiftly sent Pompeia notice of divorce, prompting his and Clodius's enemies to ask whether his action was an acknowledgment that something had happened. Pressed on the point, Caesar responded with one of the all-time bests in political equivocation. He wasn't accusing his wife of anything. He divorced Pompeia, he said, "because I thought my wife should not even be under suspicion."[4]

The prospect of an extraordinary court to try Clodius sparked controversy. Many of the most powerful senators were keen to see Clodius tried and convicted, none more than his former brother-in-law Lucullus, whose army Clodius had led to mutiny years before in Armenia. Joining Lucullus were his close friend Catulus and his kinsman Cato, both of whom would savor the chance to add to Caesar's embarrassment. But the well-connected Clodius also had his supporters, including one of the consuls of 61, Marcus Piso. After having been compelled by the Senate to sponsor the bill, Piso now worked to defeat it.

Coming on the heels of the execution of the Catilinarian conspirators, the senatorial plan to establish a new court—with jurors handpicked by the praetor rather than drawn by the usual method of lottery—could be cast as another unwelcome encroachment of Senate authority. Quite early on, senators started to hesitate over the whole scheme. Only Cato "presses and prods," Cicero wrote in a letter to his good friend Atticus.[5] Clodius himself began organizing crowds to protest, and the fate of the bill grew uncertain.

Voting day for the bill arrived. Consul Piso, in charge of the proceedings, spoke out against the law. Clodius's youthful friends in the nobility, conspicuous because they had embraced a new fashion for wearing neatly trimmed beards, mingled among the crowd and also urged rejection. When the voting tablets were handed out, according to Cicero, there was blatant irregularity. Normally each citizen was given two tablets, one inscribed *V* for "yes" (*Vti rogas*, "as you ask") and the other *A* for "no" (*antiquo*, "I vote for as things are"). Only one was to be dropped into the ballot box. On this occasion, only tablets marked *A* were distributed. "At this, Cato flew onto the Rostra and administered a spectacular beating to the consul Piso—if it was a beating, those words of such solemnity, power, and, in the end, salvation. Our friend Hortensius joined him and many good men besides," wrote Cicero.[6] So upset was he by the irregularities, Cato felt he had to break the law and seize the speakers' platform.

After his intervention, the assembly was shut down and the Senate summoned to meet. At a packed session, Piso once more argued against the bill, and Clodius went down on his knees, pleading with senators. The patrician stirred little sympathy. Only about fifteen voted to withdraw the bill, against a good four hundred on the other side. Cato had Clodius pinned.

Eager to press on with prosecution, Clodius's opponents agreed to a compromise. The extraordinary court would be established, but with jurors drawn in the normal way, by lot, from pools of senators

A citizen drops his ballot into a voting receptacle. This ballot is clearly marked *V* for "yes" (*Vti rogas*, "as you ask"). *Credit: Courtesy of the American Numismatic Society*

and wealthy nonsenators. Thus it would be up to Clodius and his supporters to save his skin by force of argument.

When the trial itself got underway, Clodius's lawyers relied on a simple defense. He had had nothing to do with the Bona Dea, they said. The night of the celebration, he was far from the city, staying at the villa of an equestrian, who offered sworn testimony to that effect.[7]

The prosecution had a much stronger case, backed by formidable witnesses. Lucullus took the stand and told of how Clodius had been caught committing incest with his own sister, Lucullus's ex-wife. That established a pattern of conduct. Cicero came forward with material evidence that broke Clodius's alibi: just three hours before the rites for the Bona Dea began, Clodius had paid a visit to Cicero's house on the Palatine, in Rome. Most damaging of all was Caesar's mother, Aurelia, who gave a full account of the night's events, which was then confirmed by her daughter, Caesar's sister, Julia. Fortunately for Caesar, he was spared from hearing any of the testimony, having left Rome for the command the Senate had finally assigned him in Spain.[8]

Throughout the proceedings Clodius filled the Forum with rowdy supporters who tried to drown out damaging testimony with shouting. The jurors demanded a bodyguard, which the Senate was happy to supply. The request appeared to be a sign that the jurors wanted to convict. In the face of such a flimsy defense and such patent intimidation, how could they not?

Jurors cast their judgments with marked tablets—A for absolvo ("I acquit") or C for condemno ("I condemn"). A simple majority was enough to convict. When the votes were tallied, there were twenty-five for conviction. But for acquittal, thirty-one—a shocking result. As Cicero explained in a letter to Atticus, following the Senate's vote of the bodyguard, a number of jurors had been summoned to secret meetings and offered bribes by a friend of Clodius's. "Then—good gods, the disgrace of it!—nighttime assignations with certain ladies and introductions to noble youths were given to some jurors as a bonus payment."[9]

When Caesar's old foe Catulus ran into one of the jurors, he asked, "Why did you ask us for a guard? Were you afraid that your purses would be snatched?" It is the last known remark of the acidic senator, who died shortly afterward of unrelated causes.[10]

Also furious was Cato, who lived on to continue his fight against Clodius. After the trial, Clodius persisted in appearing at public meetings, at which he denounced the pontiffs and the Vestals. Cato responded with another of his tongue-lashings.[11] In the Senate, Cato got a decree passed authorizing legislation that would make any juror who accepted a bribe liable to public prosecution.[12] Until then, only senators had faced such charges. With the new measure, the nonsenators on the jury, the equestrians, would as well. If he did not actually say it, Cato was implying that the blame for Clodius's acquittal lay not with the jury's senators—four hundred senators had come out against Clodius after all—but with its other members. They must now be held accountable.

The proposal had its merits. Bribery in the courts had been a long-standing problem, and reforms like Cato's had been suggested before, once even by Cato's uncle Livius Drusus. The effort always foundered on the fierce resistance of the financially powerful equestrians. Only men who had entered public life should face the glare of public trials, they said. They did not enjoy any of the pleasures of the highest rank—the magistrate's chair, the fasces, commands, provinces, and priesthoods. Senators sought the honor they had. Equestrians were compelled to serve on juries.[13]

The politics of the proposal were complex. For their part, the equestrians were angered by Cato's proposed law. Had they not stood by the Senate during the Catilinarian conspiracy, only to be insulted like this? As Cicero rightly pointed out, for Cato to alienate this important group just after Clodius's victory—when the Senate needed more support, not less—was imprudent.[14] As opposition to the bill emerged, it faltered and failed to pass.

The Bona Dea affair had all the salaciousness needed for a perfect political scandal: sacrilege, sex, jury tampering, and more. It also encapsulated essential differences between Caesar and Cato that underlay their growing conflict and the outcome of that conflict. Caesar extricated himself from a perplexing situation with skill, placing political considerations above all else. Cato's principled stance throughout the crisis impressed senators, but his actions following Clodius's acquittal overlooked political realities and led to problems for the Senate. An inability to compromise won him the unflagging support of a few but alienated more and fueled partisan struggle.

Cicero rendered a memorable verdict. "As for our friend Cato," he wrote Atticus, "I have as warm a regard for him as you. The fact remains that with all his patriotism and integrity he is sometimes a political liability. He speaks in the Senate as though he were living in Plato's Republic instead of Romulus's cesspool."[15]

Cato was, to put it more starkly, making lots of enemies. Not only was he needling Caesar, Clodius, and the equestrians; at the same time he also found ways to antagonize Pompey. Cato was driving all these men to fish around for new alliances, alliances that he was not going to like.

Pompey had returned to Italy at the end of 62, just as the Bona Dea scandal was breaking. Immediately upon landing, he dismissed his army and thus put an end to the rumors that he was planning to march on Rome. Senators had no choice but to let him celebrate a triumph for his victories over the pirates and Mithridates. When the triumph took place, in September of 61, two days were needed for the victor to parade through Rome all the impressive spoils, among which were the golden throne and scepter of the Pontic king as well as other curiosities from the royal collection, such as a gigantic gaming board made of precious gemstones. Pompey, who celebrated his forty-fifth birthday on the second day of the celebration, rode in a special jewel-encrusted chariot and is even said to have worn a cloak that had once belonged to Alexander the Great.[16]

The challenge Pompey faced was in gaining approval in the Senate for the administrative arrangements he had made in the east, and in having farmlands awarded to his veterans in recognition of their service. Lucullus seethed with resentment at how Pompey had usurped command in the Mithridatic War and how Pompey's allies had managed to delay Lucullus's triumph until 63. Though more inclined to wallow in one of his sumptuous villas, Lucullus could be counted on to return to the Senate and try to settle the score.[17]

And he would be joined by his kinsman Cato. Cato could never pass up a chance to cut Pompey down to size, but larger issues were involved. Traditionally after a major war ended, the Senate sent its own commission to settle the region. This time, Pompey had insisted on doing everything himself. To wave the whole settlement through the Senate would set a terrible precedent, especially when vast amounts of money were at stake. It could lead to future commanders taking measures to benefit only themselves, not the people. Pompey's arrangements, Cato felt, should be combed through as carefully as the lowliest scribe's ledger.

Pompey had anticipated trouble and formed a plan to win over his opponents. Shortly before landing in Italy, he had divorced his wife of seventeen years, the mother of his three children, Mucia. There were reports that she had been unfaithful during his long absence. Pompey apparently believed so and went so far as to refer to the alleged seducer—Caesar—as "Aegisthus," the Greek who had taken up with King Agamemnon's wife, Clytemnestra, while Agamemnon was off fighting the Trojan War.[18] Infidelity was an acceptable, though not automatic, reason for ending the marriage, but it was not Pompey's only consideration. The divorce was also to be understood as a break with Mucia's relatives, especially her half brother Metellus Nepos, who had so spectacularly repudiated the Senate's authority in the final days of the Catilinarian conspiracy.

Marriage and politics could rarely, if ever, be separated in the lives of senatorial families. While it was agreed that marriage could bring great happiness to wife and husband, the couple themselves and their relatives could not overlook the assets and liabilities a spouse brought to the grueling business of politics. Marriage announced an alliance of a couple and their families—and divorce, a split, sometimes acrimonious. Ancient writers, almost all male, can sometimes make it seem as if women were simply pawns in men's political games, but reality was more complicated. Girls could indeed be married at a young age, with little if any real choice. Fathers enjoyed legal authority over daughters (as they did over sons). But women could make choices about how much to support a husband and his family as opposed to her own. Women could initiate divorce. Older women helped to arrange marriages for the younger generation, and in that way they also shaped political outcomes.[19]

After Pompey's divorce from Mucia, his next step was to send for Cato's close friend Munatius and have him relay a marriage proposal. According to one version of events, it was Cato's two nieces, almost certainly the daughters of Servilia, whom Pompey sought, the elder one for himself, and the younger for his own son. The alternative story says that Pompey sought Cato's own daughters. Both accounts might be true, or some combination of them. The particular bride did not matter at this point in the matchmaking. It was Cato whom Pompey was wooing.[20]

Munatius reported Pompey's interest not just to Cato but also to Servilia and other women of the family—which suggests the importance of their role—and the women are said to have been enthusiastic. An alliance with the returning hero would increase the family's power, and Servilia might even have hoped to reconcile her brother and Pompey, not merely for her own and her family's sake but for Rome's. Cato would not listen and sent a response to Pompey that would be sure to end the matter at once: "Go, Munatius, go, and tell Pompey that Cato is not to be captured through the women's quarters, though he does appreciate Pompey's goodwill and, if Pompey acts justly, will grant him a friendship more secure than any connection by marriage."[21] These words are almost certainly a paraphrase, but their bluntness is pure Cato: if Pompey wanted the respect of the good men, he should try acting like one.

Whatever Cato said about higher friendship, the truth is that he did use marriage alliances to bind men closer to him. It is no coincidence that a list of Cato's in-laws is practically a who's who of *optimates*. There was Lucullus, married to the daughter of Cato's beloved late brother, Caepio. There was Lucius Domitius Ahenobarbus, a prominent noble who was to become one of Caesar's fiercest opponents in the 50s—married to Cato's sister. There was Marcus Calpurnius Bibulus, Caesar's disgruntled colleague in the aedileship—married to Cato's eldest daughter, Porcia.

Even stronger proof of Cato's propensities comes from his bizarre relations with his second wife. His first wife, Atilia, he had divorced after discovering she had been unfaithful. He then married Marcia, a much younger woman from a far more prominent noble family (her father would be consul in 56 BC). Marcia bore two children to Cato in quick succession, even as his daughter from his first marriage, Porcia, began having children of her own. Cato's close friend, one of the staunchest *optimates*, Quintus Hortensius, could not help but notice both women's fertility. Eager for a new heir after a falling out with his son, Hortensius came to Cato and asked for the hand of Porcia. Cato replied that while he admired Hortensius, he thought the proposal out of place. Hortensius then asked Cato for Marcia herself, even though she was pregnant at the time with a third child for Cato. Cato, when he saw Hortensius's enthusiasm, did not object, but he did make sure to say that Marcia's father, Philippus, must approve. Cato did not wish to lose the goodwill of Philippus, who, when approached, did consent. What Marcia herself thought goes unrecorded; legally her consent was required.[22]

Inevitably, the divorce of Cato's young, pregnant wife became a source of gossip, later made only worse when, after Hortensius's death, Marcia and Cato remarried. Caesar happily dredged up the whole story in his *Anticato*, a long and catty pamphlet he wrote following Cato's death denouncing his old enemy. The only explanation for Cato's strange behavior, Caesar said, was that Cato was secretly trying to get Hortensius's immense fortune through Marcia. This is unlikely, though money was perhaps a consideration for Marcia and her father. What Cato really gained was a stronger alliance with Hortensius, without losing Philippus.

In the light of general practice among the nobility as well as Cato's own proclivities, then, Pompey's hope of a marriage alliance with Cato made sense. Unfortunately for him, he was rebuffed, and he made little progress on having his eastern arrangements approved in 61. The Senate was consumed by the Bona Dea scandal, and the consul on whom Pompey had counted for support, Piso, lost credibility with many of the senators by intervening on Clodius's behalf.

Pompey needed a consul he could depend on for the following year and settled on a fiercely loyal officer of his, Lucius Afranius. A new man lacking name recognition and connections, Afranius would struggle to get votes, but, as Cicero wrote to Atticus, Pompey was able to rely on "those means by which Philip [King of Macedon] used to say that all fortresses could be stormed, so long as an ass weighed down with gold could enter them."[23] True to form, Cato was disgusted by the bribery, as was Servilia: if Pompey could buy elections for a new man, what would happen to the nobility? When word got out that Consul Piso himself was keeping agents at his house to distribute bribes, Cato and his brother-in-law Domitius Ahenobarbus pushed through two Senate decrees, one permitting searches of magistrates' houses and the other making it an offense against the Republic to have distributing agents at one's house.

Afranius was elected anyway. Cato seems to have made no effort to prosecute him, perhaps foreseeing that Afranius would be of no use to Pompey: a strong soldier, Afranius had little skill in political infighting and preferred to spend his time in Rome dancing at parties. The decrees served their purpose in providing new tools to fight corruption and in publicizing Pompey's underhanded tactics.[24]

Cato and his allies easily outmaneuvered the new consul. At first, Cato blocked discussion by dragging out debate on another matter. The corporation in charge of collecting the taxes of Asia, a powerful equestrian interest, after realizing that it had overbid on its contract, had come begging the Senate to renegotiate. A majority of senators were prepared to work out a compromise, but Cato was determined to stop them. A favorite tactic of his was to ask the presiding consul to recognize him and then to speak until sundown, after which no valid decrees could be passed.[25] For several months he carried on in this way, and finally the equestrians gave up.

When Pompey's arrangements did come up for discussion, Lucullus appeared in the Senate to demand that the acts be reviewed one by one. Nobody knew exactly what the arrangements entailed, Lucullus told the senators, and it was wrong to confirm them with a single vote, as if Pompey were their master. Cato enthusiastically supported Lucullus, as did the other consul elected alongside Afranius for the year 60, Metellus Celer. Half brother of Mucia, Celer bitterly resented Pompey's treatment of her.

Getting nowhere in the Senate, Pompey turned to the Plebeian Assembly. His first hope was to get a bill passed to distribute land in Italy, paid for by the influx of wealth his campaigns had brought to the Treasury. A friendly tribune, Lucius Flavius, proposed the legislation, which also set aside additional lands for members of the urban poor. Including the urban poor addressed the growing crowding and discontent in the city—while also, of course, increasing the chances that the bill would pass. The assembly might then go on to ratify all of Pompey's eastern settlement, taking it out of the Senate's hands. Led by Cato and Metellus Celer, the Senate expressed strong opposition to the agrarian law. However much the land distribution might help citizens, a majority of senators accepted the view that it was just a scheme to enhance Pompey's power.

Celer contested every point of the law with Tribune Flavius and attacked so persistently that Flavius exercised a traditional right to have the consul imprisoned. Celer then summoned the whole Senate to meet in the jail. To block anyone from entering, the tribune placed his bench at the doorway and sat on it. Celer ordered the wall of the jail cut open to allow in senators. It was the theater of power at its best, embodying not just the clash of two magistrates but also larger disputes that Cato had done much to inflame over the preceding few years as the champion of inflexibility.

Embarrassed by the whole spectacle, Pompey instructed Flavius to release Celer, and he ultimately dropped the legislative proposal. The divorce of Mucia, far from solving Pompey's political problems, had only worsened them. Frantically he cast about for new allies, and by June of 60 an excellent prospect was due back in Rome, his reputation enhanced by military success: Caesar.

While politicians in Rome squabbled over the Asian tax contract and Pompey's eastern arrangements, Caesar had been hard at work in Further Spain, the province he had been assigned by the Senate as the second stage of his praetorship. Raising a legion in addition to the two that were already there, he marched to the craggy mountains of central Portugal, from where (or so Caesar claimed anyway) bandits had been launching raids on more settled agricultural communities in the plains. The hill peoples promptly took up arms, and Caesar had his pretext for war. After he defeated them in battle, some of their neighbors, fearing they would be the next victims of the Romans, fled across the Douro River, and soon Caesar was at war with them too. Refusing the temptation of the cattle the hill peoples had left behind—they were valuable plunder, hard for a Roman army to resist—Caesar again attacked and won.[26]

He chased the enemy all the way to shores of the Atlantic, where they escaped to an offshore island. With only a few ships at his disposal, Caesar appeared to be stuck. He put together some rafts and had some troops cross over, but when their commanding officer's ship was carried away by the strong tide of ocean, they were cut off. All the soldiers died fighting, except one who managed to swim away. Caesar had to summon a fleet from Gades, the great maritime city where he had earlier spent time as quaestor and had powerful connections. After the fleet arrived, he crossed to the island, swiftly reduced the enemy, and then sailed along the rugged coastline of northwestern Iberia all the way to Callaecia (modern Galicia), where he demanded submission from peoples never before ruled by Rome.

Caesar had shown military flair. He had also proved his talents as an administrator. After the campaigning season concluded, he resolved a debt crisis that had been engulfing his province for years, caused, at least in part, by heavy taxation imposed by Rome. For his effort, he won a reputation in Spain that would prove useful to him later in his career.

In traveling to the edges of the known world, Caesar had moved a step closer to fulfilling his own ambitions to win a consulship and become a great man in Rome, Pompey-style. So lucrative was the Spanish war that he had funds to pay off his creditors. And so substantial were his victories that his soldiers hailed him as imperator. The title, which can be translated as "victorious general," was a signal to the Senate that Caesar's accomplishments were worthy of a triumphal procession.

Yet just as Pompey had discovered, a laurel wreath did not spare you the politics of the capital. The Senate agreed with Caesar's army that he had merited a triumph, which meant he had to wait outside the city gates until all the preparations were ready, including the muster of his troops, who would parade with him. The hitch was that Caesar also wished to stand in the consular elections of 60 BC. That required declaring his candidacy in person in the Forum—and the deadline fell before Caesar's triumph would be ready. If Caesar wanted the triumph, he had to postpone the consulship for a year.

Cato and his allies in the Senate sought to create, or at least contribute to, this painful choice. Just before the candidates had to declare, Caesar sent a request to the Senate that he be allowed to do so through a proxy. While a majority of the senators were willing to honor the request, Cato would not allow it and stood speaking until sunset, making it impossible to pass a binding decree.[27]

Time had run out for Caesar. Judging the consulship worth far more than the triumph, he crossed into the city and declared himself in the usual way. There was little doubt he would win, and so the real question became who would serve with him. The other two candidates were Lucius Lucceius and Caesar's old antagonist Cato's son-in-law Bibulus. Lucceius had far less influence than Caesar but lots of money, and so Caesar made a pact with him: they would run jointly, with Caesar offering his endorsement of Lucceius and Lucceius distributing bribes on behalf of Caesar. Concerned about what Caesar might achieve with a complaisant colleague, the *optimates* authorized Bibulus to promise the same amount to supporters. Cato winced but agreed that under the circumstances bribery was for the good of the Republic.[28]

On polling day Bibulus squeezed out Lucceius and secured the consulship alongside Caesar. That meant trouble for Caesar, since one consul had the prerogative to block the actions of the other. On top of that, the Senate had preassigned the incoming consuls commands of minor importance to take up after their year of service in Rome. There would be no second chance for a triumph.[29]

Cato and the Senate were frustrating Caesar, just as they had obstructed Pompey before him, with deleterious consequences for ordinary citizens waiting for land distribution. However much Pompey groaned about "Aegisthus," it was nearly inevitable that the two would resume their former partnership. With typical boldness, Caesar went further. It was not just he and Pompey who needed to overcome senatorial opposition. There was Crassus. He had been a strong backer of the corporation in charge of collecting Asian taxes that had been so desperate to renegotiate its contract. (While, as so often with Crassus's affairs, the details are obscure, it seems likely that he was a silent partner in the company.) Crassus stood to lose credibility, and probably cash too. When Caesar approached him and suggested he reconcile with his old rival Pompey, he agreed. The three men made a pact not to harm each other's interests and to cooperate on getting what they each wanted.[30]

Although he had been unsuccessful in convicting Clodius in the Bona Dea affair, in the year or so since those events Cato had come close to running the Republic by his mastery of the Senate. Through vigorous oratory and a manipulation of senatorial procedures, he won key votes and delayed others on such matters as new bribery legislation and Pompey's eastern settlement. So distinctive was his approach that younger senators started to emulate it. Cicero went so far as to call one of the youths a "pseudo-Cato" and another an "imitator."[31] Closest of all to Cato was Senator Marcus Favonius, who tried to outdo even Cato in rudeness. Pompey—either to cover a wound or simply to be fashionable—had taken to wearing white leggings. "It doesn't matter on what part of your body you have your diadem," Favonius said caustically, referring to the headbands eastern kings wore to denote their power.[32]

Together with his friends and kinsmen, Cato was a formidable force. In the eyes of Caesar, stopping Cato was so vital that he proposed the triple alliance with Pompey and Crassus. Despite old as well as recent resentments and rivalries among the three, Cato had driven them into partnership. With their popular favor, with their individual relationships with senators and equestrians, with Pompey's impatient veterans ready to exert influence, they would be able to overwhelm the *optimates*. Only Pompey, who despite his cold treatment by the leading nobles still sought their acceptance, would hesitate.

And when Pompey did, Caesar took up one of Cato's favorite weapons. He promptly broke off the engagement of his daughter,

Julia—his only child, from his beloved first wife, Cornelia—and betrothed her to Pompey. "It was unbearable, Cato shouted out; the men were pimping out the empire in marriage alliances; they were helping one another to provinces, armies, and powers—and using females to do it."[33] There was truth to that but also potentially a consolation for Cato: with alliances sealed by marriages of convenience, there would be more bids for power to come.

CHAPTER 7

THE CONSULSHIP OF JULIUS AND CAESAR

A ROMAN MAGISTRATE COULD ENTER OFFICE ONLY WITH DIVINE approval. On the first day of his term of office—January 1 for consuls—he was to be up at dawn and out of the house so that under the open sky he could seek a sign of Jupiter's sanction. Typically a reliable assistant was on hand to report the sort of lightning strike considered most favorable. Still, there was always a chance that something would go wrong, and that Jupiter might even give an adverse omen, such as a loud clap of thunder.

It was a ceremony of the greatest importance. If the gods were opposed to an action, it was believed, they would make it known. For any deed the magistrate would undertake while in power—whether calling an assembly, holding a Senate meeting, or fighting a battle—he would need to seek Jupiter's approval by watching for signs, what the Romans called auspices. If the auspices were un-favorable, the only option was to wait until the next day and try again. An adverse portent on the first day in office, however, was deemed something far worse: a bad omen not just for the day but for the whole year. It was a sign that the incoming magistrate should not be entrusted with the auspices.[1]

So far as is known, Caesar's first auspices were positive. After he secured them, custom dictated that he go back to his house and, dressed in the purple-bordered toga that consuls were privileged to wear, receive friends and supporters. With them and his lictors, he processed through the Forum and up the Capitoline Hill to the great sanctuary of Jupiter. There he and his colleague Bibulus each sacrificed a young white ox and offered a prayer for the welfare of the Republic. A Senate meeting in the Temple of Jupiter followed.

It was probably at this meeting, or otherwise still early in the year, that Caesar informed the senators that he intended to pass legislation distributing land to citizens. In the recent wars in the east, Pompey had captured a great haul of plunder and also had established new taxes that would bring in a stream of income. It would therefore be possible to purchase privately owned land and also to parcel out some publicly held lands, the rents from which were no longer needed. As Caesar said, it was only right that wealth won by the dangers incurred by citizens should be spent on citizens. And not only those who had toiled in the campaigns would benefit. The swelling population of the city of Rome would be eligible for land too.[2]

This was an ambitious bill. If passed, it would have far-reaching effects. Tens of thousands of ordinary citizens stood to gain farms that, though small, could provide families steady subsistence and dignity. To own land gave you honor in Rome, and this legislation would distribute honor far and wide.

Cato balked. It wasn't so much the land distribution itself that worried him, but what Pompey and Caesar would do with the power the bill gave them. What payback might they demand later? he wondered.

Previous land bills had often failed to gain the customary senate authorization and as a result died. Caesar was careful to avoid obviously objectionable measures. In the list of public lands to be distributed, he excluded the especially fertile Campanian territory, since many senators thought it should not be relinquished. Another stipulation was that land should be purchased only from those willing to sell, and only at its previously assessed value; there was to be no profiteering. The commission in charge would consist not of a few men handpicked by Caesar but of twenty chosen by election, and Caesar himself would be ineligible to serve. He would be satisfied with proposing the legislation, he said.

Caesar had the bill read out in the Senate and then called on the senators one by one to ask if they had any criticisms. Any clause not to their liking, he said, he would alter or even strike out altogether. Nobody asked for a change. Not even Cato could find a fault. Even so, Cato was determined to stop the law. His best hope was to delay voting long enough to wear down support. And so he demanded the floor and began one of his interminable speeches, in which he warned about the dangers of upsetting current arrangements.

Caesar was not about to let Cato talk away the land legislation as he had the Spanish triumph. Caesar had given Pompey his promise to help Pompey's veterans. Furthermore, Caesar saw his own standing and the people's at risk. As Cato droned on, Caesar summoned an attendant and ordered Cato to be taken to jail. A consul had the right to temporarily imprison somebody who obstructed his exercise of power—a man blocking the consul's way on the street, for instance. Caesar's action was more extreme.

Cato made little protest, knowing that this sort of overreach from Caesar was sure to win him some sympathy from fellow senators and perhaps ordinary citizens too. As the attendant started to drag Cato off, a number of senators followed him. When Caesar rebuked one of them for leaving before the meeting had been dismissed, the senator replied, "I prefer to be with Cato in prison rather than with you here."[3]

It was already clear that this incident might end up favoring Cato, so Caesar stepped back, ordering Cato to be released and then adjourning the meeting. He reminded the senators that they had been given a chance to change anything in the law before it went to the assembly, "but since you refuse to pass a preliminary decree, the people shall decide for themselves."

Caesar next went to the Tribal Assembly, a near twin of the Plebeian Assembly except that it included all citizens, patricians as well as plebeians, and consuls could preside over it. After submitting the bill, he began hosting the public meetings that were a typical part of the mandatory review period before voting. This was a chance to rally support and weaken the opposition. Caesar first called Bibulus to the Rostra and asked if he disapproved of any of the law's provisions. Bibulus echoed his father-in-law Cato's stance in the Senate and said that he refused to tolerate any innovations during his year in office.

Caesar urged his colleague to reconsider and coaxed the crowd to join in. He shouted out to the citizens, "You shall have the law, if only he is willing."

Bibulus roared back, "You shall not have this law this year, not even if you all are willing," and then stormed off.

Next Caesar called up Pompey and Crassus—the first sign the public had that the old rivals had reconciled and were both cooperating with Caesar. Pompey was glad to address the citizens and began by reminding them that, years before, the Senate had approved land for the soldiers but a lack of funds had prevented distribution. "Now," he pointed out, "the treasury has become very rich through me."

Pompey then went through the law detail by detail and approved everything in it. As the crowd cheered on the general, Caesar asked him if he would help defeat the opposition—and once again Caesar urged the people to join his request. Pompey was elated. "If anyone dares to take up a sword," he said, "I also will take up my shield." Crassus nodded his approval.

The words were not just a metaphor. Pompey, Caesar, and Crassus were signaling that if opposition persisted, it would be overcome by force. And Pompey's veterans, direct beneficiaries of the bill, would stand with him. There was not to be a repetition of the rout Caesar and Metellus Nepos had suffered at the start of 62, when they had failed to control the assembly long enough to pass their proposed legislation on the command for Pompey.

A showdown on voting day was looming, and Bibulus prepared three tribunes to interpose their vetoes persistently, just as Cato had in the fight with Metellus Nepos. Before it came to that, there were other tactics for the *optimates* to try. As consul, Bibulus had the authority to schedule feasts and thanksgivings for the gods that did not occupy a set date in the calendar. These celebrations made it impossible for the assembly to meet, and so by stacking them up one after the next, Bibulus could delay voting.[4]

Caesar refused to adhere to his colleague's schedule and set a day for voting. But his opponents had another, even more powerful, weapon: the all-important auspices. As the presiding magistrate, Caesar would take them the day he intended to pass his law. Yet it was also the custom that, if another magistrate happened to notice an inauspicious sign, he would report it to the presiding magistrate before the assembly convened, and no voting would take place that day: Jupiter did not approve.[5]

The night before the planned meeting, Caesar occupied the Forum with his supporters, some armed. By the time Bibulus arrived with his lictors as well as the three tribunes and Cato, Caesar was already speaking at the Temple of Castor. Bibulus forced his way over to the temple and onto the podium. Before he could report an inauspicious sign or say anything else, he was thrust back down the steps. His fasces were broken to pieces, and a bucket of shit was dumped all over him. Two of the tribunes with him were wounded, and he ended up seeking refuge in a nearby temple. Only Cato tried to make it back onto the temple platform to denounce the illegality of what was happening, but when he did so he was lifted up and carried away by Caesar's men. Voting began, and the law was passed.

The opposition's hope now lay in the Senate. The day after the assembly, Bibulus called the senators to an emergency session. Yet neither he nor Cato could win any support for action against Caesar. Not only had yesterday's violence been intimidating. Even more bone-chilling was the alliance of Caesar, Pompey, and Crassus. Senators who spoke out had to fear political or even financial retribution.

In addition, Caesar had included in the final version of the law a clause requiring all senators to swear to uphold it. Any who failed to do so faced severe penalties, including exile. Almost everybody took the oath, remembering how, years earlier, a tribune friendly with Marius had used a similar provision to banish a prominent senator. Cato's friends and family members begged him to comply, but he struggled. To swear obedience was to admit defeat, even to become the slave of Caesar. Yet to go into exile would leave Rome defenseless. Cato in the end yielded and was the last to take the oath except for his friend Favonius.

Caesar had, it seemed, brought Cato and his friends to their knees. Bibulus retired to his house and would not appear in public again for the rest of the year.[6] The three tribunes loyal to him stopped carrying out their duties. And most shockingly, Cato stayed away from the Senate, in contrast to his usual zealous attendance. The boycott was intended to increase the opprobrium of Caesar's mistreatment of his fellow magistrates—although Caesar himself probably just laughed.

The dispute over land distribution was a dangerous escalation of the feud between Caesar and Cato—dangerous because people had been hurt, and because new, more bitter grievances had arisen. In the ferocity of battle, each side had responded to the other by adopting increasingly devastating strategies. Cato and his friends' mulish resistance had served as a justification for Caesar and Pompey to use violence. Extreme partisanship had revealed its perilous potential.

In addition, changes to political structures increased the likelihood of future clashes. By making the position of consul far more independent from the Senate than it had ever been, Caesar eroded the ability of the Senate to adjudicate future disputes. And yet the chain reaction of partisanship was not the creation of one politician alone. Cato's obstruction and boycotts were in their own way revolutionary and damaging, both inciting Caesar's escalation and precluding any alternative solution.[7] In trying to throttle Caesar, Cato had throttled compromise, an essential feature of politics. Both sides had reasons for what they were doing, but together they were undermining the Republic.

With the opposition at bay, a flurry of further legislation to benefit Caesar and his two allies was passed. For Crassus, the corporation in charge of collecting taxes in Asia finally had its liability reduced—by a full one-third. For Pompey, on top of the agrarian legislation, all of his treaties with the cities and kingdoms of the east were ratified. Caesar did not bother to consult the Senate on any of them. More and more, it was said, he looked less like a consul than like the most radical tribune of the plebs; he wasn't so much passing legislation as waving it through.[8]

To help get all of this done, he relied on one of the year's tribunes, Vatinius, who was among the toughest politicians ever produced by Rome. Slightly crippled, he also suffered from a bad case of scrofula that caused large swellings on his neck. He was endlessly mocked. Once, the story went, when he was giving a show of gladiators and some stones were thrown at him, the aediles declared he should only be pelted with fruit. A spectator asked a distinguished lawyer in attendance whether a pine cone was fruit, and the lawyer ruled that it was if it was thrown at Vatinius.[9]

The abuse he endured only made Vatinius more unpliable. In the very first days of his tribunate, in December of 60 BC, he brazenly told the Senate that he would not let any pronouncements of the augurs stand in the way of his plans. The augurs ruled on all things having to do with the auspices, and so this is a hint that Vatinius foresaw at least some of the moves Bibulus and Cato would make and was ready to fight them. It was Vatinius who controlled the Forum for Caesar on the day the agrarian bill was passed, and quite possibly Vatinius who suggested the finishing touch of the bucket of shit. Vatinius had even tried, unsuccessfully, to drag Bibulus into prison that day but was blocked by the other tribunes. It was convenient for Caesar to get Vatinius to do his dirtiest work for him, while Vatinius in exchange was given a free hand to pursue his own schemes. Vatinius did nothing in his tribunate gratis, Caesar later remarked.[10]

The goals that Pompey and Crassus had each brought to the pact had been fulfilled. It was now time for Caesar to look after himself, with help from Vatinius. Thanks to a Senate decree passed at the insistence of the *optimates* the previous year, Caesar had been assigned a trivial province after his year in office: police duty in Italy. It offered no chance for the glory Caesar had dreamt of since boyhood. He wouldn't even qualify for a regular triumph.

And so Vatinius introduced legislation that would grant Caesar an extraordinary command, similar to those Pompey had received against the pirates and then Mithridates. For five years Caesar would govern the province of Cisalpine Gaul, in northern Italy, as well as Illyricum, just across the Adriatic. He would be provided with three legions and the funds to maintain them. And he could choose whichever officers he wished to serve on his staff—without the customary Senate approval.[11]

While Illyricum offered possibilities for military campaigning, the real significance of the historic legislation lay in the assignment of Cisalpine Gaul. It encompassed some of the most productive land in Italy, yielding bumper crops of grain as well as wine produced in such abundance it had to be stored in wooden jars almost as big as houses. Many fine recruits for the army came from these prosperous lands, and Caesar would be able to enroll them in his legions. And these troops would be in proximity to Rome. The illegality of Caesar's first months in office had made it clear he would be vulnerable.

If Cato tried to ruin him, for instance by putting him on trial, not only would he have the immunity from prosecution that commanders in the field generally enjoyed; he would have an army in Italy.

Cisalpine Gaul mattered for other important reasons. Many in the area, especially north of the Po River, still lacked Roman citizenship. As governor for five years, Caesar would be able to fulfill earlier plans of his and Crassus's to extend the franchise and secure a powerful block of voters in future elections. Each winter, after the year's military campaigning season, Caesar could cultivate citizens in the area, new and old alike, while also meeting with senators visiting from Rome.[12]

Being in Cisalpine Gaul would let Caesar stay in touch with the capital and sway politics there; furthermore, the area also faced the other Gallic province, Transalpine Gaul, which lay across the Alps. Vatinius's law did not assign that region to Caesar, but almost certainly Caesar intended to acquire it when the opportunity presented itself. Transalpine Gaul had seen fighting in recent years, and a flare-up of trouble could be expected. It would be only natural for Caesar, with his legions stationed in northern Italy, to have his command extended over the mountains.

Caesar's critics foresaw the potential this command had to swell Caesar's power and wealth, but they had no way to stop the bill. Not a tribunician veto, not a decree from the Senate, not a magistrate's report of an adverse sign would deter Vatinius. All Cato could do was issue a typically harsh warning to citizens stating that "by their own votes, they were themselves installing the tyrant in the citadel."[13]

Although Bibulus had retreated to his house, he had not entirely surrendered. As consul, he could still watch the skies, and he did. Every morning that Caesar planned to transact business, Bibulus sent a messenger to report an adverse omen.[14] Normally a magistrate submitted such reports in person, and so it was unclear if

Bibulus's notices had validity. Caesar ignored them all. But neglect of the gods made Romans nervous, and Bibulus was thereby able to increase unease concerning Caesar's actions. Once again, partisan war forged a dangerous new weapon.

Bibulus also issued a stream of edicts berating Caesar and his allies. Cicero characterized them as "Archilochian," after the Greek poet renowned for his vicious attacks. Of course Bibulus dragged up the Nicomedes affair, but with a sinister twist: whereas Caesar had once lusted for a king, now he lusted for kingship. Another charge held that shortly before Caesar had entered his aedileship back in 65 BC, he had formed a conspiracy with Crassus to enter the Senate at the start of the new year and carry out a massacre, with Crassus then to assume the dictatorship. Romans crowded the streets whenever a new edict from Bibulus was posted, fascinated by their lurid contents.[15]

Bibulus's aggressive pronouncements caught the mood of a growing number of senators who were outraged at how three men seemed to have taken over the whole Republic. They were acting like tyrants, ramming laws through the assembly, handing out eastern kingdoms as if they were personal gifts, disregarding the auspices, demanding oaths. There was even talk, when a vacancy in the college of augurs opened, that it would go to Vatinius. Cicero for one groaned with disgust imagining the special robe worn by the priests draped over the tribune's scrofulous tumors.[16]

Cato still made protests in public but the great political run he had enjoyed for a couple of years had come to an end. Foes of Caesar and Pompey started to look with greater hope to a bold young noble, Scribonius Curio. Curio had a natural gift for oratory, as even Cicero—who sniffed about the youth's lack of instruction—conceded. Seemingly without effort Curio could pound his opponents with a barrage of attacks, and he relished the publicity he won for it. He and his high-spirited friends, who included Clodius, enjoyed mixing in the Forum, where their sharp dress and fashionable beards attracted admiration.[17] Gleefully they fanned the murmurs of protest they heard. This wasn't the consulship of Bibulus and Caesar, it was grimly joked, but of Julius and Caesar.[18]

The wheel of politics was turning full circle, suggested Cicero, who was vacationing at his several villas in southern Italy, in an April letter to Atticus. Through "Cato's fault" the Senate and its leaders had lost favor, but now support was coming back through "the shamelessness" of those in charge.[19] The assessment was somewhat wishful, but a reaction was setting in against Caesar and his two allies, and Pompey especially did not care for the abuse.

Cicero mused that Pompey would grow more violent when he realized just how hated he was, but in fact Pompey was likelier to extend olive branches to the Senate now that he had secured his goals. And for Caesar, that possibility was more ominous than any of Bibulus's reports. If Pompey could be reconciled with the *optimates*, a deal might be struck to annul the year's legislation on grounds that it had been passed illegally, and then to reenact the measures in a way that undercut Caesar. For all his success over the preceding few months, Caesar's immediate position was starting to look dangerous.

It was time to counterattack, and as so often in his later military career, Caesar did so with speed and surprise. His daughter, Julia, was shortly to be married to a young man named Servilius Caepio, probably a distant relative of Servilia. In the struggles with Bibulus over the last few months, Caepio had faithfully helped his future father-in-law, but Caesar now called off the betrothal and arranged for Julia to marry Pompey. Caepio, of course, was disappointed, and to appease him Pompey offered his own daughter in exchange. It is unclear if Caepio accepted, but it hardly mattered. Caesar had secured the far greater prize of lasting goodwill from Pompey, who quickly became enchanted with his young bride.[20]

Cicero was shocked. The political wheel had already turned once in the last few months, and with this "sudden marriage alliance" Cicero saw that it was already lurching again. Caesar and Pompey were closer than ever. Caesar even started calling on Pompey to give his opinion first in the Senate, although he had been in the habit of beginning with Crassus. A defection by Pompey seemed far less likely now.[21]

Father and son-in-law pushed through with new projects. Caesar introduced a second agrarian bill, making available for distribution the fertile Campanian territory, which had been excluded before. Perhaps the program of purchasing land was proving too time consuming or expensive. Many citizens must have been elated.

In the Senate, Pompey proposed that Transalpine Gaul be added to Caesar's province, with command of an additional legion. The current governor apparently was Metellus Celer, but he had never actually left for the province and then died unexpectedly, a bad loss for the *optimates*. But there was no point in putting up a fight in the Senate over the province. The assembly would give it to Caesar if the senators refused, and likely on more generous terms.[22]

Caesar gloated in his victory. A few days after the vote, in a packed meeting of the Senate, he bragged, "Against the wishes of my enemies and over their moans, I got what I longed for. From now on, I will mount all of their heads." He meant they would have to perform oral sex. It was a very Roman taunt—but an extraordinary one to use in the Senate. Along with the bending and breaking of institutions, another consequence of the escalating partisanship was a willingness to hurl insults that would be hard to forgive.

In response to Caesar's vicious remark, one senator shot back that what Caesar proposed "would not be easy for a woman." To which Caesar replied, "In Syria, Semiramis was queen and the Amazons once held sway over a large part of Asia."[23] To be dominated by a woman: the notion only added humiliation to the senators' defeat.

The marriage alliance with Pompey did not address all of Caesar's problems by any means. There was a danger that magistrates hostile to his interests would be elected for the following year and would find a way to rescind the Gallic command. And so Caesar took

further precautions. In his second installment of agrarian legislation, he included another mandatory oath: any candidate running
for office had to swear to uphold Caesar's land laws. All but one
did, a principled man who preferred to give up his candidacy for the
tribunate.[24]

Another marriage alliance helped to solidify Caesar's position
further. Among the candidates for the consulship for 58 BC was
Lucius Calpurnius Piso, member of a distinguished noble family.
Unmarried since his divorce from Pompeia in the Bona Dea scandal, Caesar now gained the hand of Piso's daughter Calpurnia, a
highly cultivated woman who enjoyed Epicurean philosophy. Piso
would be pledged to uphold Caesar's interests, if elected, and in exchange would gain help from Pompey, Caesar, and their allies in
obtaining what he wanted, a plum provincial command. In vain
Cato fumed that the Roman empire was being bargained away in
marriage alliances.[25]

Cato was not entirely wrong. Although Pompey and Julia did
go on to enjoy great love together, these marriages were contracted
for quite naked political reasons. For love, Caesar might have married Servilia, whose husband, Silanus, had almost certainly recently
died. But doing so would give little to Caesar politically; Servilia
was not going to bring Cato and the others to Caesar's side. Also,
she was just past the age of forty, too old to be regarded as likely to
give Caesar the son he still must have hoped for. Like other Roman women at that stage of life, she would never remarry. Yet she
and Caesar stayed close, and probably at the time of his marriage
to Calpurnia he gave Servilia as compensation a pearl said to have
been worth a staggering 6 million sesterces.[26]

As the elections, scheduled for July, approached, the *optimates*
and their allies poured abuse on Caesar and Pompey especially. Curio received hearty rounds of applause in the theater and flatter-
ing attention in the Forum. Still shut in at his house, watching the
skies, Bibulus pumped out his salacious edicts. Whenever one was
posted, wrote Cicero, who was back in Rome, so many crowded

round to read it, there was a traffic jam. "Nothing is so popular now," Cicero insisted, "as hatred of *populares*."[27]

Resentment of the new regime was clearest at the games, Cicero said. When Caesar entered the theater, hardly a hand clapped. When young Curio came in next, there was the sort of ovation that Pompey used to get, "when the Republic was intact."[28] Still, after the games, Bibulus issued an edict postponing the elections to October. This suggests that the *optimates* had some doubt about how the vote would go if it were held on schedule. Pompey and Caesar were incensed. Pompey stepped onto the Rostra to complain about the "Archilochian edicts" in a speech Cicero judged pathetic. A more aggressive Caesar tried to stir a crowd in the Forum to go with him to Bibulus's house but failed.[29]

With more time, Bibulus and Cato must have hoped, hostility to Caesar and Pompey would increase. The efforts of Curio and his friends seemed to be bearing fruit. Cato's brother-in-law Domitius Ahenobarbus was all but certain to win a praetorship. There might even be a chance that the *optimates* could get one of their candidates, Lucius Lentulus Niger, elected to the consulship.

Suspicion and hatred smoldered. The city became a fever swamp of ever more sensational allegations. The surest sign of this was when the old informer Vettius, who had once tried to implicate Caesar in the Catilinarian conspiracy, reappeared on the scene. Before the elections, Vettius wormed his way into a friendship with Curio and told the hotheaded young man of a plan to murder Pompey. Perhaps this was an effort at entrapment, but if so, it failed. Curio told his father, his father told Pompey, and the whole matter was taken to the Senate. Vettius was brought in and, after first feigning ignorance, asked leave to turn state's evidence. He produced a list of young men allegedly plotting with Curio against Pompey. Among them were the son of the consular candidate Lentulus Niger (according to Vettius, Niger himself also knew about the plot) and Servilia's son Brutus.[30]

As the story poured out it seemed less and less believable, and the senators laughed outright when Vettius claimed that the dagger to kill Pompey had been supplied by a scribe of Bibulus. As if daggers were so hard to come by in Rome! Young Curio was swiftly brought in and poked even more holes in the allegations. The senators then passed a decree ordering Vettius to be imprisoned.

The next day Caesar brought Vettius to the Rostra, and again Vettius told of the conspiracy. Key parts of his story had changed. For one, Vettius now left out Servilia's son, making it clear that "a night, and a nighttime entreaty, had intervened," as Cicero remarked archly. The pearl was not Caesar's only gift to his mistress in 59. Also, Vettius listed many people he had failed to mention the day before, all firm *optimates*, including the praetorian candidate Domitius Ahenobarbus. Then, at another public meeting, this one hosted by Vatinius, Vettius volunteered even more names. Vatinius announced plans for a full investigation, but, to complete the scandal, Vettius was soon found dead in prison.

Clearly Vettius had hoped to bring the enemies of Caesar and Pompey—Curio above all—under suspicion. It also seems clear that, at least once Vettius came forward, Caesar was happy not just to do his mistress a favor but also to inflame the situation, to damage his rivals. Cicero, for one, believed that Caesar had been working with Vettius from the start, and some suspected that Vettius's death had been arranged by Caesar, out of fear of exposure. Caesar countered that it was his opponents who had silenced the informer.

In the end, the truth never was established. Charges of conspiracy by "the other side" were another manifestation of the year's reckless partisanship. Baseless as they might have been, over time they warped the way Caesar, Cato, and other key politicians looked at each other.

The elections proceeded as planned in October, with all the candidacies intact. Caesar's new father-in-law, Calpurnius Piso, secured one of the consulships, and the other went to Pompey's close friend Gabinius. This was a relief for Caesar. Still, he would face trouble from two of those elected to praetorships. As expected, Cato's brother-in-law Domitius Ahenobarbus secured one of the positions, and along with him another outspoken critic of Caesar, Memmius. After they assumed office in the new year, these two demanded an inquiry into Caesar's conduct as consul. Vatinius, meanwhile, was charged with having passed legislation by illegitimate means and was summoned to Memmius's tribunal to answer.[31]

Caesar had secured protection beyond what was provided by the two consuls of 58 BC. Powerful as the consuls were in the Roman system, in moments of true danger a politician needed the help of a tribune, and the more aggressive the better. Early in the year of his consulship, Caesar had made it possible for Clodius—the man who had caused him so much embarrassment in the Bona Dea scandal—to fulfill a long-cherished plan to transfer from patrician to plebeian status so that he could be elected tribune of the plebs. Clodius won the tribunate, which commenced in December of 59. On the last day of the year, Clodius prevented Bibulus from giving the customary farewell address as consul. Then in 58, on the day Vatinius's trial was to start, Vatinius appealed to Clodius to intercede. Clodius summoned the people to support him, and a large crowd came to Memmius's court and shut it down, knocking over the benches and the urns used by the jurors to cast their votes.[32]

Clodius's plan for Cato was his most clever gambit of all. Immediately upon entering office, the tribune had introduced an ambitious package of legislation to secure the loyalty of the plebs, and by January voters had approved it. Its most breathtaking measure was a plan for the free monthly distribution of grain in the city of Rome. To help pay the steep costs, Clodius introduced another bill confiscating the island of Cyprus, which had long been a possession of the Ptolemaic kings of Egypt. The king then ruling Cyprus was to be deposed and his vast treasure seized and sold. Initially Clodius probably had one of the consuls of 58 in mind for overseeing the annexation, but he then had the inspired idea of giving the task to Cato.[33] Not only would Cato be sure to squeeze every ounce of silver from the island; accepting the assignment would forestall him from challenging the legality of Clodius's program—and of Clodius's transfer to plebeian status in 59. This, in turn, meant it would be hard for Cato to maintain that all of Caesar's acts as consul were illegitimate.

When Clodius first approached Cato about the possibility of taking over the commission to Cyprus, Cato replied that it was a trap. That did not deter Clodius, who proceeded to pass yet another law formally appointing Cato. Now Cato could not easily refuse. Wringing out all the territory's treasure, not for himself but for the Republic, would at least be an enjoyable task.

After Cato left the city, Clodius read out at a public meeting a letter from Caesar—who had by then left for Gaul—full of congratulations. Not only had Clodius rid Rome of Cato; he also had taken away Cato's right to complain about extraordinary commands in the future. It was as if Cato's tongue had been ripped out, Clodius said.[34]

Early in his tumultuous consulship, Caesar had tried to imprison Cato and failed. Cyprus, with its great natural beauty and ample vineyards, was not exactly a jail. But from Caesar's point of view, it might be even better: a place of exile that would end up keeping Caesar's dangerous enemy out of day-to-day politics in Rome for two years. Caesar would be gone, too, in Gaul, pursuing the glory of conquest, while Cato audited financial accounts on Cyprus.

CHAPTER 8

CATO'S TRIUMPH

A s Cato set out for Cyprus, he can only have felt uneasy. To auction off the kingdom of Cyprus was an act of blatant unfairness and aggression, a blot that could long stain the Republic.[1] The basis for the island's annexation was flimsy, a will said to have been written by an earlier king of Egypt bequeathing his whole realm to Rome. It was quite possibly a forgery, meant to help the Romans lay their hands on Egypt's fertile lands and its vast accumulated treasures. Beyond that, Cyprus and Egypt were not being treated consistently. Amid the vicious power struggles of the royal house of Egypt, it was common for one member of the family to hold Egypt itself, another Cyprus. In 58 BC, Ptolemy XII—nicknamed the "Flute Player," after his favorite hobby—sat on the golden throne of Egypt, while his younger brother ruled Cyprus. The Flute Player had secured his position the year before by paying a massive bribe to Caesar, Pompey, and Crassus. The tighter-fisted Ptolemy of Cyprus was to be ousted.[2]

Distasteful as the situation was, Cato still hoped to make the best
of it. If he could liquidate the kingdom with as little turmoil as possible, he would spare the people of Cyprus what they would face
under a less scrupulous governor. On top of that, he could set new
standards in Rome for dealing with public money. And so he sent
ahead a member of his staff, Caninius, to try to persuade the king
to relinquish the island without a fight. If Ptolemy did, he was to receive a priesthood in the famous sanctuary of Aphrodite at Paphos—
where the goddess was said to have first risen from the sea.[3]

But would the king be so easily fobbed off? As Cato held back
on the isle of Rhodes to learn the result of Caninius's mission, the
other Ptolemy, the Flute Player, decided to pay him a visit. He had
just been driven out of his kingdom by subjects irate that the bribe
promised the year before, which ultimately they had to pay for, had
not spared Cyprus, the last shard of the once glorious Ptolemaic
empire. The Flute Player was on his way to Rome to secure military
support to restore his throne.

After landing on Rhodes, he sent a messenger to Cato, expecting
that Cato would come to him, as any of his subjects in Egypt would,
at least when they were not rebelling. Cato happened to be purging
himself at that moment, as Romans sometimes did for reasons of
health, and sent a message back: if the king wanted a meeting with
Cato, *he* needed to come to the Roman. When Ptolemy did come,
Cato refused to stand up, and he greeted the king like an ordinary
visitor. And after Ptolemy poured out his recent troubles, Cato gave
him a blunt lecture. The king's previous life would look idyllic, Cato
said, once he had to face "the bribery and greed of the chief men
of Rome, whom Egypt could scarcely glut, even if it were all converted into cash."[4] Cato advised the king to sail back to Alexandria
and reconcile with his people. Ptolemy recognized the truth in what
Cato said and was tempted to follow the advice but in the end was
deterred by his advisors. When he later reached Rome and came to
the doorstep of the first magistrate he had to see, he groaned as he
recalled the warning.

Cato's reprimand followed a fine tradition of Romans refusing to be dazzled by the great kings of the east. It also pointed out real failings in the Republic, failings that had worried Cato before. For all the wealth empire brought, the Roman state did a poor job of claiming much of it.[5] The treasury itself was a weak institution, with few champions. Tax collecting was subcontracted to firms of equestrians, who took a large cut for themselves. Senators raked in even bigger profits. As provincial governors, they precipitated unnecessary wars to bring in plunder that they kept. They forced large loans at usurious rates on communities. They demanded enormous bribes. Empire was inherently exploitative. The problem Cato saw was that the more individuals benefited from it, the feebler the Republic became.

After the Flute Player's departure, the grim but welcome news came to Rhodes that Ptolemy of Cyprus, unable to bear life without his kingdom, had taken poison and died. Liquidation of his holdings on behalf of the Roman people could begin in earnest. Cato first had to take a detour north since Clodius had also entrusted him with the time-consuming task of restoring some exiles in the city of Byzantium—who, at least according to Cicero, had paid Clodius a bribe.[6] Cato did not entirely trust his staff member Caninius, so he sent his nephew, Servilia's son Brutus, to Cyprus to keep a watch on the proceedings there. Although much given over to intellectual pursuits, the young man had a head for business—perhaps more than Cato realized. Brutus secretly drew up a loan with some of the Cypriots at an interest rate of 48 percent per annum.[7]

After Byzantium was settled, Cato sailed to Cyprus. A portion of the king's wealth must have lain in estates across the island, but all the paraphernalia a Ptolemaic king needed was also available—goblets, furniture, jewels, purple robes. The whole lot needed to be auctioned off. Cato was determined not only to confiscate every last item possible but also to drive prices up as high as he could. He made a point of speaking with prospective buyers and encouraging them to bid. He also insisted on handling every detail himself. There was nobody he thought he could trust fully—not staff, not auctioneers, not purchasers.

Cato became so quarrelsome that he took to squabbling even with old friends. Munatius was the last of Cato's helpers to arrive on Cyprus, where he found that he had been put in very basic housing. An abuse of expense accounts never happened when Cato was on government business. Munatius went to see Cato but was turned away at the door; Cato was too busy with Caninius, who was now back in favor, to see Munatius. Munatius insisted and Cato snapped. He was with Caninius, he said, because Caninius had gotten to Cyprus first and Cato could trust his honesty in dealing with the public accounts. Stung, Munatius refused to dine with Cato and eventually left the island altogether. Later, back in Rome, Cato's wife, Marcia, pleaded with her husband to forgive his friend. She persuaded Cato to send a note to Munatius asking him to come over to discuss something. Munatius arrived early in the morning and was detained by Marcia until all the other visitors had left, at which point Cato appeared and hugged Munatius. As Marcia understood, her husband, when wrapped up with public duties, was likely to treat even those he loved rudely.[8]

The Cyprian auctions ended up realizing an impressive 7,000 talents of silver (equivalent to 168 million sesterces). Everything had been sold off, even some poison Cato had found among the royal property—poison there was every reason to think effective, considering the king's suicide. There were only two exceptions. One was the slaves of the late king, who were themselves to become the public property of Rome. The other was a bronze statue of Zeno, the founder of the Stoic school of philosophy, who had been born on Cyprus.[9]

Fearful of the lengthy sea journey to Rome, Cato devised a plan to keep the spoils from Cyprus safe from disaster. Cato's cargo of three thousand chests was attached to long ropes with large corks at the end. In the case of a shipwreck, the corks would act like buoys and show where the treasure lay.

The money made it back safely, but a more symbolic loss embarrassed Cato. On Cyprus he had had two sets of accounts written out, which doubtless documented every transaction down to the last drachma. One set, entrusted to a freedman of Cato, was destroyed when the freedman's boat capsized after departing from the harbor of Corinth. The other set, in Cato's possession, made it safely as far as Corfu. It was a cold night, the sailors built a fire to stay warm, and the fire accidentally spread to the tents and engulfed all of Cato's records. It was galling. Cato had created the reports not so much as proof of his own integrity—who could doubt that?—but rather as an example of the scrupulousness he desired in all public accounts. If questions did come up, the late king's stewards would surely vouch for Cato. But, true to form, Cato did not believe that anyone should be able to rely on such a loophole, not even himself.

As the treasure-laden ships sailed up the Tiber River to Rome in the early summer of 56, magistrates, senators, and ordinary citizens came out to meet the returning hero. Punctilious to the end, Cato refused to disembark until the whole fleet was safely at anchor in the dockyard. The treasure chests were unloaded from the ships and carried through the Forum to the treasury, to the gasps of the crowds gathered. The procession felt like a great military triumph, except that no Romans had lost their lives, nor had the Cypriots been defeated in battle. The only captives were men already enslaved.[10]

Cato wanted it to feel like a triumph. Abstemious as he was, Cato was still too much of a noble to be completely immune to public recognition, especially for services to the Republic. He also knew that increased popularity would help him in the fight against Caesar, which he was eager to resume. Beyond that, the parade of the silver chests publicized a new and better way of running the Roman empire. Senators did not have to start unnecessary wars, did not have to demand bribes, did not have to divert imperial profits from the treasury. In earlier days, nothing had conferred more glory on a Roman than winning battles, but now, Cato believed, wars were being fought only to enrich commanders. So rife was bribery that it was more of a distinction to overcome avarice than to vanquish even the most barbaric enemy.[11]

Shocking events in Cato's absence lent support to his views. Ptolemy the Flute Player had arrived in the city in the fall of 58 and ended up spending nearly a year in a sumptuous villa owned by Pompey in the Alban Hills outside Rome. As Cato had warned, the king was forced to disburse large bribes to senators to secure military assistance in recovering his throne. At least some of the loan contracts were signed in Pompey's villa. To add to the scandal, in 57 the Alexandrians sent envoys to Rome to upset the king's plans for restoration. On Ptolemy's orders, members of the delegation were brutally murdered. Safe through his bribes, Ptolemy meanwhile slipped away to Asia and was eventually restored by Pompey's old associate Gabinius—reportedly for a further bribe of 10,000 talents.[12] In the face of this flagrant corruption, Cato's rectitude looked appealing.

In Gaul, meanwhile, Caesar had been waging the kind of war that so dismayed Cato. In 58, when the Helvetian people began a mass migration out of what is modern Switzerland, Caesar claimed that the security of Rome's province in southern Gaul was at risk, and he defeated the Helvetii in a long and hard battle. He then drove the German king Ariovistus, who had been harassing Roman allies, back beyond the Rhine. The next year, after the northern Belgae mustered a vast array of forces against Caesar, he systematically defeated their armies. Thousands of men, women, and children were taken captive and sold into slavery. Vast amounts of plunder were seized. In profits, Caesar's campaigns dwarfed Cato's mission to Cyprus, though the proceeds were drenched in blood.[13]

By late 57, Caesar could claim that all of Gaul, to the Atlantic and the Rhine, had been subdued. It was a remarkable feat, and the Senate, despite lingering anger over Caesar's consulship, could not fail to vote a thanksgiving to the gods for the people to celebrate.[14] This did not have to mean an end to Caesar's campaigns. Quite possibly Caesar was already making plans to take his army all the way to Britain, where no Roman general had gone before.

Yet as Caesar spent the winter recess in northern Italy, worries started to mount about the situation in Rome. In 59, Caesar, Crassus, and Pompey had managed to dominate the Republic, but they had also stirred up fierce opposition, led by Cato. After Caesar's departure, the three-way alliance came under strain—it was really Caesar who had held it together—and leading senators, even with Cato gone, found ways to frustrate Caesar and Pompey especially.[15] In early 56, as Cato's return loomed, the political attacks gained momentum. The consuls elected for the year were no friends of Caesar and Pompey. One was the distinguished noble Gnaeus Lentulus Marcellinus, an intelligent and eloquent man with a strong voice and a quick wit.[16] The other was Lucius Marcius Philippus, Cato's father-in-law.

Even as a new war broke out in Gaul along the Atlantic coast, perhaps connected with Caesar's British plans, he remained in Italy to deal with ominous developments. Tribunes put forward laws to provide him with additional officers and funding but were thwarted by Consul Marcellinus.[17] Other tribunes floated measures that were downright hostile to Caesar. One proposed ending the program of land distribution in Campania that Caesar had established as consul.[18] Another even tried to recall Caesar to Rome to put him on trial for the illegalities of his consulship.[19] That attempt at least was defeated by the other tribunes. But Cato's brother-in-law Domitius Ahenobarbus, who had already during his praetorship of 58 attacked Caesar, announced that, if elected consul in 55, he would see to it that Caesar was stripped of command. After all, had not Caesar himself claimed that all of Gaul was pacified? Scion of a great noble family, Domitius would be hard to defeat in the polls; a "consul from the day he was born" was how Cicero described him.[20]

And then there was Pompey. Over the previous couple of years, he had grown miserable as clever attacks by his opponents, as well as his own blunders, had robbed him of his former preeminence. So desperate was he to recover his standing, it seemed that he might turn on Caesar and make an alliance with Caesar's enemies. To do so would require Pompey to divorce Julia; Caesar was fortunate that Pompey had grown so attached to his young wife. In a sense, Caesar's single most powerful supporter in Rome was now his daughter. Still, even if Pompey did not abandon Caesar, he might quietly abet efforts by Domitius, Cato, and the others to diminish Caesar.

In April of 56 Crassus made his way from Rome to Ravenna, where Caesar was staying. Crassus informed his old associate of the latest developments, including efforts by Cicero to stop the Campanian land distributions. Caesar and Crassus then traveled together to Luca, just within the boundaries of Caesar's province, for a meeting with Pompey. Caesar complained bitterly about Cicero and impressed on Pompey the need to stick with his old allies. The only safe course of action, the three ultimately decided, was to band back together. Pompey and Crassus would stand jointly for the consulship of 55. Once in office, they would secure for themselves provincial commands to match Caesar's, each to last five years. Caesar would be renewed in his provinces for five years as well.[21]

Caesar's future depended on victory in the upcoming elections— or at least he had come to believe as much. If held at any point in 56, the elections would be presided over by the year's consuls, both of whom favored Domitius and would do everything they could to see him win. But if the new year opened without consuls, then temporary magistrates, holding power just five days each, would be in charge. That would make it easier to ensure the outcome that Caesar desired, especially since he could send troops from his winter quarters to sway the vote. As would gradually become clear back in Rome, Caesar, Pompey, and Crassus devised an intricate scheme to be certain of success—as elaborate as any military operation Caesar was planning to prosecute in Britain.

No great public announcement followed the April meeting at Luca, and details were only released as needed. Pompey informed Cicero, for instance, that the attacks on Caesar had to stop. Soon Cicero was promoting Caesar's interests and gave a speech in the Senate recommending authorization of additional funding for Caesar.[22] Senators, a number of whom allegedly had just been offered bribes by Caesar, were willing to go along. Cato was not back yet to stiffen spines, and it fell to Favonius to denounce the proposals. When he got nowhere in the Senate, he rushed out of the chamber and railed to a crowd in the Forum. Again it was in vain. Caesar received his additional funding and officers.[23]

Favonius, Bibulus, and the others had carried on the condemnation of Caesar in Cato's absence, but none could strike like Cato. His return and the parade of the silver chests gave them just the reinforcement they needed after Caesar's victory over funding. It would have helped them even more to elect Cato into a praetorship for the following year, but Cato appears to have just missed the deadline for declaring his candidacy. Consuls Philippus and Marcellinus proposed that, in view of the long and meritorious service that had kept Cato from Rome, the Senate should grant an exception and allow Cato to stand anyway.[24] Cato must have been tempted, but he refused and even spoke against the measure. For a privilege to be granted to him alone, he said, would be unjust.

It was demonstrable self-restraint like this that made Cato so powerful. And Cato knew it. After he returned, Clodius complained that all the praise for the Cyprian mission had fallen on Cato alone. To regain some credit, Clodius proposed that the slaves who had been brought back should be referred to as the "Clodiani," after his own name. Cato objected and said the slaves should be called the "Cyprii." Some of Cato's friends suggested they should be the "Porciani," after Cato's distinguished family name. Cato stomped out that plan too.[25] In anger Clodius then demanded that Cato produce the accounts of his administration, even though Clodius knew that they had been lost to shipwreck and fire. From Gaul, Caesar lent encouragement to Clodius and allegedly sent letters containing further accusations to make against Cato. One of the attacks maintained that Cato had persuaded the consuls to present their proposal on the praetorship and then pretended to give it up voluntarily, knowing that he would lose.[26]

Cato almost certainly did not fully grasp what Caesar and his allies had planned for the elections for the following year's consuls. Pompey and Crassus let the deadline for declaring candidacies pass without indicating that they intended to run. Only afterward did they start to express interest publicly. The consuls, especially Marcellinus, insisted that they would not recognize the candidacies—which was just what Pompey and Crassus wanted. This allowed them to claim that they were being robbed of the opportunity to compete. On their behalf, a tribune repeatedly used his veto to block elections. The plan was now becoming clear: Pompey and Crassus would delay proceedings to the following year, when Marcellinus and Philippus would be out of office.[27]

Many senators, including Cato, exploded in anger. Pompey and Crassus, if successful, were sure to make great demands once in office, and their move threatened everyone's chances to win elections in the future. The senators voted to change into mourning and soon returned to the Senate in their dirty clothes to try to intimidate the recalcitrant tribune. The tribune refused to change his position, and the senators marched out into the Forum to arouse sympathy. Marcellinus won some cheers for his eloquent pleas. "Applaud, citizens," he cried out, "applaud while you may. Soon you won't be able to freely."[28]

The Senate reconvened to take measures against the tribune, and while they deliberated Clodius appeared in the Forum, in ordinary dress, and attacked Marcellinus. Word reached the Senate, the senators complained, and Clodius rushed to the Senate house, but the senators would not let him in. An angry mob ran to his aid, torches in hand, and threatened to burn the building down. That more or less put an end to official business for the year. A majority of senators refused to attend any more meetings. As an additional form of protest, they stayed dressed in mourning and boycotted public games and religious festivals.

The illegality and violence of Pompey's and Crassus's actions scared off everyone planning to stand for office—except for Cato's brother-in-law Domitius. Cato persuaded Domitius that he could not back down or yield. This was a struggle not just for political office, Cato said, but for the freedom of Rome. And skewed as his ideas of freedom might have been by senatorial interests, Cato was right. Crassus and Pompey were not just running for the consulship. They, along with Caesar, were in the process of seizing practically all the provinces and armies of Rome. The problem Cato saw of senators concentrating power and wealth into individual hands had reached a grotesque level.[29]

After the year ended, the temporary magistrates took over, and finally Pompey and Crassus were ready for the elections to be held. Domitius still refused to back out and kept campaigning as if it were a normal contest. Many promised him their votes and told him there were even more who supported him but just would not say so publicly.

Early on the morning of election day, Domitius proceeded with Cato and other friends by torchlight to the Field of Mars. As they made their way in the still-dark streets, suddenly a gang fell upon them. The torchbearer at the head of the procession tried to protect Domitius, was struck, and fell down dead. Others were injured, and soon all but Cato and Domitius fled. Cato, even though he had been wounded in his right arm, tried to hold Domitius back, urging him to stay in the fight. But Domitius was afraid. He returned home, and Pompey and Crassus were elected consuls.[30]

It is not impossible to guess who made up the gang. As the elections got underway, soldiers of Caesar could be seen on the Field of Mars. They had been brought to Rome by one of the officers on his staff, Crassus's son Publius.

As always when he encountered injustice, Cato was prodded to fight back. And as always, he refused to resort to physical force himself. He could never condone the violence he had seen growing up. Instead, he announced that he would be running for the praetorship after all.[31] Because of the long delay in the elections, there was no longer any legal obstacle.

Pompey and Crassus were alarmed but responded this time by distributing lavish bribes on behalf of other candidates. At a meeting of the Senate, supporters of Cato demanded that those who won election should remain private citizens for two months afterward. Since it was already February of 55, the victors otherwise could step straight into office and so avoid prosecution for electoral malpractice. The proposal threatened the new consuls' plans, and they ruthlessly crushed it. "They control everything and want everyone to know it," wrote Cicero, aghast.[32]

The citizens were summoned to vote, and Cato took an early lead. It looked as if he would win after all. Pompey blurted out that he had heard thunder and dismissed the assembly. He and Crassus handed out yet more bribes and also took measures to exclude certain voters from the Field of Mars when the assembly was reconvened. Cato was defeated, and to make it worse, one of those who edged him out was Caesar's scrofulous tribune, Vatinius.

Immediately afterward, Cato's voters started to gather angrily, and a tribune summoned a meeting. Cato delivered a speech telling of all the disasters that would come. Pompey's and Crassus's intentions could only be evil, Cato said, if they were so afraid to have Cato as praetor. Citizens should withdraw all support for the two men. A large crowd accompanied Cato home—bigger, at least according to Cato's admirers, than the crowds of all the elected praetors put together.

The subsequent elections for aediles brought new scandals. Out-and-out violence occurred. Pompey, presiding, was bespattered with blood and had to change garments. When Pompey's slaves carried the stained clothes to his house, Julia, who was pregnant, fainted at the sight. So great was the shock that she miscarried.[33]

Julia's collapse and miscarriage was a blow to Caesar and Pompey, but otherwise they and Crassus had gotten everything they wanted. It was now time for the final part of their plan to be enacted: commands for all three. A tribune who was friendly to them, Gaius Trebonius, introduced legislation allotting provinces to Crassus and Pompey for five years each. One would have the Spanish provinces, the other Syria. Each could recruit armies the size of their own choosing and make war with whomever they pleased. No law could have disgusted Cato more.[34] Other leaders regarded opposition as hopeless and did not even try to speak against the measure. But Cato, along with Favonius, was determined to resist, and two tribunes, Gaius Ateius Capito and Publius Aquillius Gallus, were willing to help.

At a public meeting during the standard review period for new legislation, Trebonius granted Favonius one hour to speak from the Rostra. He spent it uttering vain protests against the time limit. Cato was then given two hours. He devoted his speech to an attack on the present situation rather than getting into the specifics of the law. He did this so that when Trebonius told him to stop speaking, he could complain that he still had much left to say.

Asked to be silent, Cato did not stop. Trebonius ordered an attendant to step onto the Rostra and have Cato dragged off. But even once he was standing at ground level, among the crowd, Cato kept shouting, finding men who were still willing to listen and share his anger. The attendant grabbed him and drove him from the Forum. No sooner was Cato released than he returned, rushing back onto the Rostra and bawling to the citizens for help. This happened again and again until finally Trebonius, furious, ordered Cato taken to prison. A crowd followed him. Much like Caesar in 59, Trebonius quickly realized how much sympathy his opponent was attracting, and he had him released.

Meanwhile, the day had ended before Cato's tribunes Ateius and Gallus had had their chance to speak on the proposed law. Out of fear that he might be shut out of the Forum, Gallus spent the night in the Senate house, from where he planned to leave at dawn to join the people outside. But Trebonius locked the building's doors and stationed armed men to occupy the Forum.

Ateius, Cato, Favonius, and their friends were barred from entering the Forum. Yet somehow Favonius managed to wriggle his way in, while Cato and Ateius climbed onto the shoulders of some of their followers at the Forum's edge and shouted that they heard thunder. This was the same claim Pompey had made to stop Cato's election, but the difference was that Pompey was a member of the augural college, and augurs enjoyed the undisputed power to interrupt proceedings if they observed an adverse sign.[35] A report coming from a tribune, much less a nonmagistrate (as Cato was), was not binding. It was a desperate measure by Cato, and it failed.

Attendants proceeded to drive Cato and Ateius out. Some in their group were wounded, a few fatally. One senator was punched in the face by Crassus himself and driven bleeding from the Forum. The law passed.

Cato had failed in his bid to get Domitius and himself elected, and had also failed to stop the Trebonian law. Pompey and Crassus had resorted to appalling measures—bribery, physical intimidation, even murder. The obstruction engaged in by Cato and his allies had no chance of succeeding against such tactics, yet it was powerful as a demonstration against illegality. As a symbol of resistance, Cato called upon a different kind of strength than Pompey and Crassus: a tenacity that evoked the heroes of Rome's early days, who bravely sacrificed their lives for the Republic. He was Horatius at the bridge. Catonian obstructionism, especially when carried to an extreme, could be damaging to republican government, but in the face of what was happening in 55 BC, it seemed a bulwark. Yet anyone looking clearly would have had to conclude that, in the face of force, the bulwark of obstruction could only do so much.

All that remained was for Caesar to get his command renewed by the Senate, and the plan agreed on at Luca the year before would be fulfilled. When Crassus and Pompey introduced the necessary legislation, Cato and his allies naturally opposed it.[36] But the bill was popular with voters, and the consuls would be sure to overcome any obstruction. So Cato changed tactics. He went to Pompey.

Caesar might not have been in Rome since his consulship had ended, but the bribery and especially the violence of the preceding months was most plausibly attributed to him. It was Caesar's forces who had come to Rome, Caesar whose position was most vulnerable, Caesar who had been able to persuade Pompey to renew their old alliance. At heart, Pompey opposed the use of violence in politics.

Though Pompey did not realize it, Cato said, he was carrying Caesar on his shoulders. The time would come when Pompey would feel the weight too much, but by then he would be able neither to carry it nor to put it down. Pompey and Caesar together would crash down on the city. Then Pompey would remember Cato's advice and realize that "it contained not only what was good and just, but also what was advantageous to Pompey."[37]

Pompey refused to listen and went forward with the bill on Caesar's behalf. Cato, with the doggedness he showed whenever he believed something was right, kept making his plea. Perhaps, he hoped, Pompey would turn against Caesar before it was too late.

CHAPTER 9

GAUL

S HORTLY AFTER MIDNIGHT, IN THE VERY EARLY HOURS OF A LATE-
summer day in 55 BC, Caesar's fleet set sail from Gaul to Britain. The weather was favorable, but with their unpredictable currents
and surging tides, the cold Atlantic waters were still a source of
dread for the ten thousand or so soldiers. Even more dismaying was
the landmass that came into view after the nine-hour voyage. Atop
cliffs plunging nearly straight down to the sea, armed troops were
posted, prepared to hurl weapons onto the narrow stretch of shore
below. There was nowhere for the Romans to safely disembark.[1]

Caesar waited at anchor until mid-afternoon, by which time all
his eighty or so transport ships had joined him. He then gave the
signal, hoisted the anchors, and, making use of a favorable wind
and tide, sailed about seven miles further to a wide and open beach.

The Romans stepped ashore into an ambush. According to the
account Caesar later wrote—in one of his famous third-person commentaries, by which students still learn Latin today—the Britons

Caesar's conquest of Gaul, 58–50 BC. He redefined Gaul to include the massive area beyond the old Roman province. A few locations are conjectural.

had seen what Caesar was planning and sent ahead cavalry and charioteers to prevent the Romans from disembarking on the beach. The transport ships, because of their large size, could only anchor in deeper waters. Forced to jump down into water practically above their heads, the legionaries, weighed down with heavy armor and weapons, struggled to find their footing in the current while volleys of javelins whizzed toward them.

Caesar saw that the soldiers were not going to make it out of the water on their own, so he ordered the more compact warships to withdraw a bit and then row hard to shore. From the decks of the ships, his men started shooting at the enemy with slings, arrows, even catapults. Amazed at the weapons, the Britons halted, then retreated a little. Still, the Romans hesitated because of the depth of the water, until the soldier who carried the silver eagle of the Tenth Legion plunged in and moved to land, eagle aloft. Others began to jump down and follow.

After hard fighting, the Britons were finally put to flight. But Caesar was unable to pursue. The eighteen transports carrying his cavalry, having set out from a different harbor in Gaul, had been blown off course. "This was the one thing lacking," Caesar wrote, "for Caesar's usual success."[2]

The Britons sued for peace. This annoyed Caesar. Just earlier that year, British leaders had sent envoys to the continent offering to surrender—and then they had attacked him. Almost certainly he would have preferred to continue to fight, but without his cavalry it was too risky, even for him. He accepted the capitulation, on condition that the Britons turn over hostages, which some promptly did.

A week later, nature again intervened. The eighteen cavalry ships had once more set sail, this time on a gentle wind, but as they approached Britain a huge storm arose. Some of the vessels, just in sight of the Roman camp, were driven back to Gaul immediately. Others cast anchor but found themselves overwhelmed by waves and had to sail off. There was a full moon—which brings, as the Romans did not yet understand, a very high tide. The surge swamped the Roman warships, which had been beached, while storm winds dashed the larger transport vessels, tied at anchor, one against another. Some were so damaged they would never sail again.

Near panic set in among the troops. There were no other ships to take them back, no supplies to repair the ships they did have, no store of grain to get them through the winter. Their commanders had planned and provisioned a brief reconnaissance, nothing more. The British leaders who had gathered in Caesar's camp saw the Roman predicament and one by one left and began secretly to summon men from their farms. If they could defeat Caesar's army, the Romans might never return.

Caesar suspected what was underway and immediately made counterpreparations. Every day, he sent his men out to bring in grain from the fields. He salvaged pieces of the most damaged ships to repair the others. When the Britons tried to attack his camp, he overpowered them in battle. Once more they sued for peace. Caesar demanded twice as many hostages as before and ordered them taken to the continent. The equinox was approaching, and he did not want to wait longer and expose his battered ships to the treacherous winter sea.

Taking advantage again of a spell of fair weather, a little after midnight his fleet set off. All arrived safely in Gaul. Then, after a fight with some of the Gallic peoples living on the Channel coast, Caesar established his men in camps. It was not to be a winter of resting by fires, however. The soldiers were ordered to build as many new ships as possible and to repair the old ones. Caesar would be returning to Britain the following year.

Whatever Caesar felt was left to be accomplished, his expedition in 55 was already sufficient to fill Romans with admiration and awe. Britain lay at the edge of the known world, and much about it remained mysterious. Some thought Britain an island, others a whole continent. Rumors held that it was a land full of wealth, and Caesar had gone there in hope of gathering the pearls that so fascinated him. Some small and dingy pearls were found, but Britain proved to be disappointingly poor. Still, to have sailed an army there at all, through the tidal ocean, and then to have made it back safely was a feat.[3]

The Senate voted twenty days of thanksgiving to the gods—five days more than had already been granted to Caesar at the end of his campaigns in 57, and ten days more than Pompey had received back in 63. Thanksgivings were important because they paved the way for a full triumph after the commander's return to Rome. They also redounded to Caesar's immediate reputation. Throughout the city, men, women, and children, garlanded and in their best attire, went in procession to the temples to offer wine, incense, and sacrificial animals.[4]

In the Senate's deliberations there was, however, one dissenting voice. Cato, far from thinking that the people should thank the gods for the general's victory, demanded that Caesar be turned over to the German enemy at once for having broken a truce.[5]

Earlier in 55, before the expedition to Britain, Caesar had overseen a massacre of thousands of Germans. Even by Roman standards it was a terrible bloodletting. According to Caesar, who clearly sought to justify his actions, during the winter of 56/55 a large population of Germans, under pressure from their neighbors, had crossed the Rhine and seized land in Gaul. Worried that some of the Gallic peoples might be urged on by these invaders to rebellion, Caesar left northern Italy in 55, earlier in the year than was his practice, and marched straight for the Germans. During several rounds of talks, he grew suspicious that the German envoys were only trying to buy time as they waited for some of their cavalry to return from a raid. An attack on his own advance cavalry, in which he lost seventy-four men, convinced him to break off negotiations altogether. When the German leaders came to see him the next morning, Caesar had them all detained. He hurried with his army to the German camp before anyone there could realize what had happened. Leaderless and unprepared, the men resisted for a short time. The women and children started to flee. Caesar sent cavalry to chase them all down. "The enemy numbered 430,000 persons," Caesar wrote—and few survived.[6]

That number is almost certainly exaggerated, but for Cato, even a fraction of it would have been an unacceptable toll. As a Stoic, he believed in a worldwide community of all human beings, each of whom deserved just treatment. It was the duty of the Roman government, especially the Senate, to provide it. That meant senatorial commanders needed to keep their hands clean of provincials' money. It also meant fighting a war only when a fair cause existed. So suffused was the Gallic War in Caesar's own ambitions, it was, as far as Cato was concerned, tainted from the start.[7]

Cato's aversion to war was unusual. He knew that, whatever his own feelings, most Romans sided with a victor, especially over barbarians. He therefore rested his attack against Caesar in 55 on a more specific charge. Among ancient states it was widely accepted that ambassadors were sacred and inviolable. To detain them against their will or to break a truce that had been enacted with them would bring the offense of the gods onto one's own state. According to Cato's version of events, that was just what Caesar had done: he had attacked the German envoys during a truce. For his crime, the commander should suffer the traditional penalty of being handed over to the enemy he had wronged.

Cato had to have realized that the Senate would never go along with his demand. Caesar, enriched with plunder and elevated by his astonishing exploits as well as his alliance with Pompey and Crassus, commanded too much power in late 55 BC to fall based on so murky an allegation. Still, Cato's intervention allowed him to raise doubts about the general's conduct. The war in Gaul was impious, Cato was suggesting, just like Caesar's consulship—and neglect of the gods always stirred anxiety in Rome.

Cato's motion showed that his hatred for Caesar was as strong as ever. If anything, it had grown even fiercer: The Gallic War was, in Cato's eyes, worse than Caesar's earlier crimes. It had showered Caesar in bloodstained gold to be offered in bribes. It had given him an army that might shield him from the law, just like Sulla's.

Even though they were hundreds of miles apart, the two men's wrestling match continued, with throw and counterthrow. After Caesar learned of Cato's proposal, he sent a letter to the Senate full of insults against his old enemy. The letter was read aloud, and then Cato rose to his feet and spoke with deliberate restraint. Caesar's insults were childish, Cato said. The real issue was Caesar's scheming for absolute power, the plans for which Cato listed. "It is not the children of Britons or Celts you have to fear," he told the Senate, "but Caesar himself."[8]

As was so often the case, Cato's conspiratorial rhetoric went too far. Each burst from him only made it harder for Caesar and his senatorial opponents to reach a truce, which damaged the Republic. Still, it was true, as Cato suggested, that the war in Gaul was a continuation of Caesar's political career. Just as Caesar made his already fit body stronger in year after year of fighting, he also took his power to a new level dangerous to the Republic.

One way Caesar did this was through the wealth he acquired. His commentaries on his own profiteering are, understandably, spare in detail, but they do record, for instance, that approximately fifty-three thousand captives were sold into slavery after the fall of just one fortress in northern Gaul.[9] As always with Caesar's numbers this one may be exaggerated, but there is no doubt that he auctioned off thousands of prisoners at great profit. He stole valuables from defeated peoples or those who resisted, including horses, cattle, weapons, and the gold jewelry with which Gallic warriors were so fond of adorning themselves. Sanctuaries were stripped of gold and other treasures accumulated over the centuries.

Plunder was supposed to go to the soldiers or the state, but Caesar stretched the regulations. His own finances were transformed. No longer was he at the mercy of his creditors. At his Gallic triumph Caesar's soldiers chanted verses about how he had had to borrow money in Rome to pay for all the women he slept with in Gaul.[10] But jibes like this were typical at a triumph and cannot be taken seriously. In truth, Caesar went from being debtor to lender. And like his old mentor Crassus, he made shrewd investments. To Cicero, for example, who was chronically short of money because of his expensive taste in villas, Caesar lent the small fortune of 800,000 sesterces. In exchange, Cicero was expected to help Caesar by defending Caesar's allies in court.[11]

Caesar was able to steer his new fortune toward consular campaigns. In the elections of 54, Caesar backed the candidate Memmius with substantial resources. As praetor four years earlier, Memmius had demanded an investigation into Caesar's conduct and attacked him in speeches full of salacious tidbits. Memmius even claimed that Caesar had been cupbearer to Nicomedes, a role normally held by young and scantily clad male slaves expected to provide sex on demand. But desperate for high office, Memmius could not resist Caesar's money and influence, while Caesar was eager to have the aggressive politician fighting for him. Wins by Caesar's own candidates blocked his enemies from holding office.[12]

Throughout the Gallic war, Caesar worked hard at staying in touch with the political scene in Rome. His commentaries, almost certainly written at the end of each year's campaigning season, were just one tool. He regularly sent dispatches to the Senate reporting his successes, as well as countless letters to individual senators. On his annual winter visits to northern Italy, he met with important politicians; the Luca summit of 56 was the most high-stakes example of something Caesar often did. Confidants in Rome sent him reports of all the news there and handled important business for him. Especially valuable were two men of equestrian rank, Gaius Oppius and Lucius Cornelius Balbus. Both were devoted to Caesar and after his death produced memoirs on which later biographers of Caesar drew.[13]

Such was the scale of Caesar's new wealth that he was able to go beyond buying individual politicians and supported building projects that benefited whole communities in Italy.[14] Naturally he did not forget the plebs of Rome. By 54, Caesar was at work on an audacious plan to widen the Forum. Oppius was in charge of the project, and he was able to rely on Cicero's help in working out the legal details. The two men spent 60 million sesterces just to buy the land needed. Simultaneously Caesar also rebuilt, in costly marble, the massive wooden building where voting took place on the Campus Martius. The old Sheepfold, as it was known, was now to be surrounded by an elegant portico—a mile in perimeter, Cicero boasted to his friend Atticus.[15] These were amenities for the Roman people—amenities that they would appreciate, not coincidentally, when they were voting or listening to debate. The projects also meant jobs for ordinary Romans.

A second way Caesar amassed power in Gaul was through patronage. Positions on his staff gave a bulge to purses—and to reputations. Both of Crassus's sons commanded troops, and Caesar paid tribute to them in his commentaries. Caesar told of how young Publius Crassus once was outmatched by a numerically superior enemy in western Gaul. Learning in the course of battle that the rear gate of the enemy's camp was not properly defended, Publius boldly stripped his own camp of its defenders and sent them on a long and secret march so they could make a surprise attack from behind and rout the Gauls.[16]

Some of Caesar's closest political partners in Rome came to Gaul for a tour of duty. Trebonius, after pushing through legislation so helpful to Caesar, Pompey, and Crassus in 55, was in command of three legions in Britain the very next year. Scrofula-ridden Vatinius, Caesar's faithful partner during the consulship of 59, intermittently served as a lieutenant in Gaul during the eight-year war. The new man Titus Labienus, who as tribune in 63 had worked closely with Caesar, served as second-in-command throughout all the campaigns. In warfare, Labienus had a talent for deception from which even Caesar could learn.[17]

Careful study of Caesar's commentaries reveals that many of his officers belonged to new senatorial families who were just making their way onto the political scene. And for the more junior positions on the staff, as well as essential positions in logistics, Caesar looked beyond senatorial circles altogether to the country towns of Italy. *The Gallic War* bristles with names unfamiliar in Roman history before then. New men, he must have considered, were likelier to stay loyal to him in later years than the willful sons of the nobility.[18]

One especially notorious appointment made by Caesar was his chief engineer, Mamurra, who hailed from the seaside town of Formiae, south of Rome. It did not go unnoticed that the walls of Mamurra's townhouse on the fashionable Caelian Hill were sheathed in marble; its columns too were single shafts of marble, some from the newly opened quarries at Carrara in northern Italy.[19] An attack by the poet Catullus appeared, probably late in 55:

> *Who can watch this, who suffer it, unless*
> *He's shameless and a glutton and a gambler*
> *Mamurra having all the fat that long-haired*
> *Gaul and remotest Britain used to have?. . .*
> *Was it for this, o generalissimo,*
> *You've been in the far island of the west,*
> *So that your pal, that multifucking tool,*
> *Could eat his way through twenty or thirty million?*[20]

Caesar was incensed. Not only would Catullus's lines be a permanent blot on Caesar's and his ally's reputations; they were a betrayal of Caesar's goodwill. Caesar was on friendly terms with Catullus's father and stayed at the man's house in Verona. Caesar made his anger about the insult known to the elder Catullus, and the son was forced to apologize. Caesar invited the poet to dinner that same day.[21] Caesar could, if he thought it opportune, put aside hard feelings. But Catullus was not the same kind of foe Cato was.

Catullus's verses bothered Caesar because they struck at his reputation, his *dignitas*, which he worked hard to grow in Gaul with the aid of the dispatches he sent back to Rome and through his commentaries. Describing an elaborate bridge he had built over the Rhine for a brief foray into Germany in 55, he remarked that he could not possibly have crossed by boat; it would have been beneath his *dignitas*.[22]

But words alone were not enough to win glory. Caesar pushed himself physically harder than he ever had before. There was no danger he would not face, no work he shirked. He could march in glaring sun and rain alike, moving so fast that he beat his own advance messengers. He attacked his enemies when they least expected it—immediately after a march, even in bad weather. He thought nothing of camping in the open. Oppius in his memoirs told of how when he was traveling with Caesar, they were forced by a storm to take shelter in a poor man's hut. It consisted of one room only, barely large enough for a single person. Caesar insisted that Oppius, who was ill at the time, take it. Caesar would sleep outside.[23] In battle, if his army started to give way, he would rally the men, laying hold of them one by one, catching them by the throat, forcing them to face the enemy. Once, when his Twelfth Legion was on the point of giving up, Caesar grabbed a shield from a soldier in the rear, rushed to the front, and restored the men's courage.[24]

Caesar's soldiers won his approval not by their character or private life but by their ability to fight. Service under him was a mixture of leniency and the strictest discipline, mirroring his own lifestyle. He made it a habit of not letting the men know in advance when they would march or fight; they always had to be ready. Deserters and traitors were severely punished. To more minor transgressions, however, Caesar often turned a blind eye. After a victory, he let the men celebrate with abandon. He was generous in sharing plunder, and before the war was over the soldiers' base pay was doubled. In between the rigors of training and battle they could enjoy a lavish lifestyle. As Caesar liked to boast, "My soldiers can fight well, even when they reek of perfume."[25] They were fanatically loyal to Caesar, impressed by his toughness, by the rewards he gave, even no doubt by his womanizing.

Paradoxically, it was by being away from Rome that Caesar's power over Rome grew—just as Cato had suspected would happen. Caesar now commanded the loyalty not only of the plebs but also of a battle-tested army, a corps of officers, many politicians, and whole

Caesar's success in Gaul is emblazoned on this coin, which shows a tree-trunk trophy made up of Gallic arms and armor, including a war trumpet on the right.
Credit: Courtesy of the American Numismatic Society

Another coin proclaims Caesar's success. Here is seen a Gallic warrior with beard, taken captive.
Credit: Courtesy of the American Numismatic Society

A female Gallic captive. Like her male counterpart, she is a haunting reminder of the war's toll.
Credit: Courtesy of the American Numismatic Society

towns of Italy, bound to him by his benefactions. Years and years of command give him unprecedented opportunities to enrich himself and his supporters. The glory of subduing Gaul, crossing the Rhine, and sailing through the ocean to Britain transformed his reputation. His achievement was summed up in the mind-numbing statistics Romans used to mark martial success: in less than ten years of fighting, eight hundred cities had been taken by storm, three hundred nations subdued, a million people killed, another million taken captive.[26] Caesar's exploits in Gaul put him beyond the ranks of ordinary politicians. He had far eclipsed his old mentor Crassus and caught up with Pompey in rank if not surpassed him.

Yet before the war was over, it all came very close to crashing down.

Over the winter of 55/54 Caesar's army built, for the second expedition to Britain, twenty-eight new warships and six hundred transports with a modified design that could accommodate rowers as well as sails. In the late spring of 54, Caesar ordered the armada to assemble at Portus Itius (perhaps modern Boulogne) while he set out for the country of the Treviri, a people who lived just west of the Rhine and were constantly in touch with their German neighbors over the river. The Treviri had stopped attending the periodic councils of Gallic leaders that Caesar held, and he was worried they were concocting mischief with the Germans. As was true in much of Gaul, Caesar's arrival had split the Treviri into pro- and anti-Roman factions, each headed by a rival leader. Caesar's sudden appearance in 54 led the anti-Roman leader, Indutiomarus, to submit. Caesar did what he could to strengthen Indutiomarus's rival but then hastened back to the coast.[27]

At Portus Itius Caesar found most of the ships ready, along with a large assemblage of cavalry and leaders of the various Gallic nations. Caesar would be taking many of the leaders with him, out of fear that there might be an uprising in his absence.

Unfavorable winds, and then trouble from one of the leaders, delayed Caesar for weeks. Finally in July he set sail with five legions, three more than in his previous expedition, and two thousand cavalry. The fleet landed in Britain with greater ease than it had the previous year, and Caesar marched inland. By this point it must have been clear to him that hostility against the Romans was mounting in Gaul, and he would have to limit his objectives. Full conquest was impossible, but if he could terrorize the Britons who were most in contact with the Gauls into greater submission and win some plunder doing so, it would be a successful campaign.

In this strange British land Caesar always seemed destined to be thwarted by nature. An unexpected nighttime storm mauled much of his fleet, which lay at anchor, and the army had to work continuously for ten days and nights to repair the ships and haul them onto the beach for safekeeping. In the meantime larger British forces gathered, but after failing to defeat the Romans in battle they reverted to guerilla warfare. The hit-and-run attacks of their chariots were hard for Caesar to counter. With difficulty he made it to the chief enemy stronghold and was able to storm it and seize many cattle. The last hope of the Britons was a surprise attack on the Roman naval camp; when it failed, the Britons sought terms, and Caesar readily assented. The fall equinox was approaching, and he wanted to return to Gaul before sailing became harder and any disturbances there broke out.

Just as he was about to make the crossing, a letter came to Caesar from friends in Rome with terrible news. His daughter, Julia, had died while giving birth, and the child, a girl, had also died a few days later. Caesar was devoted to Julia, and though outwardly he bore up, he grieved terribly. Since he had left Rome, his mother, Aurelia, had also died, and with both women gone he had lost his strongest defenders in Rome.[28] His wife, Calpurnia, remained, as well as Servilia.

More bad news was on the way. The harvest in Gaul that summer had been poor, which forced Caesar after his return to spread out his winter camps more widely than he liked among the hostile Belgic peoples. Indutiomarus, aiming for supremacy over the Treviri with his anti-Roman policy, in Caesar's absence had resumed preparations for war. On Indutiomarus's urging, Ambiorix, king of the Belgic Eburones, launched an attack on one of the new camps that housed a legion and a half, about seventy-five hundred men. Ambiorix realized that the camp could not easily be taken by force—no Roman camp ever fell during the whole Gallic War—and so he resorted to treachery. He convinced one of the Roman officers that all of Gaul was now alight with rebellion and the Romans must flee for safety. The legionaries set out at dawn, after staying up all night packing, and were caught in a well-planned ambush. No amount of bravery could save them, and they were slaughtered nearly to the man.

Caesar was devastated when he learned of the loss of so many of his soldiers. This was not just a blow to his *dignitas* but a source of deep anguish. He loved his men. As a sign of mourning, he stopped shaving and would not cut his beard until he had taken revenge.[29]

Ambiorix, empowered by his stunning success, persuaded neighboring peoples to launch further attacks immediately. A Gallic force swooped down on a Roman camp that was under the command of Cicero's younger brother, Quintus. For days and nights on end Quintus Cicero and his soldiers bravely held out until Caesar arrived with reinforcements. Caesar drew the enemy away and tricked them into a battle on unfavorable ground. The Gallic forces were routed. News of Caesar's victory inspired Indutiomarus to break off his plan to attack another of the camps.

Caesar would have to stay in Gaul through the winter. After the disastrous loss of his legion and a half, almost all the Gallic peoples were contemplating rebellion. Caesar summoned their leaders and managed to frighten most of them into submission, at least temporarily. The Senones, however, a powerful nation living southeast of modern Paris, tried to kill their king, one of many Caesar had placed on the throne. The plot failed. When Caesar summoned the entire council of the Senones to appear before him, they refused. In an unusual first-person intrusion into his commentaries, Caesar wrote, "I do not know whether the Gauls' rebelliousness is especially surprising, for several reasons but especially because they, who used to be held superior in bravery to all other peoples, were deeply pained that they had so forfeited this reputation that they submitted to orders from the Roman people."[30] The comment reveals much about Caesar's own values: the loss of standing could drive a man to anything.

All through the winter of 54/53, the enemies of Rome were on the move. Indutiomarus and the Treviri kept sending embassies across the Rhine to the Germans. The Germans could not be induced to cross the river, but Indutiomarus managed to increase his forces with Gallic recruits. Both northern and central Gaul had by then risen up, and in between lay Labienus's camp, a tempting target for the Treviri. As they drew near and started to prowl around, Labienus had his men feign panic. The Gauls were taken off their guard. Labienus then launched a surprise attack and overwhelmed them. Indutiomarus's head was carried back to the Roman camp on a pike—the first act of revenge for the destruction of the legion and a half.

While Caesar remained in Gaul, he had officers in northern Italy raise two new legions, and at Caesar's request Pompey lent a third. Simultaneously the forces against Caesar also gained strength. Indutiomarus's relatives made fresh alliances with Germans across the Rhine and also contracted a formal treaty of alliance with Ambiorix, butcher of the Roman legions. The Senones made plans with other disaffected peoples in central Gaul.

Caesar next devastated the lands of the peoples who had attacked Quintus Cicero's camp. Large numbers of cattle and prisoners were captured—and handed over to Caesar's soldiers. With more of his stratagems, Labienus was able to inflict similarly harsh revenge on the Treviri west of the Rhine. Ambiorix, though, the man Caesar most wanted to capture and punish, always eluded the Romans.

Caesar sent out a large number of cavalry to lay waste to Ambiorix's homeland. Every village or building they spotted was burned, and cartloads of spoils were taken off. Captives would tell the Romans that they had just seen Ambiorix on the run, a huge search would be made, but he kept slipping away into the next forest or ravine. Only two years later did Caesar give up the search for the king. The next best thing, he decided, was to strip bare his territory of inhabitants, buildings, and cattle. Ambiorix would never return to power.[31]

Caesar's reprisals, far from quelling hostility in Gaul, only inflamed it. At the start of 52, leaders everywhere began holding secret meetings in the woods. They spoke bitterly of the most recent Gallic council Caesar had convened, at which one of the chieftains had been scourged and beheaded. They poured out complaints about the loss of so many lives, so much wealth, and their freedom. That winter Caesar had returned to northern Italy, and when news reached Gaul that terrible disturbances had broken out in the city of Rome, the rebel leaders spread stories that Caesar would be long detained because of the unrest. This was their chance. A plan took shape to prevent Caesar from returning to his camps in Gaul. His armies could then be picked off one by one, as had nearly happened a couple of years before.[32]

The Carnutes in central Gaul agreed to take the lead and fixed a day to massacre the Roman traders at the important Loire river port of Cenabum (modern Orléans). From village to village, word of the grisly act of revenge against the war profiteers whipped through Gaul like a fire. What had happened at Cenabum at dawn was known that same night in the country of the Arverni, 150 miles away. There the uprising would find its true leader, the worthiest opponent Caesar faced in the Gallic War, perhaps in all his wars.

Vercingetorix was a young and powerful Arvernian whose father had once held a leading position in Gaul but was killed by his own countrymen for trying to make himself king. It was not hard for

Vercingetorix, who had a charismatic personality and was physically imposing, to stir the family's old retainers with denunciations of Rome. His followers proclaimed him king, and soon much of central and western Gaul fell into his grip. As supreme commander, Vercingetorix demanded hostages, set quotas for soldiers and arms production, and, above all, built up cavalry forces. His discipline was iron. According to Caesar, if a serious offense was committed, the offender was burned or tortured to death; for a minor offense, a man's ears were cut off or eyes gouged out, and he was sent home as a warning.[33]

Caesar was still in northern Italy when he learned that rebellion was breaking out. He surely would have liked to linger so that he could track political developments in Rome, but it was impossible. Everything he had worked for over the previous six years was at risk. After crossing the Alps he realized just how grave the situation was. If he summoned the legions to him from the winter camps, they might be destroyed on the march. If he tried to make it to the legions, his own life was in danger, so unsettled had Gaul become. Vercingetorix had sent some of his forces to threaten the old Roman province in the south while he himself had gone north to coerce more peoples into joining the uprising.

Caesar fortified the province's defenses and then made an unexpected move. Directly between Caesar and the king's homeland were the Cevennes Mountains, over which lay a thick blanket of snow that blocked the passes. Caesar had his soldiers clear drifts up to six feet deep and break a path through. The Arverni were taken completely by surprise. They had thought the mountains as good as a fortress wall.

This was like a match of *latrunculi*, the two-person strategy game Romans enjoyed playing, only the board was all of Gaul. Vercingetorix felt he must return to his homeland. While he proceeded there, Caesar crossed back over the Cevennes, moved up the Rhône Valley, and, after picking up fresh cavalry he had sent ahead days earlier, rejoined two of his legions. Soon the whole Roman army was reunited before Vercingetorix even knew where Caesar was.

Vercingetorix had to adopt a new strategy. The Gauls needed to do everything they could to cut the Romans off from forage and food. This meant burning their own villages and farm buildings in every direction. The Gauls would keep enough supplies to see themselves through the campaigning season, while the Romans and their animals would either starve or be forced to go far from their camp, exposing them to the superior Gallic cavalry. Even the Gallic towns that were not well fortified must be burned, Vercingetorix insisted, to separate the Romans from supplies there.

Despite some setbacks for the Gauls, and much unhappiness at the necessity of destroying their own homelands, the plan was effective. Caesar put Gergovia, the hilltop capital of the Arverni, under siege, but he was unable to take it and ultimately had to flee. His position weakened further when the town where he was holding his hostages, as well as supplies of grain and money, fell. Even the Aedui, the wealthy people who lived in what is modern Burgundy and had been allied to Rome for decades, were on the verge of revolt. There was talk among Caesar's staff of retreating to the old Roman province. But as Caesar wrote, to do so would bring *indignitas*—the very opposite of *dignitas*—and it would strand four legions that Caesar had sent north under the command of Labienus.[34] In truth, if Caesar retreated, the uprising might spread further, and he could lose all of Gaul and some of his army. And that, in turn, could spell political ruin. Back in Rome, Cato was scheming to strip Caesar of his command, and a devastating loss by Caesar would strengthen Cato's position immeasurably.[35] All the power Caesar had built up would be as ruined as the villages of Gaul.

By marching day and night Caesar was able to rejoin Labienus. A pan-Gallic council, meanwhile, met at Bibracte, the ancient seat of Aeduan power. Vercingetorix ordered all the cavalry to assemble there. His plan was to continue cutting off the Romans from food and forage and to launch attacks on the old southern province to force a weakened Caesar to return there. Unexpectedly, however, Caesar managed to win a cavalry battle against the Gauls.

Vercingetorix then retreated to Alesia, a well-fortified hilltop settlement in northern Burgundy. Caesar turned what should have been a stronghold for the Gauls into a deathtrap. Through prodigious effort the Roman soldiers began building a ten-mile ring of fortifications around Alesia. And then, to counter the massive reinforcing army that the Gauls would send, the soldiers constructed another, outward-facing ring of fortifications, about thirteen miles in circumference. Adjacent to the palisades on both sides they dug trenches and set traps. Sharpened tree trunks were firmly sunk into ditches, with only their pointed ends sticking out; the unprepared Gauls would be impaled. The Roman soldiers nicknamed the stakes "grave markers." Even more ghoulish were the "daisies"—pits with sharpened logs arranged in patterns of five, concealed on top with twigs and brush.[36]

Inside Alesia the Gauls began to starve. When some emerged to surrender, Caesar left them out to die, ratcheting up the psychological pressure. The massive relieving army did finally arrive and rallied spirits on the hilltop. In the middle of the night, Gallic relief forces drew near the Roman fortifications, carrying ladders, grappling hooks, and wicker screens to throw across the trenches. Vercingetorix sounded the horn, and his men poured out of the city. From both sets of fortifications the Romans pounded the Gauls with artillery, and the Gauls who made it closer fell into the traps and were impaled. The Gauls had to withdraw from the fight, and after one last desperate effort ended in failure, they knew they were beaten. Vercingetorix and the other Gallic leaders surrendered.

According to later authors, Vercingetorix put on his most beautiful armor, decorated his horse, and rode out through the gates of Alesia. Three times Vercingetorix circled Caesar, who was seated, before he leapt down from the horse, threw off his armor, and sat at Caesar's feet, silent.[37] Caesar's own account was in the sparer style of Roman military dispatches: "Caesar took his seat within the fortifications in front of his camp. The leaders were brought to him.

Vercingetorix was surrendered. The weapons were thrown to the ground."[38]

For Caesar, the surrender of his great enemy nearly spoke for itself. When word reached Rome of the victory in Gaul, twenty days of thanksgiving were decreed by the Senate.[39]

Though a versatile author, Caesar never wrote a full autobiography. Stories told by memoirists such as Oppius are essential for piecing together a complete picture of the man. Yet Caesar's most important qualities are on display in *The Gallic War*. On page after page the reader can see Caesar's ruthlessly clear mind at work as he explains his decisions—why it was necessary to show caution in one situation, to attack vigorously in another. Even more striking is Caesar's tenacity, as he grabs the shield and rushes to the front line of battle, lands the army on the British beach, pushes through the snow-filled Cevennes, prevents all of Gaul from falling.

Years of campaigning, on land and sea, in many styles of warfare, tested Caesar, strengthened him, and made him into a great general. To the next political struggles, he could bring military power.

CHAPTER 10

CATO'S MEDICINES

IN THE EVER-GROWING ANNALS OF ROMAN CORRUPTION, THE consular elections of 54 BC broke all records. Of the four men who were running, Cicero wrote to Atticus, "I've never seen candidates so evenly matched."[1] Two of the contenders, Gaius Memmius and Marcus Aemilius Scaurus, were firmly backed by the influence and wealth of Caesar and Pompey. Besides that, voters gratefully remembered the marvelous shows Scaurus had staged as aedile featuring five crocodiles and a hippopotamus, and Scaurus also had plunder from his recent Sardinian governorship to strew around. The other two candidates, Domitius Calvinus and Messalla Rufus, enjoyed the support of the enemies of Caesar, Pompey, and Crassus. As tribune in the year of Caesar's consulship, Calvinus had opposed Caesar and won great credit among the *optimates* for helping Bibulus to watch the skies. Also to Calvinus's credit was a show he had put on, even if, as Cicero conceded, it had not been hugely popular.

By early July, Memmius, worried about his prospects of victory, persuaded Calvinus to join forces and make a deal with the consuls currently in office. In exchange for help in distributing bribes at the upcoming election, the consuls were to be awarded desirable provinces to hold after their year in office. To seal the pact, Memmius and Calvinus agreed to pay the outgoing consuls 4 million sesterces if they failed to deliver the provinces, a promise they put down in writing.

It proved impossible to keep so sensational an arrangement hidden, and as word leaked out more bribes were promised by all the candidates. Such large sums of money were needed that interest rates doubled in Rome. Memmius's position became untenable. On Pompey's advice, he made a full confession in the Senate, even reading out the text of the agreement with the consuls. The openness did him no good: Calvinus felt betrayed and severed ties, and Caesar was also annoyed by the disclosure. The public revelation naturally also discredited the two sitting consuls, especially Domitius Ahenobarbus, Cato's brother-in-law, who had been elected into high office for 54 after his earlier loss to Pompey and Crassus.

Cato was disgusted. For years he had been complaining about the dominance of money in elections. Voters rewarded candidates who fed and entertained them lavishly. The politicians, in turn, racked up such debt that they needed to plunder the provinces they governed. Increasingly it seemed that only by handing out cash, whether to the people or to the power brokers, could a man step up the ladder of office. Laws against bribery and extortion had been passed, but obtaining convictions proved hard: the jurors themselves could be bribed! A further problem was that electoral malpractice was normally prosecuted after elections, and as soon as winners entered office they enjoyed legal immunity, immunity that continued as they went on to overseas governorships. The window of time for netting wrongdoers was narrow, especially if elections were delayed for any reason. With good reason, Cato believed that unless changes were made, there would be a total breakdown of politics. Corruption was a disease that threatened the very life of the Republic, and new remedies were needed to treat it.[2]

He had his first success with the tribunician elections in the summer of 54, held while the scandal of the consuls' pact was still unfolding. All the candidates for tribunician office agreed to swear an oath to have Cato serve as umpire for the campaign, and they each deposited 500,000 sesterces with him to ensure honesty. Anyone caught bribing would have to forfeit the money. As Cicero wrote to Atticus, "If the elections [for tribune] go through without handouts, as it is believed they will, Cato will have done more on his own than all the laws and jurymen."[3] On election day Cato did have to announce that one candidate had violated the law, but otherwise the threat of immediate loss of the deposit had proved effective.

For the consular election, after the revelation of the shameful pact, Cato recommended a different cure. He persuaded the Senate to pass a decree requiring that a so-called silent process be instituted. Here the idea was to require candidates to submit a full set of accounts to a panel of jurors before the elections, thereby allowing anyone engaged in bribery to be excluded in advance of voting. This novel proposal was disliked by the candidates—and disliked even more by the people, who feared the loss of the usual perquisites of a consular campaign, such as free meals and seats at games. Thanks to tribunician opposition, the proposal failed to gain passage into law.[4]

Meanwhile, though, as president of the extortion court, Cato could administer another dose of his medicine. Scaurus, one of the consular candidates in 54, had returned from Sardinia in June of that year. In early July—at the same time that Memmius and Calvinus were making their pact—Scaurus was indicted on extortion charges by a young senator with Sardinian connections, who also happened to be a friend of Cato's. Cato proved very sympathetic when the prosecutor insisted that the trial must be held promptly, before the consular elections. Otherwise, the argument went, Scaurus would be able to buy the consulship with stolen money, enter office before the case was decided, and then go on to plunder other provinces; the poor Sardinians wouldn't get a single sestertius. To see justice done, Cato also agreed to substantially shorten the normal period granted to the prosecution to collect evidence. Scaurus ended up winning acquittal, but the trial brought publicity to what he had done, and he never did hold the consulship.[5]

Many ordinary people found Cato's cures hard to take. The games, meals, and handouts candidates offered were a refuge in lives of deprivation. Nor were the rights of Sardinians likely to arouse much concern in the city's taverns or at the street fountains and altars where men and women gathered. One morning, as Cato was walking to his praetorian tribunal, an angry crowd fell upon him and even started throwing stones. Cato barely managed to make his way over to the Rostra, where he gave a speech that quelled the disturbance. The Senate passed a motion praising his resolute action. "But I do not praise you," he replied, "for leaving an endangered praetor in the lurch and not coming to his aid."[6] Cato's abstemiousness and his calls for reform were costing him popularity.

By the start of 53 no consuls had been elected, which left the temporary magistrates known as *interreges*, who held power for just five days at a time, in charge. They were empowered to hold elections but month after month were blocked from doing so. Adverse omens were reported. There was violence in the Forum. Above all, the tribunes of the year—elected separately from the consuls, and so able to take their office—tried to manipulate the situation to help themselves and their allies. One of the tribunes, a cousin of Pompey, went so far as to propose that Pompey should be appointed to the dictatorship, the emergency magistracy last held by Sulla. That was not an encouraging precedent, and Cato launched a vigorous attack on the tribune and defeated the plan. Pompey, who was away from Rome at the time, had some of his friends come forward to say that he did not desire the office anyway. Cato applauded Pompey's disavowal.[7]

As late as July of 53 there were still no consuls—and because new praetors could only be elected after new consuls, the courts were also frozen. Finally that month the impasse was broken when the Senate passed its emergency decree and asked Pompey to restore order and hold the elections. Even without a dictatorship, Pompey had military resources on hand. Since 55, he had been in command of the Spanish provinces, but he governed them through deputies, which allowed him to stay behind in Italy with men under arms. Although Cato had denounced this unconventional arrangement, he was starting to see Pompey's leadership as necessary for the Republic to move forward, and he encouraged Pompey to pursue "law and order."[8] From Cato that was almost high praise. Pompey took up the Senate's call and soon held the elections. Domitius Calvinus and Messalla Rufus—the two candidates from 54 whom Pompey had not favored—were elected.

Perhaps there was a chance that Pompey and Cato could work together further. It is likely that the impetus behind the rapprochement of the Senate leadership with Pompey was the arrival of shocking news from the east.[9] Late in 55 Crassus had set out from Rome for Syria, determined to launch a war against the great Parthian empire that would bring him new wealth and glory to match Pompey's and Caesar's. But in early June of 53, Crassus found his army encircled by a huge force of enemy archers on the plains of Mesopotamia near the city of Carrhae. Crassus's son Publius, who had brought a detachment of Gallic cavalry from Caesar, was overwhelmed, and soon Crassus and thousands of his legionaries were too. The stunning loss of three legions gave sudden urgency to the warnings Cato had been issuing for years about politicians' greedy exploitation of the empire. Just as important, Crassus's death instantly ended the three-way alliance he had shared with Caesar and Pompey.

And with the death of Julia the year before, whether Caesar and Pompey would stay together was a real question. There had been no immediate breakdown in their relationship following Julia's death— Pompey, after all, lent Caesar a legion at the start of 53—but Caesar was eager to renew a marital connection. First he offered the hand of his grand-niece to Pompey. Pompey declined. Then Caesar asked for the hand of Pompey's own daughter for himself. Pompey again said no.[10]

Cato surely took note. Already a critic of Pompey in the 60s, Cato had attacked the great general even more fiercely for his alliance with Caesar in 59 and afterward. The pimps of empire, Cato called the two, as they traded armies and women. But Cato had no doubt that Caesar was the greater threat to republican government, and senatorial government especially. Pompey had resorted to bribery and violence but with more reticence than Caesar. Pompey was keener than Caesar to work with the Senate and win its leaders' approval. He had not blatantly insulted the Senate, as Caesar had. Pompey shared Cato's interest in providing just government for the empire and the world. Had Caesar been entrusted with the command against the pirates, Cato must have thought, it would not have been the quick and merciful campaign Pompey had planned and executed. The Gallic War, far from offering solutions to the interlocking problems of violence and bribery at home and misgovernment abroad, had only worsened them. Hand in hand with his desire to rid public life of dirty money went Cato's other dream: to rid the Roman world of dirty Caesar.

With the deaths of Julia and then Crassus, as well as Pompey's refusal of the dictatorship in 53, new possibilities were opening, possibilities that were exciting for Cato, alarming for Caesar and Caesar's friends. Pompey might not have been ready to turn on his old partner yet. For Cato's other goal of curing the state from corruption, however, cooperation with Pompey was possible—and that might prepare the way for Cato then to do something about Caesar.

After the new consuls of 53 finally took office, Rome remained unsettled, but the consuls did pass a decree that no ex-praetor or ex-consul should assume a command abroad until five years had elapsed following their time in office. The hope was that by cutting magistrates off from power and plunder right after holding office, they would curtail the frenzied struggle surrounding elections, especially all the bribery and the occasional violence that occurred.

The intention, in other words, was to break the vicious cycle of electoral malpractice and exploitation of the provinces that was destabilizing to both the city of Rome and the empire—and which Cato had long denounced. The consuls' proposal was a gratifying acknowledgment that Cato had been right. Perhaps because of ongoing unrest in the city as well as popular opposition to a reform that could sweep away much of the campaign system, the decree was not immediately enacted into law.[11] But like a doctor who has recommended a treatment, Cato must have hoped the patient would follow through on it and finally recover.

The Republic had to go through a near-death experience first. The campaign for the consulship of 52 was marked not just by open bribery but also by horrific violence. Among the candidates was Milo, a close friend of Cicero who years before had organized professionally trained fighters to take on Clodius and his gangs. Clodius himself, now running for the praetorship, was determined to keep Milo out of the top office. As their supporters beat each other up in the streets, the elections kept being postponed. Like 53, the year 52 opened with no consuls or praetors.[12]

Milo was desperate for the elections to be held. He had ample support, thanks in no small part to the theatrical shows and gladiatorial games he had staged—on which he used up three inheritances, Cicero claimed.[13] But Milo's two opponents, who were supported by Pompey, were determined to keep postponing the elections, as was Clodius, until they could be sure Milo would be defeated.

On January 18 Milo left Rome on a brief trip, and as he and his entourage made their way down the great Appian Way, they unexpectedly ran into Clodius, who was traveling on horseback with around thirty slaves. A couple of Milo's gladiators got in a fight with these slaves, and Clodius himself was wounded with a spear and carried to a nearby inn. Thinking that Clodius, if he survived, would be more dangerous than ever, Milo had his old enemy taken out of the inn and killed. Clodius's body was left lying on the road until another traveler found it and took it to Rome.

At dawn the next morning the corpse was displayed on the Rostra, naked so that all the wounds could be seen. Clodius's followers went wild. They carried the body into the Senate house, heaped the wooden benches there into a pyre, and lit a fire for the man who had given Rome free grain. The Senate house went up in flames and with it the nearby Basilica Porcia, built by Cato's great-grandfather. The angry mob then made an attack on Milo's house and finally went to Pompey's residence on the Field of Mars and called on him to take over as consul or dictator.

Weeks of violence followed. The Senate, unable to meet in its own ruined building and forced to use other temples, passed an emergency decree, just as it had the year before. And once again it entrusted Pompey with the task of restoring order, authorizing him to raise new troops to do so. Yet even after Pompey returned with the troops, the *interreges* proved unable to carry out the election of new consuls. Tribunes who were determined to avenge Clodius's murder insisted that Milo had to stand trial first.[14] The city seemed to be slipping into anarchy. Cato was alarmed.

Cato came to a realization: only a compromise would save Rome from civil war, and the compromise would have to infringe on that most fundamental principle of the Republic, the sharing of power. Pompey was to become sole consul. This would avoid the hateful associations of Sullan dictatorship and ensure that Milo would be tried before he had any chance of the consulship, a necessary step for restoring law and order. Not Cato himself but the higher-ranking Bibulus introduced the proposal to the Senate. When it came Cato's turn to speak, senators felt sure he would oppose it. To their surprise, he said that although he could not introduce such a motion, he did support it. Any government was better than none, and for the Republic's present illness, Pompey would have to become the physician. His comments swayed the Senate. The resolution was passed, and after a formal vote by the people, Rome had a sole consul.[15]

The compromise never could have been struck without Cato's support, and to acknowledge that fact, Pompey invited his old critic over to his house. When Cato arrived, Pompey grasped his hand warmly, thanked him, and asked him to serve as an advisor in a private capacity. Cato replied that in a private capacity, he would do so—but on public affairs he would always make his opinion known, whether asked or not.[16]

The two men would hardly agree on everything. Very soon after becoming consul, Pompey proposed new legislation on bribery and violence. Trial procedures for both offenses were radically streamlined, and as a safeguard against bribery the final panel of jurors was selected at the very end of the trial. Cato largely approved, but he and his friends did attempt to arrange for Milo to be tried by the old procedures—in vain.[17] Pompey was determined to remove Milo from Rome, and when Milo's trial took place in early April, with Pompey's soldiers posted around the Forum, not even Cicero could save his old friend.

Cato also clashed with Pompey over Caesar. During the riots that followed Clodius's murder, Caesar was in northern Italy, and there was some discussion of his assuming the consulship alongside Pompey. But Caesar needed to be in Gaul, especially after he learned of the massacre at Cenabum that started the great uprising of 52. So instead he asked the tribunes, all ten of them, to pass a law that would help him obtain his second consulship later by allowing him to stand for it in absentia. The law immediately enhanced Caesar's *dignitas*. It also offered him protection because he would be able to retain his Gallic command right until he entered his second consulship, meaning he could not be accused in the courts, as Cato had long been threatening to do. Furthermore, the tribunes' law would spare Caesar from the dilemma he had faced in 60, when Cato made Caesar forgo his triumph to declare his candidacy in person. Pompey agreed to support the law, against the opposition of Cato, who would never have allowed such an exemption to his best friend, much less to Caesar.[18] Cato gave one of his daylong speeches to try to stop the bill but in the end was unsuccessful.

This was a setback for Cato's efforts to get rid of Caesar, but in advancing Cato's other goal, to purge politics of money, Pompey cooperated willingly. Not only was there the new legislation on bribery itself, which proved effective at netting offenders; Pompey also had enacted into law the Senate decree of the previous year that mandated ex-praetors and ex-consuls wait five years before they take an overseas province.[19] Without any chance of an immediate payout of plunder, it would be much harder for candidates for high office to bribe. A further benefit of the law, for *optimates* like Cato, was that it broke the automatic connection between urban magistracy and governorship. It would give the Senate some discretion in choosing which former magistrates should be eligible for governorships at which time.

Even if Cato and his fellow champions of senatorial government did not get everything they had wanted out of Pompey, they still got a great deal. Pompey was not the perfect physician in Cato's eyes, but he had rapidly brought the Republic back to health and had even removed some of the sources of future illness. True to form, Cato complained when Pompey rescued his new father-in-law, Metellus Scipio, from conviction in the bribery court by having Scipio elected fellow consul in August of 52.[20] Aside from the principle of it, Scipio was the man who had stolen Cato's fiancée years earlier. Cato was also appalled when he was serving as a juror in the violence court and a written testimonial on behalf of a patently guilty defendant arrived from Pompey—in violation of Pompey's own new law, which prohibited such testimonials. With great theatricality Cato clapped his hands to his ears and managed to have the tablet with Pompey's letter removed.[21]

Cato's greatest frustration remained Caesar. Despite years of warnings, Cato believed, Pompey was not taking proper action against Caesar. Cato would have to try to do something himself. As the election for the consuls of 51 approached, Cato announced that he was running, and doing so on a platform of taking away Caesar's army from him.[22] Under the old system of governorships, Caesar could have expected that he would only be succeeded in the year 49, by a consul of 50. But thanks to Pompey's new legislation, it was now possible for the Senate to act sooner, which made Cato's threat serious.

Yet if there was any hope of persuading voters that this was the right course of action, it was nixed—by Cato himself. At his insistence, the Senate passed a decree requiring candidates to do all their own canvassing; nobody else was allowed to ask for votes on a candidate's behalf. This was highly annoying to voters. Not only were they losing free meals; they couldn't even shake the hand of the celebrity surrogates on whom candidates normally relied. Cato himself was a terrible campaigner.

It would have been hard to design an electoral strategy more likely to fail. Cato nevertheless insisted that it was more important to take a stand for clean elections. Shortly after his loss, he made a point of going to the Field of Mars to play a handball game that Romans enjoyed, and he then spent the afternoon wandering barefoot around the Forum with his friends. Outwardly he showed no disappointment or distress. In part he was saving face, but he was also trying to set an example for other candidates: life went on after defeat.

Cato probably could feel carefree for another reason. This was not like the consular election of 60, when Cato and the *optimates* so feared Caesar that they condoned bribery on behalf of Bibulus. In 52, the other two candidates were quite acceptable choices in Cato's eyes. One was the patrician Servius Sulpicius Rufus, an old friend of Cato's who had first run for the consulship against Catiline in 63, at which time he took a hard line against bribery. The other was Marcus Claudius Marcellus, a member of a distinguished family, a superb public speaker, and probably another longtime friend of Cato's.[23] As events would show, Marcellus was, besides all that, also a determined opponent of Caesar.

As the year 51 got underway, Marcus Marcellus tried to move forward with Cato's plan to strip Caesar of his army. The Gallic War was over, Marcellus said, and peace had been established. In fact, even though Vercingetorix had been defeated, there were still pockets of fierce resistance spread throughout the country, and Caesar had to spend the year pursuing a military campaign before he could impose a final settlement. Regardless, Marcellus insisted that Caesar be brought back anyway, and if he wanted his name to appear on any ballot, he should declare his candidacy in person.[24]

There was much opposition to this proposal, not only from die-hard Caesarians but from others too. The law of Pompey and Crassus that had renewed Caesar's command in 55 only allowed there to be consideration of a successor for Caesar on March 1, 50, or later—which, under the old system of governorships, meant no ex-consuls could take over for Caesar until at least 49. Pompey's recent legislation did allow for replacement of Caesar on March 1, 50, but that date still needed to be respected to satisfy legality. Tribunes friendly to Caesar were ready with vetoes if the Senate acted earlier. Even Marcellus's fellow consul, Cato's friend Sulpicius Rufus, criticized Marcellus's proposal and warned that it could lead to civil war.[25]

Marcellus had other means of humiliating Caesar. While fighting the Gallic War, Caesar had also been moving forward with his plans to extend the citizenship in northern Italy. He had, for example, recruited noncitizens into his legions. Marcellus made a motion in the Senate that thousands of the citizenship grants should be revoked. Tribunes interposed the veto. Undeterred, Marcellus had one of Caesar's new citizens beaten with the consular fasces—a punishment meant to mark him as an alien. Marcellus then told the man to go show his scars to Caesar.[26]

Cato can only have been disgusted by this brutality, but there were other developments that he would have found gratifying. In the consular election held in July of 51, Marcus Marcellus's cousin Gaius, another fierce critic of Caesar, gained one of the ivory chairs. The other victor, Aemilius Paullus, was not a friend of Caesar's either. And later that month Pompey succumbed to pressure in the Senate to say that he would withdraw the legion that he had lent Caesar at the start of 53. "Everyone ought to be obedient to the Senate," Pompey said.[27]

By September, Pompey seemed to be moving to the view that Caesar should not be elected consul while also retaining his army.

A marble bust of Pompey the Great, an ally first of Caesar and then of Cato. The thick, tousled hair evoked portraits of Pompey's role model, Alexander the Great.
Credit: akg-images

Pompey would still respect the legal requirement not to consider a successor for Caesar until March 1, 50, but after that date the Senate could and should bring up the matter. If tribunes tried to interpose a veto then, Pompey said, they would be disregarded; the Senate's authority must be respected.

And what, one senator asked, if Caesar still sought election and refused to give up his army? Calmly Pompey replied, "And what if my son wants to hit me with a stick?"[28] Seemingly the remark was meant to suggest that such behavior by Caesar was unthinkable. But as a shrewd observer wrote to Cicero (who was away from Rome at the time), "With these remarks Pompey has made people think that he is having trouble with Caesar."[29] And if Pompey and Caesar were growing apart, Caesar's opponents had less reason to make any effort at compromise.

Caesar was confronted by paradox: after defeating Vercingetorix and stomping out the last flames of Gallic resistance, he faced more domestic political peril than ever. If replaced in command on March 1, 50, and then required to declare his candidacy in person, he could be put on trial and perhaps even convicted. Or he might be made to choose between a triumph and another consulship.[30] Either was a terrible thought. It was not for his property or his life that Caesar feared, but for what he held dearer than life itself, his reputation. From his earliest years Caesar had harbored a dread of failure or humiliation. His many astonishing successes only made it worse: he had so much more to lose. As far as he was concerned, he was the first man in Rome; Marcus Marcellus should not question that, nor even should Pompey, especially after all Caesar had done for Pompey. The people had given Caesar the right to stand in absentia, and it was outrageous for the Senate to try to revoke it.[31]

Caesar had just fought for his survival in Gaul. Now he would have to fight for survival in Rome. He worked on shoring up old alliances and securing new friends. He released streams of Gallic wealth as never before. He undertook expensive contracts for the gladiatorial games and the public feast he was planning in honor of his late daughter. He gave a vast sum of money to the incoming consul Aemilius Paullus, who had gotten into financial difficulties while trying to rebuild the family's basilica in the Forum. Most important was Caesar's investment in the bold young noble Scribonius Curio, one of the tribunes for 50. In 59 Caesar had gotten a taste of Curio's talent from the bitter attacks Curio had launched against him and Pompey, and since then the enthusiastic crowds who cheered on Curio had only grown. At recent funeral games for his father, Curio had built two wooden theaters that could be used for dramatic shows and then, by a marvel of engineering, joined together for afternoon gladiatorial contests. Such extravagance had saddled Curio with substantial debts, and Caesar agreed to settle them, in exchange for the young tribune's help.[32]

It was another of Caesar's sneak attacks. Until the much-anticipated meeting of March 1, 50, nobody knew how closely Curio was working with his old enemy. When the scheduled debate got underway in March, Curio persistently imposed his veto to prevent discussion. Finally the consul Gaius Marcellus was able to force the matter and proposed replacing Caesar immediately. Paullus kept silent. Curio said he would support Marcellus's motion—provided that Pompey resign his provinces and army too.[33]

It was an ingenious proposal. If both Pompey and Caesar had to disarm, Caesar's *dignitas* would be upheld. Caesar's enemies would not be able to rely on Pompey bringing soldiers into Rome to sway elections and trials, as he had two years earlier. Above all, the proposal took Caesar off the defensive. Ordinary citizens, worried about the possibility of civil war if one or both sides refused to back down, applauded it. There was sympathy in the Senate for it as well.[34]

Caesar's most determined opponents, of course, found Curio's proposal outrageous. Pompey's command was not set to expire, as Caesar's was. Also, there could be little doubt that even if Caesar dismissed his army, he could quickly call on them for their help. The Republic must not be left defenseless. On at least one occasion after Curio repeated his demand for mutual disarmament, Cato shouted out that everything he had been warning about for years had finally come to pass. The forces Caesar had tricked the government into giving him to fight in Gaul, Cato said, were really being used against Rome itself.[35]

Cato was content to let others take the initiative in opposing Caesar. He himself was absorbed by another major issue, the state of the Roman east after the terrible defeat of Crassus in 53. A Parthian invasion of the empire was a real threat, and if it happened it would have momentous implications for politics. Caesar might seize command in a war that would bring far more prestige and profit than Gaul. To Cato it seemed more important than ever to win back the loyalty of Roman allies after years of misrule. With Pompey's help in 52 Cato had treated at least some of the illness affecting Rome; that had been the first step. Now the same had to be done in the empire. Allies of Cato's were sent by the Senate to the critical provinces—Bibulus to Syria, Cato's old tribunician colleague Minucius Thermus to Asia, and Cicero to Cilicia.[36]

Letters from Cicero to Cato reveal Cato's efforts. After hearing a report of the movement of a massive Parthian army, it was to Cato whom Cicero wrote first, even before writing to the Senate. Cicero offered the Stoic a reassurance that he would use "gentleness and restraint" to keep Rome's allies faithful during the crisis—a clear indication of Cato's own priorities.[37] A few months later, after Cicero had enjoyed a minor military victory over a mountain people on the border between Cilicia and Syria, he wrote once more. Cicero was hoping that Cato would be willing to support the vote of a thanksgiving to the gods, but again the letter was full of reassurances that spoke to Cato's policy. Cicero wrote, "I made fairness and restraint the strongest defense against the risk of a major war."[38]

Cato was one of just a few to vote against the honor (his friend Favonius was another), apparently on the strict grounds that a thanksgiving to the gods was not owed to Cicero for what Cicero had achieved by his own merits.[39] Cicero was greatly disappointed since a thanksgiving often led to a triumph. But as Cato wrote to Cicero, in the only letter of Cato's to survive, "I did what, in keeping with my judgment, I could: with my speech and with my vote I commended you for defending your province by your integrity and good judgment… and for winning back the goodwill of our allies in support of our rule." The Senate's judgment that a province was held through "the gentleness and integrity of its commander rather than by the swords of an army" should be worth more than a triumph. Cato signed off: "Goodbye and remember me kindly, and, staying on the path you have chosen, render to our allies and to the Republic a strict and careful administration."[40]

While restoring stability in the east, Cato did nothing to help broker a compromise in the more urgent crisis unfolding in Rome. For Cato and his allies, there could not be one iota of compromise with Caesar. And the consular elections held in the summer of 50 only seemed to strengthen their position: a former officer of Caesar's was defeated by two of his enemies, one of them yet another member of the suddenly resurgent Marcellus family. Caesar could take consolation that one of his officers, the immensely talented Mark Antony, was elected to the tribunate, always the last refuge for a politician in peril. An intimidating man who liked to wear his tunic girt up to his thigh to show off his powerful legs, Antony would keep up the fight in Rome. One other satisfaction for Caesar was that Antony also beat out Cato's brother-in-law Domitius Ahenobarbus in an election to fill a vacancy in the augural college created by the death of Cato's longstanding ally Hortensius, to whom Cato had handed over his wife, Marcia, several years before. Domitius was furious at his defeat.[41]

Meanwhile, Curio also inflamed the tensions. After falling seriously ill in the late spring of 50, Pompey staged a recovery that was hailed throughout Italy. Convinced that he was invincible—that, as he put it, he need only stamp his foot in Italy and armies would spring up from the earth—he informed the Senate he would relinquish his powers if the senators wished it. Certain that Pompey's statement was only meant to make Caesar look bad, Curio demanded that Pompey disarm first, and then he denounced Pompey unsparingly as the one who was truly aiming at supreme power.[42]

At a senate meeting at the start of December, Curio finally was able to force a vote on his proposal that both Pompey and Caesar step down from their commands: 370 voted in favor and only 22 against. Like the people, the vast majority of senators were worried about what civil war would mean for them and were desperate to prevent it.[43]

The consul Gaius Marcellus dismissed the meeting, angrily crying out, "You win—Caesar is your master."[44] Along with the consuls-elect, Marcellus went to Pompey's house on the Field of Mars and placed a sword in Pompey's hands, urging him to save the Republic. With no authorization from the Senate, Marcellus then entrusted Pompey with two legions that had been earmarked to fight in Parthia but were still in Italy, and also authorized him to recruit additional troops. Pompey accepted the assignment. Curio protested against these highly irregular arrangements but in vain, and after his tribunate ended on December 9, he went to join Caesar in northern Italy. Caesar's opponents, it was now clear, were prepared to resist him militarily, and Pompey had agreed to support them.

Caesar was at Ravenna, which fast-traveling messengers from Rome could reach in three days. He had just one legion with him, but probably as soon as he learned of Pompey's acceptance of the sword, he sent orders for more of the Gallic army to cross the Alps.[45] Caesar was not going to let himself be intimidated. If it came to war, he had ample resources: northern Italy with its great reserves of manpower, all the auxiliary forces and staff officers he had acquired in Gaul, above all his battle-tested and utterly loyal legions. But Pompey and his allies had considerable assets too: control of all the provinces beyond the Gauls, a network of powerful allies in the east, two legions in Italy and many more in Spain, and total naval dominance in the Mediterranean thanks to relationships Pompey had been building since the war against the pirates. Caesar was ready for war but was ready to avoid it as well. He remembered the savagery of his teenage years and knew that even still some of the wounds of those earlier battles were unhealed.

By the time the Senate convened on New Year's Day of 49, Curio had returned to Rome with a letter from Caesar. Only with difficulty did Mark Antony and another tribune supporting Caesar get permission for it to be read out. In the letter, Caesar reviewed all his accomplishments from the beginning of his career, and he reiterated his offer to lay down his army at the same time Pompey did his. Otherwise, Caesar made clear, he would defend his rights—including the right to stand in absentia for the consulship, legally voted to him by the people of Rome. The letter struck at least some in the Senate as menacing, and under pressure from the new consul Lentulus Crus, a majority voted in favor of a proposal by Pompey's father-in-law Metellus Scipio that Caesar disband his army. Antony and his colleague interposed the veto.[46]

Over the next few days negotiations continued. Cicero, newly returned from his eastern province and convinced that civil war would be disastrous, assumed a leading role. Already in December Caesar had said he would be willing to give up Transalpine Gaul and reduce his legions to two, and now his friends went further and said he would also give up Cisalpine Gaul and an additional legion. For a brief moment it appeared that Pompey might accept this compromise, but the new consul Lentulus was opposed to it—and so was Cato, who cried out that Pompey was allowing himself to be deceived.[47] As the situation grew more desperate and a few moderates in the Senate pleaded simply to send envoys to Caesar, Cato spoke against that proposal as well.[48] On January 7 the Senate passed its emergency decree. The consuls would no longer recognize the vetoes of the two Caesarian tribunes nor guarantee their safety. Along with Curio, the tribunes fled the city in disguise. The Senate had effectively declared war on Caesar.[49]

The news was carried to Ravenna. According to his own account, Caesar assembled his soldiers and listed aloud the whole series of wrongs his enemies had inflicted on him. He deplored the suppression of the tribunes' veto. Even Sulla, he pointed out, while stripping the tribunes of all their powers, had left the veto unhindered.

And the emergency decree had previously been passed only when the city was under direct threat. "Caesar," Caesar continued, "urged the men to defend, against his enemies, the reputation and the position of the man under whose command and leadership for nine years they had administered the state so successfully, won a great many battles, and pacified all of Gaul and Germany."[50]

As he had so many times before—when Sulla had ordered him to divorce Cornelia, when the pirates had kidnapped him, when the great uprising in Gaul had been unleashed—Caesar felt that his life and his reputation were in danger. He had to show he would not be daunted, whatever risks were posed by his doing so. Accompanied by just one legion he was ready to set out, and as he prepared to cross the Rubicon River, which separated his province from Italy, he was heard to utter an old Greek saying: "Let the die be cast!"[51]

In the immediate political breakdown that led to civil war, Cato's actions were less inflammatory than those of others such as Gaius Marcellus, presenter of the sword to Pompey. Cato did not want civil war, but even less he wanted Caesar dictating terms to the Senate.[52] For years Cato had been demanding that Caesar be ruined: Caesar needed to be stopped from distributing land, to be stripped of his command in Gaul, to be turned over to the Germans. Cato's refusal to compromise had now led to a crisis, and in the crisis Cato lent only encouragement to the extremists.

Cato had diagnosed some of the worse problems of politics and helped find remedies for them. Yet the idea that Caesar could somehow be removed from the Republic—as a tumor might be cut out with a scalpel—was a denial of political reality. Even before the Gallic Wars, Caesar had achieved too much and helped too many Romans. Caesar's accomplishments had to be acknowledged, not simply denounced. His *dignitas* was a fact that had to be accommodated. As many clearly saw, to force a war with him was folly. Nobody could be sure, but there was a very real chance that civil war would only make Caesar stronger.

CHAPTER 11

CIVIL WAR

Reports that Caesar had crossed the Rubicon River and was hastening to Rome with his soldiers sent the city reeling. Though Pompey had a large army in Spain, in Italy he had just two battle-ready legions, and both of them had served under Caesar in Gaul for a time, putting their loyalty in doubt. Pompey insisted that more troops would be ready soon, but not soon enough. It was too risky to try to defend the capital. The magistrates and the Senate needed to evacuate Rome. Rather unhelpfully, Cato pointed out that if only Pompey had heeded the warnings Cato had made for many years, the senators wouldn't be in such fear of Caesar now, or so reliant on Pompey. Favonius was more biting: Pompey should stamp on the ground to call up all the necessary forces, as he had once bragged he could do.[1] Nevertheless, Pompey was the Senate's best hope, and Cato in the end recommended that Pompey be entrusted with sole supreme command. "The same men who brought about great evils should put an end to them," Cato said grimly.[2] But a majority of the senators, probably upset at the proposed evacuation, refused to support the motion, preferring to let other commanders retain more latitude. That did not stop Pompey from announcing, as he left the city to join his troops in southern Italy and to raise more, that the senators needed to follow him; anyone who stayed behind would be considered a member of Caesar's camp. Cato followed, along with many other senators and both consuls.

Before he set out, Cato made arrangements to protect his household. For the preceding few years he had been unmarried, but he had responsibility for all his children: a son and a daughter from his first marriage to Atilia, and a further son and two daughters from his second marriage to Marcia. By now the children from Atilia were adults. Cato's son by Atilia would accompany him and help fight for the Republic. Of Cato's daughter Porcia, long married to Bibulus, nothing is known about this part of her life. Cato's younger son, from Marcia, around ten years old, was sent to stay with Cato's old friend Munatius in southern Italy. That left the young daughters of Marcia. At least in part to protect them, Cato quickly remarried her. Her husband Hortensius had recently died and left her a large inheritance; thus she could ensure that if Cato never returned, the girls would receive dowries. Besides that, her father, the consul of 56 BC, was married to a niece of Caesar and so was well positioned to provide help for the family if Caesar prevailed. In turn, Marcia and her family would benefit from Cato's protection if Caesar lost. In war just as in peace, marriages were a survival strategy for noble families—although one may also wonder if the stress of events helped to reawaken in Marcia and Cato an old intimacy.[3]

As usual, historical sources say less about the senatorial women, but it is clear they were making decisions about their lives and shaping public opinion in their own right. Some women who were close to the Republican opposition to Caesar decided to leave Rome, and even Italy, altogether, as if to demonstrate that any government there would be illegitimate. Among this group was Pompey's wife, Cornelia, and Cato's niece Servilia, the widow of Lucullus, who took her teenage son with her. Others stayed behind, such as Caesar's lover

Servilia, even though her son, Brutus, who was close to Cato, fought with the Republicans. Servilia might not have seen Caesar for years, but he retained affection for her, and she was ready to exploit it. She and her daughters would prove to be the family's great survivors.[4]

Cato was uneasy about the unfolding war. He was surely relieved that the Senate was finally confronting Caesar after years of failing to heed his warnings. Yet Cato was a political fighter, not a military one. He knew from his own childhood that civil conflict could mean not only deaths on battlefields but also terrible hardships for civilian populations and the empowerment of autocratic leaders—all threats to justice. To show his distress, he stopped cutting his hair and trimming his beard and wearing garlands at dinner, as if he were in mourning.[5]

If there had to be war, Cato wanted it to be a war of exhaustion. He disparaged Pompey's earlier mistakes, but he did support the strategy Pompey intended to execute. Pompey meant to evacuate Italy and go east. A full retreat might seem shocking, but it would allow Pompey to use decades-old relationships to build up large forces on both land and sea. Italy, which depended on grain imports, could then be strangled in a naval blockade that would weaken Caesar or perhaps topple him altogether.[6] There were ugly implications to the plan, perhaps not all of which Cato accepted, but full-dress battle with Caesar was risky, and it was almost certain to result in the slaughter of thousands of Roman soldiers. Cato could not abide that.

Before Cato left Rome, the Senate had assigned him the important task of taking command of Sicily, a major granary of Italy that was also rich in naval resources.[7] Yet for once in his life Cato dawdled. He lingered with other senators in the city of Capua, south of Rome, in the hope that war might be averted.

On January 25 the consuls presented to the senators a new peace proposal.* Caesar offered to give up his army in exchange for

---

* The Romans did not use a solar calendar until reforms introduced by Caesar himself in 46. All dates here follow the calendar then in effect, which in early January of 49 was about six weeks ahead. In other words, the true date was early December.

Pompey discharging his troops in Italy and going to Spain. Pompey and the consuls supported the proposal, provided that Caesar first withdraw his garrisons from the towns he had occupied in Italy. According to a letter from Cicero, the senators in Capua were hopeful that Caesar would withdraw; "Favonius alone did not approve of Caesar imposing terms on us." Cato supported Pompey and the consuls, "but he does say that he wants to be present in the Senate when there is discussion of the terms of the settlement, if Caesar is induced to remove the garrisons."[8]

Cato's sudden new willingness to consider negotiating with Caesar speaks to his ambivalence about violence. With armies marching through Italy and more troops being mustered, he cracked—but only slightly. Cicero, no doubt rightly, worried that if Cato returned to the Senate rather than proceeding to Sicily, he would squelch any hope of a settlement. Compromise was not Cato's greatest strength, and a compromise between him and Caesar would practically require the laws of nature herself to bend. Anyway, Caesar ended up rejecting the counteroffer. Cato crossed over to Sicily to take up the pressing task of recruitment.

Like Cato, Caesar also found it hard to compromise after so many years of mistrust. In the commentaries he wrote on the civil war, a continuation of his earlier series on Gaul, Caesar explained that he could not accept his opponents' counteroffer because he was being required to withdraw before Pompey had to give up anything.[9] Caesar was holding out for a face-to-face meeting with his old partner, at which he felt sure he could wheedle his way to a settlement that truly protected both his safety and his standing. After his bold gamble of crossing the Rubicon with a single legion, his position was strengthening. The towns of northern Italy were well disposed to him, or at least put up no opposition, and two more Gallic legions were on the way. He began a swift march down the eastern coast of Italy and easily seized control of Picenum, a region thought

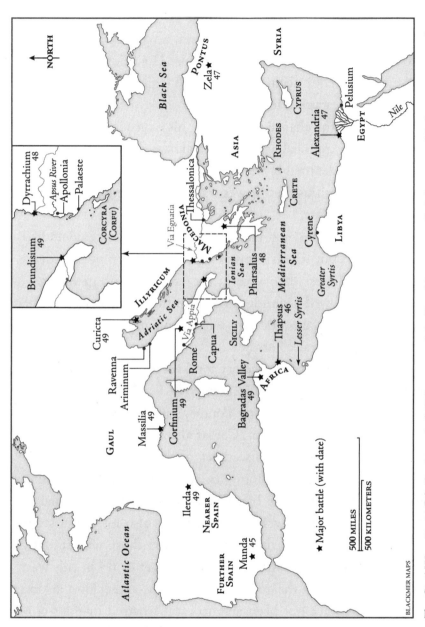

The Civil War, 49–44 BC. By the end of 49 Pompey and the Republicans controlled the eastern Mediterranean as well as Africa. The whole war then pivoted around the narrow strait separating Italy from present-day Albania (see inset).

to be a bastion of support for Pompey. Caesar was meticulous in sparing civilians undue hardship.

Only Cato's brother-in-law Domitius Ahenobarbus decided to take a stand against Caesar in Corfinium, a well-fortified town in the foothills of the Apennine Mountains. Domitius had a newly raised army, the equivalent of about three legions, many recruited off his own vast estates. He had assured Pompey he would take the forces south, but the chance of defeating his old enemy was irresistible. Domitius was probably also skeptical of the strategy of evacuation. As Pompey learned of the change of plans, he refused to send help, warned Domitius that he was walking into a trap, and begged him to try to get away.[10]

Domitius had blundered badly. Substantial reinforcements had just reached Caesar, which allowed him to put Corfinium under a tight blockade. In less than a week, the city fell. With great ostentation Caesar allowed Domitius and Domitius's son, as well as the other senators and the equestrians with them, all to go free. Caesar took over the newly raised army.

It was a highly satisfying victory for Caesar. He had robbed the Republicans of a substantial force, which he would now dispatch to capture Sicily, thereby wrecking Pompey's plans to put a stranglehold on Italy. Just as important, Caesar also showed that he had no interest in proscriptions, confiscations, or the punishment of ordinary soldiers. He was not going to be, as some had feared, another Sulla. Given his own early life, Caesar was naturally inclined to favor a policy of clemency, but clemency was also for him a strategy to win support from moderates and even those who initially fought him. As he wrote in an open letter, "Let us try in this way, if we can, to win back the goodwill of everyone and enjoy a lasting victory. Others have not been able to escape hatred in their cruelty or to have their victory last very long, with the lone exception of Lucius Sulla, whom I have no intention of imitating. Let this be a new way of conquering: to fortify ourselves with mercy and generosity."[11]

Clemency was also yet another way in which Caesar could express his superiority. "It does not disturb me," he wrote Cicero, "that those whom I released are said to have gone off so they can wage war against me again. I want nothing more than that I stay true to my nature, and they to theirs."[12]

Still hoping to negotiate with Pompey, Caesar rushed to the port of Brundisium, the disembarkation point for Pompey's troops. By the time Caesar made it there, the consuls had already sailed off with about half the soldiers. Caesar tried desperately to block the mouth of the harbor using dams and rafts but was unable to. Pompey's fleet returned, and Pompey made his way with the rest of the army across the Adriatic to the port city of Dyrrachium.

In just two months Caesar had become master of Italy, but the road ahead was difficult. To a large degree Pompey had ceded the territory to Caesar's armies. Now Caesar had to reckon with the fact that he had no real navy and would be unable to pursue Pompey until he raised one. Meanwhile, Pompey had at his disposal a large and well-trained army in Spain, under the command of loyal and experienced generals. If Caesar failed to eliminate that army first, he risked losing control of the west as soon as he headed east to confront Pompey. Caesar resolved to go to Spain personally, where he would be joined by some of his Gallic legions. Simultaneously, Curio, who had served Caesar so well as tribune in 50, was to take over Sicily and from there sail to Africa, another region vital for its grain production. Curio's task was to wrest Africa out of the hands of the Pompeian general who had seized control of it.

Before setting out for Spain Caesar spent a week in Rome. He convened what remained of the Senate and demanded that it send a peace mission to Pompey. Not surprisingly, given Pompey's warnings when he had left the city, nobody wished to go. Caesar did not compel emissaries to take up the journey, but he did opt to use coercion in service of another, more pressing goal. This was to seize a large reserve of gold and silver from the treasury, which

Pompey in his haste to leave had been unable to take with him. The people of Rome, already suffering from the disruptions of war, did not care to see their money stolen. When one of the tribunes said he would use his veto to prevent it and went to the treasury to block the door, Caesar abandoned all pretense of legality. His soldiers forced their way into the treasury and carried off all the money.[13] So much for the rights of the tribunes that he claimed to be upholding.

The episode is illustrative of how Caesar would fight the whole war. He might not have wanted war, but once war was upon him he gave everything to win. If he had to compromise his popularity with the people or be hard on his soldiers or make harsh demands of allies, he would. Again and again he would take bold risks. He was always on the offensive. The contrast with Cato, who was so passive that he seemed almost to have fallen into a state of depression, is sharp.

Organizing forces on Sicily was at least the kind of task Cato enjoyed. He busily repaired old warships and built new ones while his officers raised troops in southern Italy and in Sicily itself. Cato showed his old feistiness when news came that an officer of Curio's had landed on the island; Cato sent a message asking whether it was by order of the Senate or the people that the officer had arrived.[14] The officer was coming in advance of the army Caesar had snatched from Domitius Ahenobarbus, which would be on Sicily soon.

Cato was more comfortable writing bellicose letters than standing and fighting, however. He refused to put up any military resistance and made plans to evacuate and join Pompey across the Adriatic. He was sure, he said, that Sicily would in the end be lost to Curio, and he wanted to spare it the destruction of war. Cato was showing his usual consideration for the lives of those under Roman rule, though he could have done more to slow Caesar's advance, especially if he had gone to Sicily immediately in January.[15] Because of the numerical superiority of Caesar's troops in the region, Cato probably would have had to abandon Sicily eventually, but had he prepared more of a defense, things might have gone differently. At least according to Caesar's commentaries, as Cato left Sicily he fumed about all the mistakes Pompey had made leading up to the war—rather than considering his own responsibility.[16]

Once in the camp of Pompey, Cato continued to advocate for mustering strength and avoiding an open fight. He was all too happy to encourage Pompey in the strategy of gaining vast forces on land and sea and risking nothing unless victory looked overwhelmingly likely. As Cato's biographer put it, Cato, with typical doggedness, held to one view: "to deliberately protract the war; he hoped for a peaceful conclusion and did not want Rome to be worsted in the struggle and, by its own hands, suffer the most awful fate, settling its conflict with the sword."[17] This was really just a militarized version of Cato's old political tactics: victory by filibuster.

But the Senate and the battlefield were not the same, and avoiding a fight was not a guarantee of victory. As such, Cato's military vision left a lot to be desired, though Cato did provide useful service by undertaking a mission to the coast of Asia Minor to collect ships and troops.[18] On the island of Rhodes, where Cato had spent time before, he was able to persuade the local population to side with Pompey. The fleet of the old maritime state was a vital contribution to the navy that the Republicans were amassing. Cato's niece Servilia and her son Lucullus accompanied Cato to the island, where he ended up leaving them. Presumably Cato thought they would be safer there, but Servilia could also keep Cato informed about developments on Rhodes and throughout the whole eastern Mediterranean; the island was a communications hub.

As the year 49 wore on, the Republicans gained impressive strength. Pompey built up an army of nine legions and filled his followers with confidence as he personally trained with the soldiers. Though he was almost sixty, Pompey still fought and rode with skill. The navy swelled to five hundred, perhaps even six

hundred, warships. In Thessalonica, at the eastern end of the Via
Egnatia, the great military highway that stretched across the Balkans, the Republican leadership maintained what was effectively a
government-in-exile. The senators met and issued decrees. On the
motion of Cato, it was agreed that no Roman should be put to death
except on a battlefield, and no ally of Rome should be plundered.
This action suited Cato's high standards, and it counteracted any
claim that only Caesar cared about clemency. The Republicans
also showed punctiliousness in electing no new magistrates for 48,
which for procedural reasons would have been hard to do outside
the city of Rome. Belatedly, it was agreed to entrust the supreme
command to Pompey.[19]

By the end of the year Pompey was massing his forces in the
western Balkans, at the other end of the Via Egnatia. The port city
of Dyrrachium was turned into a great supply depot, with mag-
azines full of grain. Further south, a naval base was established
on Corfu, and the fleet was transferred here. Pompey reportedly
planned to put Cato in overall command of the naval forces but
then began to waver, suspecting that Cato, once in control of the
fleet, would demand that Pompey give up authority as soon as Caesar was defeated.[20] In the end, Pompey appointed as admiral Caesar's old antagonist Bibulus. As events would show, Bibulus was
willing to fight more aggressively than Cato, and that might have
been Pompey's real consideration.

"I go to an army without a leader, and I shall return to a leader without an army," Caesar confidently told his friends as he set out for
Spain.[21] But his advance was unexpectedly delayed when the leadership of Massilia (modern Marseilles) refused to let him into the
city—and then shortly afterward admitted Domitius Ahenobarbus,
who, undeterred by his defeat at Corfinium, had arrived with seven
warships. Clearly the Massiliotes expected the Republicans to win.
Caesar, refusing to accept the coastal city's decision, ordered three

legions to transfer to Massilia and warships to be built in nearby
Arelate (modern Arles). Massilia was put under a punishing siege
by land and sea, which Caesar left in the hands of his officers while
he moved on to Spain.

A large army awaited him just south of the Pyrenees at Ilerda,
but an even greater problem loomed in his glaring lack of supplies,
especially after a flood washed out a couple of river bridges on
which he depended. Reports of a victory for the Caesarian forces at
Massilia finally helped to bring some of the local Spanish communities over to Caesar's side, and Caesar was able to turn the tables
on the Pompeian army. Cut off from food, forage, wood, and even
water, they surrendered. As at Corfinium, Caesar had won a major
victory without bloodshed and was able to reinforce his policy of
clemency.[22] The Pompeian leaders were allowed to go, their army
was discharged, nobody was put to death. Caesar traveled to southern Spain, where he swiftly secured control, and then returned to
Massilia, which after months of fierce resistance had succumbed
to several defeats in battle, famine, and epidemic. The Massiliotes
were ready to surrender to Caesar and negotiate terms, while their
defender Domitius slipped away.

Not everything went Caesar's way, however. Curio had easily secured Sicily but suffered a terrible defeat in Africa, masterminded
by the Numidian king Juba, who held an old grudge against Caesar.
Even after the surviving Caesarian forces surrendered, Juba slaughtered many of them in cold blood. Caesar lost two legions, while
Africa, with its rich supplies of grain, remained in enemy hands.
Another setback came on the Adriatic island of Curicta, where two
legions sent by Caesar to control Illyricum were blockaded and then
captured.

A far worse crisis confronted Caesar as he made his way from
Massilia to Rome: a mutiny of his own Gallic veterans. Caesar
might have needed to fight civil war to save himself, but the soldiers
were finding the experience an ordeal. They had expected to be discharged after the Gallic War, but were now being dragged this way

and that across the whole Roman world. There was no opportunity for plunder, and even the bonus Caesar had promised at the start of the year remained unpaid. When Caesar made it to northern Italy, the soldiers in one of his legions, the Ninth, told him they refused to go on.[23]

A mutiny could ruin Caesar. To stop it from spreading, he responded brutally. He announced that he was going to carry out a decimation, the traditional punishment in which all the soldiers of a mutinous army, regardless of their own individual guilt, drew lots for execution. The veterans, shocked, immediately begged for mercy. They had not really wanted to abandon Caesar; they were just seeking better terms. Caesar yielded, but only slightly, and ordered the 120 men thought to be ringleaders to draw lots, of whom 12 were selected for death. Perhaps something like this had been his intention all along. He could not afford to lose men, but he also had to establish that he would not be blackmailed.

Relentlessly Caesar pressed on. In advance of his arrival in Rome toward the end of 49, he was appointed dictator. Caesar held the office for just eleven days and mainly used it to conduct magisterial elections. In the elections he gained one of the consulships for 48, a great boost for him politically, since anybody who opposed him now, citizen or provincial, would be defying a duly elected consul. While in Rome Caesar undertook measures to try to settle a debt crisis brought on by the outbreak of civil war and arranged for a grain distribution. He also restored full civic rights to the sons and grandsons of the men proscribed by Sulla. That fulfilled a long-standing political goal, but at this particular moment it had the additional benefit of yet again reinforcing his reputation for clemency. It was his enemies who were Sulla's true heirs, he maintained. And thus, it was he who was fighting for the people against brutal authoritarians.[24]

On January 4, 48, Caesar set sail from Brundisium. Caesar's naval capacity was limited, and he could only take about half the troops he had assembled, around twenty thousand men. Miraculously he made it across the Adriatic without losing a single ship and safely landed near a little town called Palaeste. The Republicans apparently had not expected Caesar to attempt a crossing until spring. As soon as Bibulus learned of his enemy's arrival, he put out from Corfu to try to intercept Caesar's fleet, but it was too late. He only ran into empty transports making their way back to Italy. Bibulus seized about thirty of the ships and burned them all, along with the captains and crews aboard. Cato could never have condoned such a brutal act, but the stark reality was that the Republicans needed to show some ruthlessness if they were going to defeat Caesar.

After landing, Caesar established a bridgehead and began a forced march to the great supply depot at Dyrrachium. Pompey rushed to defend the city and cut Caesar off just in time. Former son-in-law and father-in-law now camped on opposite sides of the River Apsus. Caesar was desperate for the rest of his forces to join him, but Bibulus maintained a viselike blockade. So hard did Bibulus push himself that he became exhausted and ill, but he refused to abandon his storm-tossed ships and eventually died. For several months, his heroic efforts, along with the bad weather, kept Caesar's reinforcements locked in at Brundisium. Pompey, however, failed to exploit his numerical advantage.

At last the Caesarian reinforcements made it across the Adriatic under the leadership of the fearless Mark Antony. They landed about a hundred miles north of the Apsus, and Caesar and Pompey raced to meet them. Caesar made it first.

With his army now enlarged, Caesar tried to force Pompey to battle. Pompey refused once again to fight, and so Caesar secretly marched to Dyrrachium in the hope that he might cut Pompey off from the supply depot and seize it. Pompey arrived just in time to stop the capture and was able to camp on favorable ground nearby that gave him access to the sea. Caesar then started to wall Pompey in by land with fortifications.

As Caesar later wrote, a very strange kind of warfare ensued.[25] Effectively, Pompey was under siege. But in a normal siege, it was the weaker side that was besieged. The besiegers would leverage greater numbers to cut off the food supplies of those blockaded. Here, the Republicans, with control of the sea, stayed well provisioned. "No wind could blow without them having favorable sailing from some region," moaned Caesar.[26] Caesar, by contrast, had very limited access to grain, and Dyrrachium itself proved to be too well protected for him to take.

But Caesar's men turned the difficult situation into an opportunity to show their ruthlessness. To survive, his soldiers had to dig up a kind of wild cabbage, which they managed to turn into bread. On one occasion they ran up to the enemy fortifications and threw some of the loaves inside. As long as the earth produced roots, the Caesarians taunted, they would keep Pompey under siege. Appalled, Pompey told his men they were fighting wild animals.[27]

Cato had wanted this kind of war of exhaustion. But Pompey's pride could not allow him to be blockaded forever. After two Caesarian cavalry officers defected to him and revealed weaknesses in Caesar's fortifications, Pompey made careful plans for a breakout, using both land and sea forces. In an effort to rouse his demoralized troops for battle, he asked each of his commanders to speak. Sluggishly the soldiers listened until finally it was Cato's turn.

Cato delivered what was later described as one of the great speeches of his life. He dwelled on the values that the men were fighting for: "freedom, virtue, death, and reputation." At the speech's climax he called upon the gods themselves to witness the struggle the soldiers were making on behalf of their country. The soldiers, roused at last, cried out enthusiastically.[28] One might wonder, though, if Cato was really trying to urge himself on.

The attack succeeded brilliantly. The Republicans broke the blockade, and Caesar's forces were routed. Yet Pompey failed to pursue the enemy as they ran off. He could have ended the whole civil war then and there, but the chance was lost. This miscalculation led

Caesar to make another of his pithy judgments: "The enemy might have won today—if they had a winner."[29] Still, everyone in the Republican camp rejoiced at the victory—everyone except Cato, who grieved for the death of citizens at one another's hands.[30]

Caesar had no choice but to make an immediate retreat, heading east to Thessaly with its abundant fields of ripening grain. In the Republican camp some favored returning to Italy, but Pompey rightly insisted that they pursue Caesar. Pompey's preference was to keep up a war of exhaustion—to avoid major battles and limit Caesar's access to food. There was sense in this strategy, and Cato commended it out of his desire to spare lives. Yet it was becoming worrisomely clear that Pompey had some deeper fear about confronting Caesar and his soldiers, a fear that would in the end fatally hobble Pompey's command.[31]

Even though Cato backed Pompey's plan, Pompey seems to have found Cato difficult to deal with. He ended up leaving Cato behind at Dyrrachium. With a legion and a half of soldiers as well as the naval fleet, Cato was to make sure that no additional Caesarian troops crossed over from Italy and that the restive provincial population did not rebel. Cato would also be the guardian of all the supplies and arms stored in Dyrrachium, a responsibility nobody would carry out more diligently. Not a single sword would go missing on Cato's watch.[32]

It wouldn't be long before Pompey and Caesar clashed again. Pompey worried about the Caesarian veterans, but political currents made further delay impossible. On the plains near the Thessalian town of Pharsalus, the Caesarian and Republican armies met in August of 48 (really June, but still a swelteringly hot time of year). Caesar, about to run out of grain, was preparing to move away, but Pompey was goaded into battle—by his own side. Frustrated by the seeming lack of progress and by their exile from Rome, the senators accused Pompey of prolonging the war just to hold on to power. Domitius Ahenobarbus taunted the leader, calling him "the King of Kings" (a title favored by eastern potentates) and "Agamemnon" (the peevish commander of the Greeks in the Trojan War).

The numbers were lopsided in Pompey's favor, but the battle would turn more on strategy than on size. Pompey had around forty-five thousand infantry to Caesar's twenty-two thousand, and seven thousand cavalry to Caesar's one thousand, and he set in motion a typically elaborate plan of battle. He would use his cavalry for a flanking attack while keeping the center of his infantry stationary during Caesar's initial onslaught, thus sparing them from the worst of battle.

Unfortunately for Pompey, Caesar's sense of tactics was superior. Inferring Pompey's plan from the disposition of the battlefield, he set a trap. Behind the usual three lines of infantry he hid a secret fourth line of troops who were to use their javelins to slash at the faces of the cavalry. The plan worked, and Caesar's forces won the battle decisively. Pompey fled to his camp and then quit the scene of battle altogether. By Caesar's account, around fifteen thousand men in Pompey's army fell, while Caesar lost just a couple of hundred.[33] Among the dead was Domitius Ahenobarbus. Pompey's prestige had sustained a shattering blow.

With an eye toward his larger political aims, Caesar was magnanimous in victory. He incorporated the surviving soldiers of the Republican army into his own legions and announced that he would grant pardons to the enemy leaders, except those he had already forgiven once. Another blow to the Republicans came when they learned that Cato's nephew Brutus, who had slipped away from the battlefield, had himself sent a message to Caesar offering surrender. Caesar had already instructed his officers to make every effort not to kill the young man in battle—out of regard for Servilia, it was said—and so he was delighted to welcome Brutus to his side.[34]

When news of Pompey's ruinous defeat reached Cato's forces in Dyrrachium, mayhem erupted. Some of the soldiers mutinied, plundering the granaries and setting the cargo vessels on fire. The Rhodian fleet that Cato had recruited absconded. While evacuating, Cato must have felt bereft as he watched the conflagration from aboard his ship. He sailed to the naval base at Corfu, where he was joined by more refugees from Pharsalus, as well as Pompey's son Gnaeus. Gnaeus had been in command of a fleet from Egypt, which, like that of the Rhodians, had deserted on learning the battle's outcome.[35]

With no one certain of what had happened to Pompey, the Republicans were scattered and leaderless. Cato urged Cicero, who had stayed with him at Dyrrachium during the Pharsalus campaign, to take command, since, as an ex-consul, Cicero outranked Cato. Surely it would have been wiser to appoint one of the commanders from Pharsalus, Labienus, formerly Caesar's second-in-command, but in Cato's mind, even in such a crisis, political considerations superseded military ones. Cicero, who had barely any ability as a general, had no interest in taking over and fled to Italy. Young Gnaeus Pompey wanted to stop Cicero by force, but Cato talked him out of it. They would have to fight on without him.[36]

The remaining allies sailed to Greece, taking in more fugitives from the battle. Then, as a Caesarian commander drew near, they set sail again, fleeing due south toward Libya. Having retained a good part of its fleet, the Republican side could at least move freely across the sea. They were also fortunate to maintain control of the province of Africa, which lay west of Libya, in what is modern Tunisia. Stocked with copious grain, the province was a natural base for launching an invasion of Sicily and then Italy. As word spread that Pompey had survived, Cato thought it very likely that he would end up in Libya or Egypt. The king of Egypt, Ptolemy XIII, a young teenager, was in Pompey's debt because of the help Pompey had extended to the king's late father, Ptolemy XII, the Flute Player. It should have been easy for Pompey to boss the king around and gain valuable supplies and money.[37] And with Pompey still in the war, Cato thought the Republicans should fight on.

But after they reached Libya, Cato and Gnaeus got staggering news. As Cato suspected, Pompey had indeed sailed to Egypt, with his wife, Cornelia, and his son Sextus. Worrying that Pompey might try to turn Egypt into a new base for his ill-fated war with Caesar, Ptolemy XIII's advisors had no intention of welcoming the commander with

open arms. They invited Pompey to come ashore, and after he transferred to a small boat, he was stabbed to death with his wife and son
looking on. The king's men lopped off Pompey's head and threw the
rest of the body into the sea. Cornelia and Sextus barely made it to
safety. After spending several decades as the most powerful man in
the Roman world, Pompey died an inglorious death, helpless before
the Egyptian's treachery, his remains scattered far from home.[38]

For a time, no one knew that Pompey had fallen, and Caesar hoped
he could end the war personally, meeting his rival commander face
to face. When he realized that Pompey was heading to Egypt, he
set sail with a force of a few thousand men for Alexandria. It was
the most splendid city of the Mediterranean, founded by Alexander
the Great himself and enriched by succeeding generations of Ptolemaic kings with staggeringly beautiful temples, theaters, palaces,
parks, and porticoes. A many-storied lighthouse, shimmering in
white marble, rose from atop a sea-swept rock in front of the royal
harbor and dazzled visitors as they arrived. Such a grand city would
be a fitting venue for a final meeting and settlement between the
two great men.[39]

But a settlement was not to be. As soon as he arrived, Caesar was
told of Pompey's death, which had taken place about two hundred
miles east of Alexandria at the fortress city of Pelusium. Ptolemy
XIII sent Pompey's head in a basket a few days later. Caesar was
revolted by the gift and shed a tear for his old kinsman. Inwardly,
he almost certainly felt cheated out of his final victory.

He decided it was safe to disembark, though the Alexandrians
were just as suspicious of his intentions as they were of Pompey's.
When he entered the city accompanied by his twelve lictors carrying the fasces, crowds grew furious. Egypt was not a province of
Caesar or of Rome, and the display was an offense to the majesty
of their king. Some of the king's soldiers sparred with the Romans,
and Caesar beat a hasty retreat into the royal palace. It was there

he would have his fateful meeting with Egypt's erstwhile queen Cleopatra.[40]

Cleopatra, then about twenty-one years old, was already a formidable political force. The late Ptolemy XII's will had ordered that his son, young Ptolemy XIII, was to share the throne with his older sister, Cleopatra, whom he also was to marry, in accordance with Egyptian tradition. In her first few years of power, Cleopatra had worked hard to win support from Egyptians outside Alexandria. She was the first of the Ptolemies to learn to speak the native Egyptian language. Apparently feeling threatened by this extraordinarily capable woman, Ptolemy XIII's advisors had managed to drive her off the throne and out of Egypt altogether. She had gone to Syria, raised an army, and returned to eastern Egypt. The king and his advisors had been at Pelusium with their own army to hold her off.[41]

For Caesar, the dispute between young Ptolemy XIII and his sister appeared to be an opportunity for enrichment. He decided to stay in Egypt for a while to collect money he claimed to be owed by the late king and to broker a settlement between his feuding children.

This decision compounded his initial provocation of the Alexandrians. Palace insiders and populace alike were horrified. They did not want to pay more money to the Romans, whom they hated, and Ptolemy's advisors dreaded the idea of Cleopatra being restored to power. A eunuch named Pothinus, once a tutor of the king and now serving as chief finance minister, took efforts to get rid of Caesar immediately. He exacted money from the Egyptians in ways designed to make them as unhappy as possible and provoke unrest. He served the Romans stale grain and at dinners in the palace used wooden and earthenware dishes, spitefully claiming that Caesar had confiscated all the gold and silver. He secretly communicated with the commander of the royal Egyptian army, positioned outside the city.[42]

Young Ptolemy joined Caesar in the palace. Cleopatra, on the other hand, had to communicate through agents until finally she found a way to sneak in. With just a single one of her companions, a Sicilian named Apollodorus, she came on a tiny boat at dusk. Apollodorus rolled her up in some bedding, fastened the bedding closed with a strap, and carried her into Caesar's chambers. It is said that Caesar's fascination was sparked by this unusual introduction. Cleopatra was beautiful and charming, but it was the cleverness of her entrance that he found especially appealing.[43]

Caesar lost all objectivity in arbitrating the royal dispute. He sent for Ptolemy and insisted that the king reconcile with his sister. Upon seeing Cleopatra in the palace, Ptolemy became enraged. He rushed out among the people, told them he had been betrayed, and tore off his diadem. The already restive populace began to assault the palace. Soon enough, on Pothinus's orders, the royal army was marching on the city. Caesar had worked himself into a very dangerous situation.[44]

In the months that followed, he faced extraordinary challenges while penned up in the palace and struggling for survival. The Alexandrians built siege towers on wheels and dragged them through the city's wide streets. They pumped seawater into the fresh-water channels that supplied Caesar's quarters. Fortunately Caesar discovered that new wells could be dug. Caesar captured Pharos Island, which dominated the city's two main harbors, but experienced a bad reverse on the causeway that led from the island to the main part of the city. He had to jump into the sea and swim to safety, stripping off the scarlet robe he wore as commander. According to one story, he had many papers with him at the time and preserved them by holding them high above his head with one hand while swimming with the other.

During the war a younger sister of Cleopatra, Arsinoe, escaped the palace and tried to take command of the Alexandrians. However, many Alexandrians wanted King Ptolemy XIII back. Perhaps in the hope of a respite in fighting, Caesar released him—but Ptolemy swiftly turned on Caesar. All the while, a romance bloomed between Cleopatra and Caesar, and soon after her first meeting with Caesar, Cleopatra was pregnant with his child.

Finally reinforcements came, and after some fighting along the Nile, upland from Alexandria, Caesar prevailed. While fleeing the scene of battle, Ptolemy XIII drowned in the river. Arsinoe was arrested. With the treacherous finance minister Pothinus already killed, Cleopatra's obstacles to the throne were at last clear.

Caesar now recognized Cleopatra as the ruler of Egypt, along with another, younger brother, around ten years old. At least in the short term, this arrangement benefited her since it was hard for a woman to hold the throne of Egypt alone. In time, she would hit on the even better solution of removing the brother and making her son from Caesar—nicknamed "Little Caesar" by the sharp-tongued Alexandrians—her coruler.[45]

Before he left, Caesar took a cruise up the Nile with Cleopatra. The trip would help her solidify control of her kingdom. For Caesar, it provided a chance to enjoy the queen's company as well as some of Egypt's extraordinary sights.[46] He would have liked to linger but had pressing business elsewhere: an invasion of Roman territory in Asia Minor, unrest in the city of Rome, and a resurgence of Republican military strength in Africa, to which Cato had made a great contribution.

The Alexandrian War showed Caesar at his most swashbuckling. So many of his distinctive qualities were on display: his fearlessness, his stamina, his ability to get out of a scrape, his fondness for extravagant love affairs. Yet the romance with Cleopatra overshadowed a more prosaic reality: he had blundered into an unnecessary war.[47]

His failure to understand the situation in Alexandria had almost doomed him. He had nearly gotten himself killed multiple times, his months of delay had led to challenges to his authority elsewhere, and the time he squandered allowed his opponents to regain strength. Civil war was far from over.

CHAPTER 12

"EVEN A VICTOR"

CATO WAS SAILING ALONG THE COAST OF LIBYA WHEN SEXTUS Pompey arrived with the distressing news of his father's murder. With Pompey dead and his eastern allies out of the war, the Republicans were far weaker militarily. As more and more of the empire recognized Caesar as rightful leader, and as senators who had fought him sought his pardon, the Republicans' claim to represent the one true government of Rome was crumbling. Senators and thousands of ordinary soldiers now looked to Cato for what should happen next. Was it time to give up?

Cato would no sooner surrender to Caesar than the sky fall. But continuing the fight was a wearying prospect. Upon learning of the defeat at Pharsalus, Cato had considered withdrawing into exile—"the furthest possible from the tyranny"—and that impulse must have tempted him again now.[1] To give in to it, however, meant abandoning good men who had stuck with him. And so Cato agreed to take command, at least temporarily.

With his army he went to Cyrene, an old Greek colony made rich through the export of silphium, a now-extinct plant considered a wonder drug in ancient times. The city and its territory had passed into the control of the Ptolemies and then Rome, just like Cyprus. A few days before Cato's arrival, the local leadership had shut the city's gates against Labienus. Cato they admitted. Perhaps they were reassured by his reputation for fair treatment of provincials. Or perhaps the presence of his army forced their hand.[2]

In Cyrene Cato received some encouraging news for a change. Metellus Scipio, the distinguished noble and father-in-law of Pompey who had commanded the center of the Republican battle line at Pharsalus, had made it safely to Africa and been well received by the Numidian king Juba. Also in Africa was Publius Attius Varus, a Republican general who had helped Juba to defeat the Caesarian Scribonius Curio in 49. Cato resolved to take his army to these two men, the commanders best positioned to stop Caesar. But the journey would not be easy. By sea, Libya was separated from the Roman province of Africa by the Syrtes, a pair of gulfs that posed challenges of navigation because of unusually strong tides as well as treacherous shallows and shoals. Boats trying to cross the waters could easily stray into the shallows and get stuck.[3]

The land route along the coast was hardly more inviting. The country was naturally arid, with limited agriculture: the very opposite of what a large, hungry, and thirsty army needed. Ancient writers complained about sandstorms and an abundance of snakes. One of the peoples who did manage to make their home in this inhospitable region was the Psylli, reputed for their fabled abilities to charm snakes and cure snakebites by sucking out the venom.

By the time Cato was ready to move, it was the winter season, which made sailing even more difficult, so he chose the land route. The great march across the desert, lasting perhaps thirty days, became one of the iconic moments of Cato's life, much celebrated in later years as a symbol of his resolve. Improbable as it might seem, Cato was turned into a superhero, guiding his men through a parched landscape filled with deadly serpents, able to survive on no water himself.[4]

In reality, the march was a triumph of logistics. Cato's forces numbered around ten thousand. Because of the scarcity of watering places, he divided the men into separate groups and made sure to bring along a large number of mules to carry water. Food was transported by cattle and wagons. Cato walked at the head of the forces the entire way. In solidarity with the regular troops, he never rode a horse or mule. He kept morale up, just as he had as a young officer twenty years earlier. When he ate, he refused to recline on a couch, as Romans normally did, and would only sit, to show his grief over the devastating civil war.

By early 47 Cato had made it to Africa, where he found Scipio and Attius Varus sparring over who should take command. Varus had been there longer, but Scipio, as proconsul, had the higher rank. Varus had Juba's backing, but Scipio had also begun courting the king, a violent and arrogant man who was determined to wring as much as he could from the desperate Republicans. When he met Cato for the first time, he placed his throne between the seats of Scipio and Cato, the middle position being regarded as the one of honor by the Numidians. Cato, in response, lifted his chair and moved it to the other side of the two men, placing Scipio in the center. For Cato, even in a fight for survival where help from allies was essential, the senior Roman magistrate was still owed deference.[5]

Cato and Scipio had a long history together. Scipio had stolen Cato's first fiancée from him many years earlier, but Cato would not let that get in the way now. He insisted that Scipio and Varus stop their squabbling and that overall command be awarded to Scipio, who outranked Cato as well as Varus. Cato had no intention of breaking the laws, he said, when they were fighting against the lawbreaker. Also in favor of Scipio's command was a prophecy circulating among the soldiers that Scipios were always destined to win in Africa.[6] Members of the patrician family had enjoyed almost godlike victories there before: one Scipio had defeated Hannibal

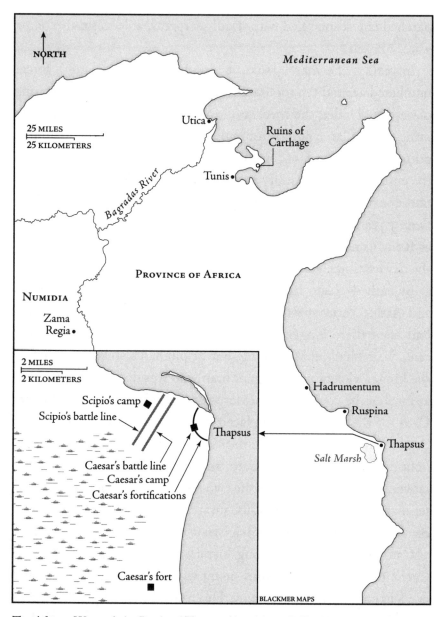

NORTH

Mediterranean Sea

25 MILES
25 KILOMETERS

Utica •

Ruins of
Carthage

Tunis •

Bagradas River

PROVINCE OF AFRICA

NUMIDIA

Zama
Regia •

2 MILES
2 KILOMETERS

Scipio's camp ■

Scipio's battle line

Caesar's battle line
Caesar's camp
Caesar's fortifications

Thapsus

Caesar's fort ■

Hadrumentum •

Ruspina •

• Thapsus

Salt Marsh

BLACKMER MAPS

The African War and the Battle of Thapsus (April 6, 46 BC). While Cato held Utica, Caesar was confined to a small area at the other end of the province. Finally, Caesar exploited the terrain around Thapsus to neutralize the Republicans' superiority in cavalry.

and his army at the battle of Zama; another Scipio razed the city of Carthage after a long siege.

Scipio almost seemed to be emulating his ancestors when he demanded that Utica, the capital of the Roman province of Africa, be destroyed. Strategically located at the mouth of the River Bagradas, the city was divided in its loyalties. The wealthy traders of Utica and its environs who enjoyed Roman citizenship were more sympathetic to the Republican side (perhaps, in part, because the Republicans had been winning in Africa). The ordinary people, however, favored Caesar, which was the main reason Scipio insisted that the city be demolished. If Caesar could land in Utica and take it over, he would have a superb base. The city boasted strong defenses and excellent harbor facilities. Cato shuddered at Scipio's demand, and at a meeting of the general's advisory council he protested loudly and called on the gods to rescue the people of Utica from this cruelty. Scipio relented, and he put Cato in charge of watching over the city to make sure it lent no help to Caesar.

Cato poured himself into his duties. He reinforced the city's walls by building new towers. He ran trenches and palisades in front of the city. He compelled the local men of military age to camp in or around the earthworks outside Utica. Within, he stockpiled weapons and grain, just as he had done at Dyrrachium. He sent out supplies to Scipio's army as needed, while always making sure that the local population was treated as fairly as possible. He kept a careful register of grain, weapons, siege equipment, and men under arms.

Cato was making Utica impregnable—and in a sense making himself impregnable. Utica would not be captured just as Cato would not be captured. The old hope of his came back: if he and his allies could just hold out, somehow they might defeat Caesar in the end. To Scipio, Cato delivered the same advice as to Pompey: to avoid battle and put their trust in time, "which weakens the peak condition in which tyranny is strong."[7]

Scipio considered this stance cowardly. He was far more willing than Pompey had been to engage Caesar in battle, at least when circumstances seemed favorable. Scipio sent Cato a message accusing him of being "not only happy to sit within a walled city himself; he would not even allow others to seize opportunities boldly and effectively."[8] Cato wrote back that he was prepared to take the forces he had brought from Libya and go to Italy, thereby forcing Caesar to change his plans. Scipio laughed at the idea, though Cato's proposal was a serious one, in line with his long-standing strategy of prolonging the war by avoiding engagement. Cato did send young Gnaeus Pompey to Spain to foment rebellion against Caesar there.[9]

But Cato's heart sank after he received Scipio's dismissive response. Cato told his friends that under Scipio's leadership any hope of victory had faded. Even if, by some stroke of luck, Caesar were defeated, Cato said that he would not return to Rome but flee from Scipio, who was now issuing terrible threats. Scipio would have to meet Caesar in battle without Cato.

It took Caesar some time to reach Africa. After bidding farewell to a pregnant Cleopatra in Alexandria, his first destination was Asia Minor, where he had military matters to attend to. Pharnaces, the son of Mithridates the Great, taking advantage of the Romans' distraction during the ongoing civil war, had moved out of his small kingdom on the northern coast of the Black Sea and seized the realms of several other kings as well as Roman territory in Asia Minor. Caesar marched with three legions and on August 2, 47, defeated Pharnaces in a great battle near the city of Zela. It was a gratifyingly swift campaign. "I came, I saw, I conquered," wrote Caesar in an official dispatch—a slogan so good he later had it painted on a placard shown at the triumph that he celebrated over Pharnaces.[10]

With Asia pacified, Caesar proceeded to Rome. After his victory over Pompey at Pharsalus, about a year earlier, he had been made dictator again, this time for a whole year. The office gave him supreme power to finish the civil war and also allowed him to control

Rome through a deputy, known as the master of the cavalry. The city was seething with violence and unrest as the debt crisis that had begun in 49 worsened. Caesar hoped his young officer Mark Antony would restore order as master of the cavalry, but Antony struggled. Romans were offended to see Antony roam through the city accompanied by a throng of soldiers. His fondness for carousing did not sit well with the war-deprived citizenry. On Antony's watch, Cicero claimed, "there was disgraceful pillaging of gold, silver, and, above all, wine."[11] Meanwhile, veterans from the Gallic War who had been promised farms by Caesar lost all patience as Caesar's return to Italy was delayed and they learned that they would need to fight one more time, in Africa. They were on the point of mutiny.

Caesar had to restore order quickly. He refused to give in to demands for full debt cancellation, knowing that to do so would cost him the support of the better-off. "I, too, owe large amounts," he told the struggling populace in an effort at appeasement.[12] He did waive all interest owed since the start of the war and also arranged for one year's remission of rent up to a certain limit. To the angry troops, stationed in southern Italy, he sent the promise of a cash bonus. Many remained disgruntled and marched to Rome to try to intimidate Caesar. He met them on the Field of Mars and told them they were all dismissed. They were stunned, especially when Caesar referred to them as mere "citizens" rather than his "soldiers," and begged to be reinstated.[13] Caesar eventually agreed, reaffirming his commitment to provide farms for the men on unused public lands and on land he purchased. He meant to avoid the politically unpalatable confiscations that Sulla had undertaken, but he began liquidating the real estate of his unpardoned enemies, including Pompey. Servilia picked up some valuable estates at a low price, giving rise to a crude joke that she had bargained Caesar down by throwing in her daughter's services along with her own.[14] Humorous gossip helped relieve the city's misery.

Around the end of November Caesar left Rome, and on December 17, 47, he reached the west coast of Sicily, from where he would sail to Africa.[15] To show his officers that he meant to depart immediately, he pitched his tent on the seashore, so close to the water that the waves almost lapped against it. For about a week, the weather proved unsuitable for sailing. Caesar made the rowers and troops stay on the ships anyway, so they would be ready to go at any hour. When finally a favorable wind arose, he embarked with six legions and two thousand cavalry. Among the men Caesar took with him was an obscure member of the family of the Scipios. The man had no military ability to speak of, but Caesar always made sure to put him at the front of the battle line, which made Metellus Scipio and his prophecies look rather ridiculous.[16] Still, as Caesar's soldiers must have known, the war in Africa was not going to be a walkover.

Three days later Africa was within the fleet's sight. Utica was too well guarded by Cato for Caesar to land anywhere nearby, so he went to shore near Hadrumentum, the major city at the opposite end of the African province. His ships had been scattered during the crossing, and initially he commanded no more than 3,000 infantry and 150 cavalry. Hadrumentum also proved well guarded, which forced Caesar to march south, harassed by Moorish cavalry all the way. With some difficulty, he established camp in the small coastal town of Ruspina, where his other transports arrived. Right away the shortage of supplies pinched. Caesar had been unable to bring much with him, and the Republican forces had stripped the countryside of grain.[17]

Vulnerable and poorly provisioned, Caesar found himself in a dire situation. After setting out with perhaps ten thousand men to collect whatever grain he could find, a couple of miles outside of camp he received word from his scouts that enemy forces had been spotted. Just as the message arrived, a huge cloud of dust started darkening the horizon. Caesar sent orders to his camp for his pitifully small cavalry to join him. When the enemy came into sight, he ordered the soldiers to put on their helmets and get ready to fight.

The enemy formation, under the command of Caesar's former officer Labienus, was like none Caesar had ever encountered. According to *The African War*, a continuation of Caesar's commentaries by an unknown author who almost certainly was an eyewitness, it was a battle line "of amazing length and densely packed, not with infantry but cavalry." Among the cavalry were interspersed "light-armed Numidians and unmounted archers, massed so tightly that, from a distance, Caesar's men thought they were regular infantry."[18] On either end were huge contingents of horsemen.

Caesar had to do the best he could with his small numbers and deployed his men into a single line instead of the usual three. On either end he placed the cavalry and told them to do everything possible to avoid being outflanked. He thought the main fight would be against the center of the battle line, which he took to be regular infantry.

At first, both sides waited. Then suddenly Labienus's cavalry began to spread out and advance. Sure enough, this was the outflanking maneuver Caesar had expected, but he soon realized it was no normal infantry he was facing. The whole enemy line was highly mobile and able to shoot from afar. Out of their densely packed squadrons the light-armed infantry together with the cavalry rushed forward and hurled their javelins. "Whenever Caesar's men made a charge against them, their cavalry turned back and fled; their infantry, meanwhile, stood their ground until the cavalry renewed their charge and returned to help their infantry."[19]

Caesar's forces were caught in a double bind. His infantry could not move forward and fight at sword point without being wounded by javelins. His cavalry could not hold off the large numbers of Labienus's horsemen. Labienus, meanwhile, was riding boldly, without a helmet, at the front of his line, encouraging his men and shouting insults at the Caesarians. Little by little, Caesar's whole line was penned in.

Caesar barely avoided defeat by having his men push their line outward to break the surrounding circle; every other cohort had to turn around so they could face the enemy on both sides. They managed to drive Labienus's forces back, but reinforcements arrived to renew the attack on Caesar's retreating legionaries. The Caesarian troops, fighting, finally made their way to the Ruspina camp, exhausted.

This was a type of battle tactic that Caesar had never dealt with before, one that made excellent use of the Republicans' overwhelming superiority in cavalry and light-armed infantry. The Republicans, in fact, enjoyed nearly every advantage over Caesar at this point. Aside from their strength in cavalry, they had far more infantry, including four legions that Juba had trained in the Roman style. Their depots brimmed with food and fodder. And they commanded strength at sea, which would allow them to hamper transport ships trying to carry reinforcements and supplies to Caesar's camp at Ruspina. It was no wonder Labienus had ridden around with such intoxication during the attack on Caesar.

Quite unusually, Caesar practically had to go into hiding. He hunkered down in his camp while Scipio arrived with eight legions to join forces with Labienus. The two men's cavalry roved around Caesar's fortifications and picked off anyone who came out for food, forage, or water. To save his starving animals, Caesar had to feed them seaweed.

With Juba's arrival imminent, and even more troops on the way, this moment might have been the end of Caesar but for an unexpected stroke of luck. A certain Publius Sittius, who years earlier had fled Italy because of his debts and become a mercenary commander under one of the kings of Mauretania in western Africa, took a gamble and decided to help Caesar by attacking Numidia. The strike forced Juba to turn back, withdrawing his whole army along with some of the troops he had already given to Scipio.

Undaunted, day after day Scipio brought hosts of soldiers out of his camp and lined them up in battle formation. Nobody advanced from Caesar's camp. Eventually Scipio had his whole force out on the plain, practically in front of Caesar's camp. Again, nobody stepped out of Caesar's camp. Shameful as it was for a Roman general to keep refusing battle, Caesar had no other choice. Day and night he kept his eyes fixed on the sea, hoping more troops and food would arrive.

After three long weeks relief did come, including more troops from Sicily, and although Caesar would remain confined to a very small part of Africa over the next few months, he was able to change his position twice. At various moments, as the opposing armies moved around, one side would line up for battle on ground favorable to it; the other was always careful to refuse.

Juba had returned from Numidia about a month after he had turned back, but luckily for Caesar the king's arrogance made it hard for Scipio to work with him and even inspired defections to Caesar's army. Labienus kept trying to use cavalry to ambush Caesar. He once came close to forcing Caesar into camping at a spot with no water. Caesar, by having his legionaries throw spears in synchronized volleys, was able to move forward in spurts and just reach his camp.

Finally Caesar decided he had to engage the battle on level ground. It was the only hope he had of winning the war. But Scipio, who still enjoyed many advantages, saw no need to take the chance. Caesar would have to force him to fight.

In the very early hours of April 4, 46, Caesar and his army left camp and marched about fifteen miles north to Thapsus, a coastal city allied with the Republicans and protected by a substantial garrison. A large salt marsh lay nearby, which meant that Thapsus could only be approached by two narrow strips of land, one west of the city and one south. Caesar placed a fort on the strip of land south of Thapsus and camped just outside the city, which he began to ring with fortifications.[20]

Scipio felt compelled to come to the defense of his allies. Blocked by Caesar's fort on the southern isthmus, he marched all the way around the salt marsh by night. Early on the morning of April 6, he appeared north of the marsh and began fortifying his own camp, not far from Caesar's. Juba, with his army, remained south of Caesar's fort. The Republicans' hope was to throw up ramparts across the two strips of land around Thapsus and hem in Caesar from both sides.

Caesar rushed with his army to meet Scipio. Scipio's battle line was drawn up in front of the camp, even as some of his soldiers frantically kept building fortifications. On either end of the line rumbled elephants contributed by Juba. Caesar was not ready to give the signal for battle, but his soldiers were impatient, and a bugler on his right wing suddenly sounded the advance. All the cohorts started moving.

Realizing that they could not be stopped, Caesar acquiesced, giving as the watchword "Good luck." His slingers and archers bombarded the elephants and drove them back. Soon the enemy's Moorish cavalry were in retreat too; the narrow strip of land on which they were fighting denied the Republican army its great advantage.

Caesar's unstoppable legions surged forward and routed Scipio's infantry. Scipio's camp and then Juba's were captured. There was nowhere for the soldiers to flee, and they tried to surrender, but as the author of *The African War* admits, Caesar's "veteran soldiers were so inflamed with anger and resentment, they could not be induced to spare the enemy."[21] According to this account, ten thousand of the Republican forces were killed. In truth, the toll might have been even higher.[22] Scipio and Juba both managed to escape, but their army was annihilated.

Given the disadvantages Caesar had faced at the outset, this campaign, along with the struggle against Vercingetorix, was the most impressive he ever fought.[23] The civil war, he expected, could now be ended quickly. The day after his victory, Caesar made a sacrifice to the gods and held an assembly of his soldiers at which he handed out much-deserved prizes for valor. He then left with part of the army and headed to Utica, about 140 miles away. His hope was to capture Cato and force his old enemy to seek a pardon. Not only would that break the opposition's resistance; it would be the most gratifying revenge possible for everything Cato had done to Caesar over the many years of their feud.

Late in the night of April 8, two days after the battle, a messenger reached Utica with news of the Republican army's destruction. Fear and anger quickly spread among the town's inhabitants. Many Uticans had wanted to support Caesar. Now they were on the side of the losers. Cato was able to restore some calm and the following day called a meeting of the Council of the Three Hundred, the prosperous Romans who did business in the town. They were told to assemble in the Temple of Jupiter, along with all the senators from Rome who were present and the senators' children, among whom was Cato's older son.[24]

Cato came in, quiet and composed, absorbed in the study of his register of weapons, supplies, and manpower. Once everyone was present, he thanked the Three Hundred for their loyalty and urged them, whatever happened, to stick together. If they ran away individually to Caesar, he suggested, they were unlikely to get the best terms possible. Beyond that, the choice was theirs. They could surrender to Caesar, as necessity might seem to dictate. Or they could keep fighting to defend their liberty. Many times, Cato said, Rome, by her greatness, had recovered from even worse disasters.

It was almost like a scene out of an earlier, more glorious age of Roman history—like the aftermath of Hannibal's celebrated victory at Cannae, when despite staggering losses of men and the defection of many allies, the Romans refused to breathe a word about peace.

There were grounds for hope, Cato insisted. The province of Further Spain had kicked out its Caesarian governor, and some months earlier Pompey's son Gnaeus had left Africa to establish control there. The city of Rome had not fully accepted "the bridle" of tyranny and was ready to rise up. Caesar took risks; they must now do so as well. And even if they failed, they would enjoy a glorious death.

Many of the businessmen were stirred by Cato's speech, and someone proposed that they take a vote to free their slaves to join the fight—just as had happened during the war against Hannibal. Scrupulous even in the hour of peril, Cato said the owners of the slaves had to give their permission first; to seize their property would be unjust. Many promised they would grant permission, and Cato ordered a list drawn up of those who volunteered.

Shortly afterward, messages arrived from both Juba and Scipio. Juba was hiding on a mountain with some men; Scipio was on a ship not far from Utica. If Cato made a stand, they wrote, they would join him. Cato felt he should confirm the attitude of the Three Hundred before he sent the messengers back. While the Roman senators were enthusiastically carrying through manumissions, the businessmen already proved to be wavering. Some were even thinking of trying to arrest the senators, in order to gain Caesar's gratitude. Cato wrote to Scipio and Juba to stay away from Utica.

Around fifteen hundred cavalrymen from Scipio's army who had escaped from Thapsus appeared outside Utica's walls, where they clashed with the Caesar-friendly townspeople whom Cato had forced to camp there. The cavalrymen sent three envoys into the city to explain to Cato that they were divided over what to do. Cato told a deputy to watch the Three Hundred and accept any slaves they manumitted while he conferred with the cavalrymen. Outside the city, Cato begged the remnant of Scipio's army not to abandon the senators and to come into Utica, "which could not be taken by force and had grain and other provisions to last many years."

The horsemen discussed their options while Cato sat on a nearby knoll. Cato's deputy arrived to report that the Three Hundred were planning to abandon Cato, and the city was breaking into tumult. Cato had to return at once.

More negotiations followed as Cato went back and forth between the increasingly angry businessmen, inside the city, and the cavalrymen, outside the city, who prudently decided they did not want to be trapped within and would flee to Juba. Cato realized that any chance of holding out in Utica was finished. The senators would have to evacuate by sea and try to make it to Gnaeus Pompey in Spain. The cavalrymen agreed to stay for one day to help the senators get out.

Nervous about the presence of the cavalrymen, the Three Hundred asked to speak with Cato again. The senators, who feared for his safety, did not want him to go, but Cato felt he must. The businessmen were apologetic. Cato had treated them and their city well. But they thought it necessary to send an embassy to Caesar and plead for forgiveness. They would plead on behalf of Cato too, they claimed, and would only accept a pardon from Caesar if Cato was pardoned as well.

Cato told them to appeal for their own safety by all means, but they must ask nothing for him. It fell only to the conquered to beg, only to wrongdoers to seek mercy, Cato explained. And not only had he remained undefeated; he was "even a victor...a conqueror of Caesar" since he had acted with honor and justice while Caesar had been caught acting against his country.

After the speech, news came that Caesar was on the way with his army. "Aha!" Cato cried out. "He treats us like real men!" He turned to the senators and told them to hurry to the ships while he stayed behind to supervise arrangements for the evacuation. At a public meeting with the Uticans, he turned over the accounts he had been keeping and asked the citizens not to spur Caesar on against the Three Hundred. Finally he went down to the sea and all through the night of April 9 and most of the next day oversaw the embarkation.

Lucius Caesar, a relative of the victor who had been fighting on the side of the Republicans, was getting ready to leave Utica and go see his kinsman on behalf of the Three Hundred. He came to Cato to ask for suggestions about what to say, and he wondered, as the businessmen had, if he might make a plea for Cato. Of course Cato would not hear of it. If he wanted to be saved by Caesar, he said, he would go in person. "I don't want to have to be grateful to the tyrant for his illegal actions."

As Cato said goodbye to Lucius, he asked that Lucius try to protect Cato's son. Cato returned to his house in Utica, called together his son and his friends, and began discussing a number of topics. He told his son that he should not engage in politics—"the situation no longer allowed it in a manner worthy of a Cato."

Toward evening he visited the baths, and he then had dinner with a large group, sitting at the table rather than reclining, as he always had after Pharsalus. Friends of Cato's who had refused to leave Utica were there, including a couple of philosophers, one of whom is likely to have written a full account of Cato's last days that informs the later, admittedly quite hagiographical sources on which we must mostly rely.[25] After dinner, conversation continued over wine. The men debated points of philosophy. Cato spoke of his concern for all those who had just left by sea and wondered whether they would have favorable weather and enough time to make their escape before Caesar arrived. The gathering came to an end, and Cato walked around with a few friends, as he usually did after dinner. He gave the officers on watch their orders, embraced his son and friends more warmly than usual, and retired to his bedroom.

He lay down and started reading a copy of Plato's dialogue *Phaedo*, which recounts Socrates's last hours in his prison cell and his drinking of the hemlock. In *Phaedo*, Socrates argues that any man dedicated to philosophy looks forward to death because it frees the immortal soul from its imprisonment in the body. A philosopher should not kill himself, however, unless the gods send a signal that they no longer require his service—as they did when an Athenian jury sentenced Socrates to death. Later Stoic philosophers, who believed that the divine lies within us in the form of reason, developed this idea by arguing that reason itself can tell us when it is acceptable to end our lives.[26] Possible grounds might be suffering from an incurable disease or having to live under tyranny. Socrates's own death remained the supreme example: although he was sentenced to execution, he actually had a chance to escape but refused to take it, determined to hold on to his convictions and face his end bravely. The gods had given him the signal.

Cato had been reading for some time when he called one of his slaves. Cato's sword was not hanging in its usual spot. Over dinner, his son had grown suspicious of Cato's behavior and removed it. Cato asked the slave who had taken the sword. There was no reply. Cato returned to reading but then a little later asked the slave to bring in the weapon. The slave did not come. One by one, Cato called the slaves in and, in tones that grew louder, demanded the sword. He hit one of the slaves across the face, bruising his own hand in the process. Angrily he shouted that he was being handed over to the enemy.

Finally his son entered the room, in tears, along with Cato's friends. Cato again protested that he would have no way to defend himself against Caesar. The sword was brought in, Cato tested its edge, and then he laid it down and resumed reading. He slept for a while, then around midnight called in his doctor to bandage his hand and asked one of his secretaries to check on the progress of the evacuation.

After learning that the ships had not been driven back to the harbor, as he had feared, Cato asked his secretary to close the door. Once the secretary left, Cato lay down on the couch. Drawing his sword, he stabbed himself beneath his chest. The thrust was somewhat feeble because of his injured hand, but the wound was grave. As Cato fell from the couch he overturned an abacus standing nearby, and the noise prompted his slaves, his friends, and his son to rush in. They were shocked as they saw the blood, the organs spilling out, and Cato, eyes open, still alive. The doctor attempted to sew up the wound, but in a final burst of strength Cato pushed the doctor away, tore open the wound with his own hand, and died.

He was forty-eight years old. The Uticans did not hesitate to give him a fine funeral. Even though they wanted to ingratiate themselves with Caesar, they recognized that Cato had saved their city. They decorated the corpse, carried it in a solemn procession, and buried it by the sea, where even centuries later stood a statue of Cato, sword in hand.[27]

A few days later Caesar arrived at Utica. At a public meeting he thanked the people of Utica for their support but sharply attacked the Three Hundred. "His speech went on at some length about their crimes," wrote the author of *The African War*, "and only at the end did he announce that they could come out into the open without fear."[28] He would spare their lives, but he would take all their property.

Caesar was angry that Cato had killed himself. Earlier, when a report informed Caesar that Cato had not left the city with the others, Caesar wondered what his old rival had planned.[29] Perhaps Cato would surrender? Now Caesar knew. There can be no doubt that he would have issued a pardon to his longtime enemy as a way of sealing his victory. He did pardon Cato's son and allow him to keep his father's property. But the defeated Cato had stolen from Caesar his greatest opportunity to show magnanimity.

Why did Cato kill himself? He could have boarded one of the ships and sailed to Spain, but that was risky; if the ships encountered bad weather, they might have been blown back to Utica. Caesar's new ally Sittius had a fleet on the coast of Africa that did end up capturing some of the fleeing Republicans, including Scipio. Scipio managed to fatally stab himself before he was taken into custody. Cato would have been unaware of those events, but Scipio's action shows how disgraceful it was for a Roman noble to suffer defeat and surrender or be taken captive. Suicide was a more honorable alternative.[30] Thus, even if Cato did not prevail, he could, by killing himself, maintain that he never was beaten. In the end, he, not Utica, proved to be the fortress that would not be stormed.

To the Roman tradition of avoiding the shame of defeat, Cato introduced new elements from the philosophy he had studied his whole life. Not only was he reading *Phaedo* the night he died; he was deliberating the morality of his situation with his friends and companions. Cato advocated a particularly Stoic view that an individual had to act in accord with human nature, with one's own personal nature, and with the circumstances at hand. Cato's nature prevented him from being able to adapt to life in a Rome in which Caesar had won and installed a tyranny, even if others, like the Three Hundred or Cato's son, could. For Cato, suicide was the right choice; for others, such as the Romans he helped to escape from Utica, it need not be. No single principle applied absolutely. Death was not always necessarily preferable to defeat.[31]

In his final days, Cato was doing more than supervising the evacuation of the senators and trying to protect Utica; he was also, with perfect integrity, working out an ethics of suicide. His thinking was new for Rome, though it would turn out to be profoundly influential in later generations. Cicero grasped the importance of Cato's example almost immediately, and in a philosophical dialogue he wrote shortly after Cato's death, he had Cato say, "When a man's circumstances are more in keeping with his nature, it is his duty to stay alive; when they are more contrary to his nature or it appears they will be, it is his duty to go."[32]

Conventional and innovative, practical and philosophical, the suicide was also, as was only fitting for Cato, political. By killing himself, Cato simultaneously denied Caesar the chance of pardoning him and marred Caesar's victory. For Cato to prefer death to any sort of life under Caesar was an indelible reproach to the nature of Caesar's victory and whatever political regime he would go on to establish. Cato chose to take his own life, but his death could be seen—was *meant* to be seen—as the final act of a martyr who suffered for the cause of freedom. He had allowed himself to be pelted with stones, dragged off the Rostra, hauled to prison—and now stabbed. When he tore out his guts, he made himself stronger than ever before.

Cato wanted to show that no tyranny, however mild, was acceptable for one who prized freedom the way Cato did, and he did so in the most vivid way imaginable. His suicide was his last, and most supreme, act of obstruction. It weighed on the consciences of survivors such as Cicero. They began to praise Cato in death as they never had in life. It infuriated Caesar, who responded by making decisions that would derail his victory.

And so maybe Cato was the victor after all.

CHAPTER 13

ANTICATO

I T'S A PROBLEM FOR ARCHIMEDES." THAT WAS HOW CICERO, IN A letter to Atticus, described the challenge of writing a eulogy for the dead Cato. How could Cicero truly pay tribute without offending Cato's mortal enemies the Caesarians? "Even if I backed away from his interventions in Senate debate, from his overall attitude to politics and his recommendations, this still would make unpleasant reading for them." Rarely was Cicero at a loss for words, and this was why he had been asked by Cato's nephew to write the eulogy. But there was no way to give Cato his due, the orator concluded, without recognizing "the way he saw in advance what was coming and strained to prevent it and abandoned his life so he would not see it, once it did happen."[1]

While Cicero vented darkly to his friend, the Senate was heaping honors on the victor. There were to be forty days of thanksgivings to the gods and special trappings at Caesar's upcoming triumph. White horses would draw his chariot instead of the usual black, and a whole host of lictors was to accompany him. At meetings of the Senate, Caesar was to sit on an ivory chair, as the consuls did, and he would always state his opinion first. In all the games in the Circus, he was to give the signal for the start of the horse races. A chariot of his was to adorn the sanctuary of Jupiter on the Capitoline Hill, and so would a bronze statue of Caesar mounted atop a globe, with an inscription to the effect that he was a demigod.

Simply to list all the honors that were voted to Caesar in the last two years of his life could fill a whole chapter. The litany culminated in the recognition of Caesar as a god, with a temple to be consecrated to him and another new deity, the Clemency of Caesar; Mark Antony was to hold the associated priesthood.[2] It is, of course, impossible to know how, or even if, all these glories would have been implemented—Caesar would not live long enough. But the decrees were more than empty flattery from a Senate increasingly stuffed with Caesar's supporters. They established Caesar as a new kind of ruler in Rome, the initiator of a modern age of Roman history, a god made by the votes of his fellow citizens.

Yet just as the honors piled up, resentment and resistance swelled. Cato was no longer able to lead the opposition, but his growing legend stirred senators to action. Inspiration also sprang from the stories of much earlier times, especially the foundation of the Republic, when the first consul, Lucius Junius Brutus—the putative ancestor of Cato's nephew Marcus Brutus—drove out the last of the city's kings and executed his own sons when they tried to restore the monarchy. A statue of Lucius Brutus, sword unsheathed, stood watch in the sanctuary of Jupiter on the Capitoline Hill.[3]

Caesar's new era would be short-lived, but those bent on toppling him would fail to win a free Republic. Both sides suffered from dangerous delusions. After Caesar's fall, civil war would flare up once again in Italy, fueled by profound disagreement over what sort of government Rome should have. Old quarrels would rage on in different forms and stir yet more anger, fear, and violence.

Key to Caesar's public profile in his last few years was his evolving dictatorship. In late 49 BC he had held the office for eleven days to preside over elections. After his victory at Pharsalus in 48, he took the office for a whole year, with a view to ending civil war and restoring stability in Rome.[4] Caesar's unexpected detention in Alexandria upset those plans, but now, after Thapsus, they could proceed. This meant reopening the courts in Rome and ending the ongoing debt crisis. It also meant passing laws to improve the moral health of the community by restricting the use of luxury goods and foods, for example.[5] Excessive ambition and greed, Romans thought, had contributed to, and been increased by, the recent civil war and needed to be restrained. And so after Thapsus, Caesar was again made dictator, but this time with the right to hold the office for ten years. He also assumed, somewhat improbably, the censors' traditional duty of overseeing morals, for a term of three years.[6]

A portrait of Caesar on a silver coin issued in 44 BC, shortly before his assassination. He relished the laurel crown seen here because it concealed his receding hairline.
Credit: Photo © the Trustees of the British Museum

Nobody in Rome had held these exact powers before, but they drew on the pattern set by the extraordinary command that Caesar had enjoyed in Gaul and Illyricum. The ten years of dictatorship, for instance, doubled the five-year term of the Vatinian Law of 59 BC. Very likely, Caesar was configuring his position to elevate his prestige and carry out the stabilization that everyone agreed was needed, but also to equip himself for what he most sought to do: fight a major war against the Parthians in the east. His new dictatorship gave him ten years of military power, superior to that of consuls. It would also allow him to control the city of Rome in absentia through deputies.[7]

In 47 Caesar had left troops behind in Syria in preparation for this new war. He had good pretexts for fighting: the need to avenge his old friend Crassus and the loss of the three Roman legions at the battle of Carrhae in 53, as well as recent instability in the eastern provinces. There were also mouthwatering opportunities for accruing wealth, patronage, and prestige. Parthia was to be a second Gaul, only better. Caesar had played up the glamor of reaching Britain at the edges of the earth, but now he would truly be following in the footsteps of Alexander. And it would all be written up in new installments of commentaries filled with the names of historic places and descriptions of exotic peoples. What a sequel they would make!

First, though, Caesar was to enjoy a proper celebration of his victories over the previous fifteen years. After returning to Rome in late July of 46, he had a series of four triumphs, probably spread out over a span of eight days.[8] The first was for Gaul, the second Egypt, the third Pontus, and the last Africa. With all his talent for showmanship, Caesar displayed magnificent spoils and high-profile captives. Heaps of gold and silver, representations of the Rhine, the Rhône, and the Nile, even a model of the great lighthouse of Alexandria with a live flame at the top were paraded through the streets. Vercingetorix himself had been carefully kept alive for the Gallic triumph and stumbled along in chains before being dragged off to the prison for execution. In the Egyptian triumph appeared Cleopatra's sister Arsinoe, and in the African, the young son of the

Numidian king Juba. (Juba himself had taken his own life in a suicide pact with one of the Republican generals, Petreius.) Each triumph was festooned with equipment made from a suitably exotic material, such as ivory from Africa and tortoiseshell from Egypt.

Caesar's soldiers were in good spirits and sang out rude songs about their general's whoring around with the women of Gaul, with Cleopatra, and even—much to Caesar's annoyance—with King Nicomedes.[9] The crowds of citizens are said to have enjoyed paintings re-creating the deaths of Pothinus the eunuch and Caesar's other enemies in Alexandria, as well as the flight of Pharnaces of Pontus. But they groaned when forced to look at Metellus Scipio stabbing himself and jumping into the sea, Petreius taking his life with Juba, and Cato tearing himself apart "like a wild animal."[10] The depictions were apparently an effort to counteract the glory those men had won for their refusal to submit to Caesar.

Following the last triumph, Caesar dedicated a gleaming new marble temple to Venus the Mother. For a time Caesar had been planning an extension to the overcrowded Forum, but now the land he had bought up was to become his own so-called Julian Forum, a vast colonnaded square dominated by the temple to Venus, the lofty podium of which could be used as a speaker's platform at public meetings.[11] Caesar filled the temple with treasures, including a statue of Venus by a leading sculptor of the day, cases of engraved gems, and a breastplate made of pearls from Britain. The lavish complex proclaimed both Caesar's devotion to the goddess from whom he claimed descent and her devotion to him. After the dedication, Caesar feasted practically the whole city at banquets with imported Greek wines, eels cultivated in artificial fishponds along the Bay of Naples, and other delicacies, all cries for moral reform notwithstanding.[12] Caesar was escorted home by a procession of elephants carrying torches—as if he were a god himself.

The citizens of Rome were given gifts of grain, oil, and cash. They were treated to the most impressive games the city had ever witnessed, combining an inaugural festival for the new cult of Venus with the funeral games that Caesar had long ago promised in honor of his much-lamented daughter Julia.[13] Crowds of spectators enjoyed gladiatorial contests and wild-beast hunts in a temporary wooden amphitheater. They marveled at the display of a strange animal that bore some resemblance to a camel, except that it had spots like a leopard, hind legs shorter than the fore, and an amazingly long neck. It was a giraffe, the first ever seen in Rome. Stage plays, athletic competitions, and dance performances were mounted throughout the city. In the Circus, which Caesar lengthened, horse-drawn chariots raced, and foot soldiers, horsemen, and even men on elephants fought each other. An artificial lake was engineered on the Field of Mars for a mock naval battle, in which banked ships from the fleets of Egypt and Tyre fought. Caesar outdid even himself when, to protect spectators from the blazing sun, he stretched awnings over the Forum all the way to his own house and up to the Capitol, all made of luxurious silk. Cato, had he been alive to see it, would have been disgusted.

Over the next few months Caesar threw himself into administrative duties with typical energy and efficiency. He launched basic measures of stabilization that senators had called for, including reestablishment of the courts. He introduced innovations as well. Caesar conducted a new type of urban census in which officials combed through the city of Rome block by block, requiring building owners to list all residents. This method helped Caesar reduce the number of those who received grain at public expense, freeing up large sums of money for other uses.[14]

Even more revolutionary was Caesar's introduction of an entirely new calendar. Until 46 BC, the Romans used a lunar calendar that required periodic insertion of a so-called intercalary month in order for the all-important cycle of religious festivals to keep up with the seasons. In recent years the system had broken down, and Caesar replaced it, lengthening the twelve existing months, removing intercalation, and adding a leap year. The Egyptians had long used a solar year, and an astronomer from Alexandria assisted Caesar with the reform. Critics of Caesar naturally complained that it was an abuse of power. Cicero, on being told that a particular constellation would be rising at the start of January in the new, Caesarian year, grimly remarked, "Yes, by decree."[15]

Colonization was another major project of Caesar's dictatorship.[16] In conjunction with the magnificent quadruple triumph, Caesar distributed vast sums of money to his veterans. He also made good on his promise of farms. Agrarian settlement was the issue that, more than any other, had driven Caesar and the *optimates* fatally apart in 59. There was an old Roman tradition of the settlement of citizens on public land, but the *optimates* were convinced that sponsors of such programs would acquire unacceptable levels of power. They could not stop Caesar now. He arranged for some of his soldiers to take over unused public land as well as land that Caesar himself purchased in Italy. He also created entirely new overseas colonies in which whole swathes of territory would be surveyed and distributed, with settlers to form their own local governments. Some of these were for his soldiers, but others were intended for the poor of Rome. The most eye-catching of the new settlements were Carthage and Corinth. A century earlier both these great maritime cities had been destroyed simultaneously in a brutal proclamation of Roman supremacy across the Mediterranean. To reestablish them was, like Caesar's new calendar and the many honors and offices voted to him, an assertion that a new historical epoch was underway.

As was almost inevitable, murmurings of complaint arose over how Caesar exercised his victory in Rome. It did not help that Cleopatra came to the city and was installed by Caesar in one of his houses even though he remained married to Calpurnia and probably hoped for a son from her. His passion for the foreign queen was uncooled. Despite criticisms, he had her and her younger brother formally recognized as friends and allies of Rome.[17]

Far more serious opposition developed in the province of Further Spain. Caesar had installed a deeply unpopular governor there, and before the battle of Thapsus, Pompey's elder son Gnaeus had sailed from Africa to exploit the discontent. He was later joined by his younger brother Sextus, Labienus, and other fugitives from Africa. They raised substantial forces, including over a dozen legions. They also gained control of much of the valley of the Baetis River, an agriculturally rich region encompassing a number of major towns with strong defenses, including Corduba, the provincial capital.[18]

Parthia would have to wait. Caesar made it to Further Spain after a fast journey of under one month. To amuse himself while on the march, he composed a poem called *The Journey*.[19] As usual, he appeared so quickly in his new theater of war that he had limited supplies. He was unable to take Corduba, held by Sextus Pompey, but he did capture or win over other settlements.

On March 17, 45, a day of brilliant sunshine, Caesar accepted an invitation for battle from Gnaeus Pompey just outside the town of Munda. Gnaeus had established himself on high ground, forcing Caesar to cross a spring and marshy land and then move uphill. On both sides the infantry fought with great ferocity. When Caesar's troops started to give ground, Caesar jumped off his horse, rushed to the front of the line, and yelled that his soldiers should hand him over to the enemy if this was the best they could do.

Finally, Caesar's veteran Tenth Legion was able to put pressure on the left wing of Gnaeus's battle line. As Gnaeus tried to move some of his troops from his right wing, Caesar's cavalry pounced there. Labienus pursued the Caesarian cavalry. The Pompeian infantry, mistakenly thinking that a full rout had begun, started to flee. Some managed to make it back into Munda, but thousands were killed. Caesar piled up the corpses to form a rampart around the town, and on top of the rampart he stuck the heads of the bodies on the points of swords, facing the town. "I have often fought for victory, never until now for my life," Caesar said as he left the gory battlefield.[20]

Labienus was killed in the fighting. Gnaeus fled to the coast but, badly wounded with a twisted ankle, was unable to escape and was also killed. His head was brought to Caesar. His younger brother Sextus fled Corduba into northwestern Iberia and there raised some forces to carry on a guerilla war. One by one, the major settlements, including Corduba and Munda itself, fell to Caesar. It had been a brutal war with atrocities committed in town after town as communities divided over which side to back. At the end of it all, Caesar imposed severe penalties on those who had supported Gnaeus and his allies. In Caesar's eyes, Gnaeus had usurped official power and was an out-and-out enemy of Rome. Far more than at the start of the civil war in 49, Caesar was embittered toward his opponents, and this contributed to the savagery in Spain.

His anger also took a literary form. Caesar was irritated by the tributes to Cato that had recently appeared. Not only was there Cicero's eulogy, which had won considerable acclaim; Brutus had ended up writing his own *Cato*. Neither work survives, but both seem to have narrated Cato's life in some detail, with glimpses of his childhood, and both commended him for virtuous conduct.[21] As Cicero put it elsewhere, Cato was "first of any people in the world for virtue."[22] Cicero's *Cato* naturally was eloquent. In a letter to Cicero, Caesar himself said that reading and rereading it had made him richer in expression; Brutus's *Cato*, on the other hand, left Caesar thinking *himself* something of a writer.[23] Of course, as so often with Caesar, the remark was tinged with irony. Cicero, Caesar was suggesting, was able to take all the warts off a verrucose Cato and turn him into a god—which made Caesar himself look like a toad.

Caesar readied his counteroffensive. First, Aulus Hirtius, an officer of Caesar's who was also an excellent writer, prepared a booklet that collected all Cato's faults while ostensibly praising Cicero. After Cicero read the document, he told Atticus to have copies made and distributed, thinking that the abuse of Cato "would invite mockery."[24]

Then came Caesar's own effort, his *Anticato*, a work so big it took up two scrolls. The imperial satirist Juvenal crudely joked that it was thicker even than the penis of the "lute girl" who had violated the ceremonies of the Bona Dea.[25] As a rebuttal to Cicero's eulogy, Caesar attacked every aspect of Cato's life. In a preface brimming with irony, Caesar "begged readers not to compare the plain speech of a military man with the cleverness of an orator who was naturally talented and had ample leisure to practice the art."[26]

Only a few quotations and paraphrases of *Anticato* survive, but they are enough to show that Caesar flexed his wit. He told a story of how early-morning callers on the streets of Rome ran into a drunk. Uncovering the dazed man's head and discovering that it was Cato, they blushed. "You would have thought not that Cato had been caught red-handed by them, but they had been caught by Cato," wrote Caesar.[27]

In places the book was downright scurrilous. Cato, Caesar claimed, was miserly and cold. Cato showed no trust for his friends, not even Munatius. After the death of his beloved half brother Caepio, he sifted the ashes from the pyre, looking for melted gold. As for Cato's marriage with Marcia: that was nothing more than money grabbing. What other reason was there, Caesar asked, for Cato to give up his wife and then take her back? "Everybody holds their family dear," Caesar charged, "with one exception—the man whom nature made different from all."[28] It was not Caesar who was the cruel and monstrous tyrant—but Cato.

Caesar's lack of generosity extended to the celebration of another triumph in early October of 45, after his return to Rome. This was a more controversial celebration than those of the previous year because there was no great foreign leader for Caesar to claim victory over—no Pharnaces or Juba—but only the son of Pompey. The traditional requirement of thousands of casualties had been met, but many of the casualties were Roman citizens.[29]

Meanwhile, new honors and powers gushed from the Senate and lifted Caesar to permanent supremacy. Any hope that he would reestablish the Republic and then abdicate from the dictatorship, as

Sulla had, was dashed. All armies and public moneys were entrusted
to the sole disposition of Caesar and his delegates. In every province
of the empire, he would hold command. All military successes were
now to be associated with him by adding an extra day of thanksgivings in his name whenever anyone won a victory anywhere. It did
not matter if he had no part in it. Caesar was authorized to wear
at public occasions the laurel crown of the triumphant general and
also the ceremonial toga of purple and gold.[30]

No privilege pleased Caesar more than the laurel crown since it
allowed him to cover his growing bald spot. But the honors were
important for far more than this. They made Caesar a perpetual
victor, a companion of the gods. In the grand processions that went
from the Capitol to the Circus as part of the major religious festivals, a statue of Caesar fashioned out of ivory was to be carried
alongside those of the other deities, including the goddess Victory
herself.[31]

In July of 45, even before Caesar's return from Spain, the statue
appeared in the great annual games for Apollo. Atticus attended
with his young daughter and reported to Cicero that the crowd had
been less than happy.[32] Normally the games for Apollo were organized by one of the year's praetors, but for most of the year 45 there
were no praetors. Caesar had arranged for himself to serve as sole
consul (as well as dictator), and aside from tribunes and some of
the aediles, no other magistrates were elected. In Caesar's absence
Rome was mostly managed by his deputy, Marcus Aemilius Lepidus, along with a board of prefects appointed by Caesar. Caesar's
long-standing personal advisors, including Balbus and Oppius, ex-
erted a great deal of power too.[33]

Free elections were dying, which displeased the people of Rome.
Upon Caesar's return to the city in the early fall of 45, he resigned
from his consulship, and consuls and the other magistrates were
finally elected. But effectively the consuls had been appointed by
Caesar, and when one of them entered the theater and a lictor demanded that the crowd recognize him, the crowd shouted back,

"He's no consul!"[34] Elections still took place, but they were turning into empty formalities. After Munda, Caesar was granted the right to nominate all the candidates himself, although he did not immediately exercise it.[35]

Some of the senators felt great frustration. Caesar had massively increased the size of the Senate and filled it with men who had supported him in his wars. They might have been happy enough to vote honor after honor, but the more independently minded resented their inability to engage in real debate. Probably hoping to dissuade Caesar from setting out immediately for war against Parthia, Cicero worked on a formal *Letter of Advice* for Caesar that drew inspiration from similar works written for Alexander the Great. Cicero had Caesar's men Balbus and Oppius read a draft, and they insisted on so many changes that Cicero abandoned the whole project.[36] Caesar never saw it. Freedom of speech was dying too.

Cicero mostly avoided Rome, but in December of 45 he was treated to a visit from the dictator at one of his properties on the coast near Naples. Caesar was staying in the nearby villa of Marcius Philippus, the father of Cato's widow, Marcia. As Cicero wrote to Atticus, two thousand soldiers accompanied Caesar, and they nearly overran Philippus's house. On the morning of December 19, Caesar admitted nobody and was busy until about one p.m.—working on accounts with Balbus, Cicero guessed. Caesar then took a short walk along the shore, followed by a bath. Ever neat with his grooming, he put on scented oil before dining with Cicero.

Caesar was on a course of emetics at the time and so ate and drank heartily, Cicero reported. The conversation flowed, though it was confined almost entirely to literary matters, "nothing serious." Clearly Caesar could still be charming. The visit was not disagreeable, Cicero decided, though it was a lot of work to entertain Caesar's vast entourage. "My guest was not the sort to whom you say, 'Please do drop by again when you're next in the area.' Once is enough."[37]

The extraordinary power Caesar had won over the preceding few years had not made him monstrously cruel. He was not a Caligula or

Nero. But he was more impatient and more inconsiderate than ever of the true feelings of others, especially old senatorial colleagues. *Anticato*, the Spanish triumph, the wearing of the laurel crown and purple toga: all spoke to his testiness and his pride. He had some sense of how hated he was becoming—and he did not care. After the senators swore an oath to protect him, probably toward the end of 45, he dismissed the bodyguard of Spaniards he had been using. When he was later urged by advisors to reconstitute the force, he refused.[38] Caesar could not seem to be afraid to walk around.

Caesar returned to the city to preside over elections for magistrates who would enter office on January 1. When he learned that a consul who had gained office a few months earlier had suddenly died, he converted the assembly into one to elect a new consul. A former officer of Caesar's from the Gallic War, Caninius Rebilus, was voted into office—for less than twelve hours. For Cicero this highly irregular proceeding captured perfectly just how little Caesar cared for the traditions of the Republic. Political life was becoming a dark joke, as Cicero suggested in a private letter to a friend: "In the consulship of Caninius, you can be certain that nobody had lunch. When this fellow was consul, no crime was committed. His vigilance was extraordinary. Throughout his whole consulship, he didn't sleep a wink!"[39]

Preparations for the war against the Parthians were advancing. Across the Adriatic Caesar was mustering sixteen legions as well as a large force of cavalry. He collected funds to pay the troops. So that the city should not fall into chaos during his absence, he arranged to have all the magistrates appointed for three years. Caesar directly nominated many of them.[40]

Caesar's opponents were filled with dread. His men would have a stranglehold on politics in the city for the next three years at a minimum. Caesar himself, meanwhile, was all too likely to succeed where Crassus had not: the Parthian conquest would bring even more glory and wealth to his name. He had used Gaul to conquer Rome; with Parthia, he very well might become master of the whole world. The warnings Cato had made years before about Caesar's tyranny and about wars of conquest must have seemed more relevant than ever.

The city grew uneasy. Rumors spread—no doubt with the encouragement of Caesar's critics—that he intended to establish himself in the east, in Alexandria perhaps, with his lover Cleopatra. Caesar's minions would be in charge of everything, and Italy would be drained of troops and money to feed Caesar's ambition.[41]

Some even whispered that Caesar sought to gain the title of king. That charge was almost certainly untrue. In the last months of his life Caesar did consent to be recognized as a god, the culmination of claims he had long been making about his divine ancestry. Yet while in the east divinity and kingship naturally went together, in Rome "king" was still a hated word. Caesar publicly rejected it. "I am Caesar, not king," he wittily said, punning on the Latin word *rex*, which also could be a name, Rex.[42] Caesar did, however, take a new title: dictator for life (*dictator perpetuo*). It recognized the permanence of his supremacy over the Roman state and allowed him to give up the consulship he was holding at the start of 44 and not seek the office again for the next few years while he was away. For some, the difference between "dictator for life" and "king" seemed hard to make out.[43]

Another spectacle for the people of Rome disgusted Caesar's opponents and heightened fears of Caesar's overweening ambition. One of the city's most ancient festivals, the Lupercalia, fell on February 15, not long before Caesar was due to set out. At dawn, in a cave where Rome's founders, Romulus and Remus, were said to have been suckled by a she-wolf, goats were sacrificed by an association of prominent young men known as the Luperci. The Luperci smeared themselves with the goats' blood and used the hide of the animals to form whips. Clad only in the scantiest of loincloths, the men ran through the city, flicking the whips at the large crowds who met them. Women who were lashed by the whip, it was believed, would become pregnant, so young wives in particular bared their bodies. It was a quintessentially Roman festival, linking the foundation of the city to its ongoing prosperity, with a lot of sexiness and partying thrown in.[44]

Traditionally there had been two teams of Luperci, one commemorating Romulus and the other Remus. This year a third group had been added, the Luperci Juliani, in recognition of Caesar as a new founder of Rome. The new team's captain was Mark Antony, a close associate of Caesar's and consul that year, who also happened to boast one of the most impressive physiques of Rome.

At the climax of the festivities, the nearly naked and well-oiled Mark Antony ran into the Forum, where Caesar, in his purple toga, was seated on a golden chair on the Rostra. Antony produced the white headband that was the traditional symbol of kingship in the east. The crowd gasped. Several times Antony tried to place the diadem on Caesar's head, but Caesar refused it. "Jupiter alone is king of the Romans," Caesar proclaimed, and he had the diadem carried to Jupiter's temple on the Capitoline.[45] Although critics of Caesar—and of Antony—would later say otherwise, almost certainly the whole scene had been staged as a rejection of kingship itself. Romulus had been king, but Caesar intended to be a different kind of founder. If that was the intention, though, the spectacle failed to achieve its goal.

Resentment of Caesar's high-handedness and monopolization of power had been simmering, even among those who had served with Caesar in Gaul. Even if he did not call himself king, they felt like a king's subjects—and the almost nude Mark Antony dangling a crown before Caesar only heightened their suspicions.

After the Lupercalia, small groups who had complained quietly to one another coalesced into a conspiracy with a single goal: to take Caesar's life. At least twenty men were involved, including Marcus Brutus, the son of Servilia.[46] The driving force was Gaius Cassius Longinus. Cassius hated Caesar and thought he must be removed, just as men who had sought undue power in Rome had always been removed, going back to the last of the kings. Yet Cassius realized that the conspiracy would need a figurehead, and Marcus Brutus fit the bill perfectly. In addition to counting Rome's first consul as an ancestor, Brutus claimed descent, on his mother Servilia's side, from Servilius Ahala, a hero of the early Republic who stopped a man aspiring to kingship by stabbing him to death with a dagger in the Forum.[47]

Brutus owed much to Caesar. As a favor to his old lover, Caesar had supported Brutus for years. Caesar had pardoned him at Pharsalus, made him governor of Cisalpine Gaul, and chosen him to serve in 44 as urban praetor, a prestigious position that entailed presiding over the great games for Apollo.[48] Brutus, there is no doubt, could have risen high under Caesar, but those words, "under Caesar," rankled him. His lineage was well known, and opponents of Caesar knew exactly what they were doing when they covered the statue of Lucius Brutus on the Capitol with a graffito: "Oh that you were alive, Brutus!" On Marcus Brutus's own praetorian tribunal, they taunted him, scrawling, "You are not really Brutus" and "Brutus, are you sleeping?"[49]

Much nearer in the family tree was Brutus's uncle Cato, the man he was said to have admired more than any other. Brutus wrote his tribute to Cato and then in the summer of 45 went a step further by divorcing his wife and marrying Cato's daughter Porcia, the widow of Bibulus and a fierce devotee of the memory of her father. The political significance of that marriage could not be missed, and Servilia was quite annoyed by Brutus's actions.[50] In the wake of Cato's passing, the next generation of politicians who were determined to resist one-man rule and uphold the free election of leaders coalesced around Brutus. It was a thrilling thought: they would become tyrant-slayers like the ones they knew from history books or the ancestor masks in their own houses.

Whether Cato would have approved of any plan to take Caesar's life is questionable. Cato's horror of violence was well known. But

Brutus and Cassius built their plot on a foundation not merely of legend but of philosophy. One of the ways the two men sounded out other possible supporters was by having Brutus, a serious student of Platonic philosophy, raise in conversation the question of tyranny.[51] Plato himself had written that life under tyranny was intolerable slavery, and so, for a Platonist, killing a tyrant must be justified. When Brutus broached the topic with Favonius, Favonius stated as his view that civil war was worse than illegal monarchy—words Cato himself might have said. Monarchy might still provide some order; civil war brought on disorder as well as illegality. Having revealed his position, Favonius was not invited to join the conspiracy. Nor indeed was Cicero. This was rather an enterprise for younger men who believed they had been robbed by Caesar of the chance of securing glory for themselves in the traditional way. They were standing up against lawless tyranny and for the free Republic.[52]

The plotters saw their opportunity with a meeting of the Senate called for March 15, the so-called Ides, just a few days before Caesar was supposed to leave for the east.[53] The meeting was to take place in the great theater complex Pompey had built years earlier on the Field of Mars, in a room known as the Senate house of Pompey. There the assassins could gather without undue suspicion and yet might inspire other senators with their historic deed.

But when the day arrived, Caesar was not at the Senate house at the appointed time. The conspirators sent Decimus Brutus, a distant kinsman of Marcus and longtime favorite of Caesar, to lure the dictator for life to his doom. Decimus persuaded Caesar to attend, while another Caesarian who had joined the plot, Gaius Trebonius, was given the job of detaining Mark Antony outside the Senate house while Caesar went in.

As Caesar entered, the senators rose to pay their respects. One of the conspirators approached Caesar to hand him a petition. Others crowded around, seemingly to support their colleague's request. Caesar tried to brush them off. But it was already too late. One conspirator pulled at Caesar's toga. Another drew a dagger. Then came

A silver coin issued by the mint of Marcus Brutus shows a portrait of the assassin. The reverse memorably commemorates the Ides of March by showing two of the daggers that killed Caesar and the liberty cap given to freed slaves.
Credit: Courtesy of the American Numismatic Society

the first stab. Then more and more. Caesar struggled to fend off the blades, but he soon saw that he was surrounded by assassins on all sides. For the first and only time in his life, he gave in and pulled his toga over his head. Stricken twenty-three times, he fell dead.

The rest of the Senate fled in panic. "Run!" the terrified men yelled. "Bolt the doors!" Brutus and the other conspirators hurried to the Forum, exultant, daggers raised high. They called out to the citizens to assert their freedom. But panic, not joy, and certainly not relief, spread through the city. Ordinary Romans slammed shut the doors of their taverns and workshops and houses. Brutus later made a speech in the Forum but won little support from it. He and the other murderers of Caesar were forced to barricade themselves in the sanctuary of Jupiter on the Capitoline Hill. Mayhem was about to break out.

CHAPTER 14

REQUIEM FOR A REPUBLIC

S EVERAL DAYS LATER, CAESAR'S BODY, BATHED AND ANOINTED, was carried into the Forum on a litter accompanied by mourners and musicians. On the Rostra, a miniature version of Caesar's Temple of Venus, covered with gold, had been erected. Inside was an ivory couch with purple and gold cloths, on which the corpse would repose while Mark Antony delivered the eulogy.[1]

As the procession made its way through the Forum, the masses that had gathered cried out in anger and sadness. Veterans of Caesar's forces, armor gleaming in honor of their commander, clashed their shields. Shortly before the funeral the people of Rome had learned that Caesar had bequeathed to them his gardens, located across the Tiber River, to enjoy as a park. The grounds housed a remarkable collection of paintings and statues. To each individual citizen he had left 300 sesterces.[2] Previous days' grumbling over the man who would be king had been replaced by laments for the truest friend and champion of ordinary Romans.

A great funeral for the dictator had never been part of the assassins' plans. They had wanted to toss his body into the Tiber, confiscate his property, and annul all his enactments. But the panic that had fallen over Rome after Caesar's death allowed Antony, Lepidus, and other political allies, backed by Caesar's veterans, to thwart those intentions, channeling the assassination into a great tragedy rather than the political triumph the conspirators had hoped for. A compromise was worked out in the Senate by which all Caesar's acts, including land grants for the soldiers, would stand, in exchange for which the assassins were to escape punishment for the murder. Further, Caesar would be honored with a public funeral.[3]

The funeral offered Antony a chance to stoke fury against the murderers even more than Caesar's will already had. "Friends, Romans, countrymen...." Shakespeare composed his own version of Antony's speech, but the playwright was not far off from the essence of Antony's words and actions. High on the Rostra he stood, in front of the gilded shrine. At first, he limited himself to reading out some of the decrees that the Senate had voted in honor of Caesar. With each decree, he looked back and gestured toward Caesar's body and gave voice to his own grief and indignation. He recited the oaths that been sworn to protect Caesar. He reeled off the wars Caesar had fought, the battles he had won, the peoples he had subdued, and all the spoils he had brought home.

The audience was already moved, but Antony meant to transfix them with grief. He lifted up, on the point of a spear, the toga Caesar had been wearing at the time of his murder, stained with Caesar's blood. As Antony pointed to the many spots on it, the crowd sobbed. "This was the unkindest cut of all," Shakespeare has Antony remark, as he claims to identify the blood from Brutus's blow in particular.

Funeral dirges sounded above the collective grief. An actor, mimicking the voice of Caesar, cried out a line from an old Roman tragedy: "Saved I those men, so they could destroy me?"[4] A bit of stagecraft hammered at the brutality once more as a mechanical device raised a wax likeness of Caesar over the bier, rotating it to reveal all twenty-three wounds to the grieving crowd.

The people could bear it no longer. With shrieks and yells, they began running through the Forum. Some grabbed the bier with Caesar's body and hoisted it onto their shoulders.

A pyre had already been built on the Field of Mars, near the tomb of Caesar's daughter Julia. Men and women had jammed the streets all day while carrying offerings to it. But now, hysterical with grief, they conveyed the bier to the eastern end of the Forum, setting it on fire there, where everyone could see it. To keep the blaze going, they heaped on it the wooden tribunals of the praetors and the jurors' benches. Musicians and actors tore off their robes, soldiers their weapons, even some of the women their jewelry, and added them to the flames. An angry mob carried torches to the houses of the assassins and nearly burned those down as well.

For days afterward, throngs of people gathered to mourn at the spot where Caesar had been cremated. Caesar's remains were interred in a tomb on the Field of Mars, but on the site of the pyre, a column of yellow marble from Africa was erected that stood almost twenty feet high. "To the Father of his Country," it was inscribed. At its base, people sacrificed, made vows, and settled disputes by swearing an oath "by Caesar."[5]

The leading assassins, meanwhile, had fled Rome. Later in the year, Brutus and Cassius forsook Italy altogether and began recruiting forces in the east. Sextus Pompey, left behind in Spain by Caesar as defeated, also gained strength. The itch to wage civil war could not be soothed. The heirs of Pompey and Cato, including Cato's eldest son and even his old friend Favonius, felt they had to take up arms against the emerging tyranny and defend the free Republic. But one by one the champions fell. Young Cato died in battle in 42 BC. Favonius was captured and executed.[6]

As Antony had shown at the funeral, too many Romans had benefited too much from Caesar's rule for him to be repudiated. He had created a political movement that would outlive him. Shakespeare's

Brutus proclaims, shortly before his own suicide at the battle of Philippi in 42, "O Julius Caesar, thou are mighty yet!"

Fifteen years after the funeral, in August of 29, a new temple of shimmering white Italian marble was dedicated on the spot where Caesar's body had been burnt. It loomed over the whole Forum, and anyone walking through the center of Rome would find it hard to resist gazing up at the massive statue of Divine Julius that stood within. As with Caesar's Temple of Venus, the front part of the new building also functioned as a speaker's platform. Crowds listening to and watching an orator there could not help but see Caesar.[7]

It fell not to Antony to dedicate the Temple of Divine Julius but to his younger rival, Caesar's great-nephew Octavian. Born Gaius Octavius and just eighteen years old at Caesar's death, he had been designated primary heir in Caesar's will and had taken the name of Caesar. Only his enemies actually called him Octavian, as do modern historians for convenience. He referred to himself as Imperator Caesar, and soon he would add the name Augustus, meaning "revered one." He and Antony, after defeating Brutus, Cassius, Sextus Pompey, and the others, had prolonged Romans' torment in civil war by fighting over the succession to Caesar's position. Antony ended up in an alliance with Cleopatra that proved a political liability in Rome and was outwitted militarily. As Octavian closed in on Alexandria in 30 BC, Antony took his own life, followed by Cleopatra.[8]

With the vast wealth of Egypt now his, Octavian returned to the capital to celebrate three triumphs, open the Temple of Divine Julius, and preside over many days of sumptuous games in honor of his adoptive father. At beast hunts, vast numbers of exotic animals were slain, even a rhinoceros and a hippopotamus. Gladiators from Germany and Scythia, which lay at the barbaric edges of the Roman world, were brought to the city to fight. The games went on without interruption even when Octavian fell sick, as he often did.

On regular citizens he showered cash gifts, on soldiers even more. Romans enjoyed countless acts of largesse. Hung for public display in the Temple of Divine Julius was a painting by a Greek Old Master that showed Venus, the ancestress of Caesar, rising from the sea.[9]

Julius Caesar's presence in the Rome of his successor went beyond the massive new temple and victory games held every August.[10] Also dedicated in 29, at the other end of the Forum, was the new Julian Senate house. On its pediment stood a statue of the goddess Victory perched atop a globe. With the fall of Egypt, spoils from which decorated the building's interior, Rome's conquest of the world felt almost complete.[11] Everything about the new Senate house, certainly including its name, would have agitated Cato had he been there to see it.

In due course, Augustus's indispensable ally Agrippa built the first Pantheon, predecessor to the more famous structure that stands in Rome to this day. In it, Agrippa placed a statue of Divine Julius.[12] Augustus himself opened in 2 BC a whole new Forum, dominated by a Temple of Mars the Avenger, which he had vowed to construct when fighting Caesar's assassins forty years earlier. The long porticoes on either side of the Forum were filled with statues of the great men of the past. One whole section honored members of the Julian family, including Julius Caesar's father and his kinsman Caesar Strabo, on whose oratory young Caesar had modeled his own.[13]

The calendar, refashioned by Caesar, was studded with holidays in his honor. The days of his six greatest victories in the civil war were celebrated: Munda on March 17, Alexandria on March 27, Thapsus on April 6, Ilerda and Zela on August 2, and Pharsalus on August 9. Caesar's birthday, July 12, was also made a holiday, and of course the very name "July" paid lasting tribute to his victories.[14]

A less overt but in some ways even more significant memorial to Caesar lay in the serial numbers of the Roman legions.[15] Throughout the history of the Republic, it had been standard for legions, after their tours of duty were completed, to be dismissed and have their numbers (for example, Tenth) reassigned to new units. In the months after Caesar's death, however, as Octavian, Antony, and others rallied the dictator's veterans, many of his former legions, going back to the Gallic War, were reinstated. From that point onward, legions became permanent institutions, with fixed numbers, emblems, and titles, many of which honored Caesar. The Fifth Legion Alaudae, for example, originally recruited in 52 in Transalpine Gaul, bore a name of Celtic origin that meant "Larks." Its emblem, an elephant, commemorated exploits at the battle of Thapsus in Africa.

The establishment of a military monarchy in imperial Rome was not inevitable after Caesar, but it certainly would have been inconceivable without him. His charisma rubbed off on his successor, Augustus. His rejection of senatorial government, his downplaying of free elections, and above all his concentration of power into his own hands through the cultivation of his soldiers led the way for Augustus. Augustus kept control of virtually all the legions until his death. He established a special military treasury to fund large payments to them when they were discharged from service.

At the same time, Caesar also functioned as an antimodel. Shortly after the Ides of March, Antony moved in the Senate that the office of dictator be abolished, a decree that was later passed into law.[16] The title of dictator, tainted by Caesar's high-handedness in his final days, never returned to Rome. The term Augustus preferred for himself was a less formal one that stretched back into the history of the Republic: *princeps*, "first man."[17]

The principate of Augustus—as his rule came to be known—consciously repudiated much of Caesar's dictatorship. At the end of the civil war, Augustus had around eighty statues of silver that had been put up in his honor melted down, and thenceforward he rejected divine accolades in the city of Rome.[18] At meetings of the Senate he always took care to greet members of the body by name without using a prompter. Whenever he entered or left the Senate house, he insisted that nobody rise in his honor.[19]

Augustus wished for the Senate to continue debating matters of policy—or at least he thought it prudent to do so. Likewise, he tried to bring back some semblance of free elections for the magistracies, while avoiding the bribery and violence that had accompanied the contests of earlier decades. Senators, many from new families but also some survivors of the nobility, could accept this because they were still allowed to compete for honors, though with less expense and hassle. Paradoxical as it may seem, in some ways the Augustan principate represented the victory of the *optimates'* vision for the Republic, in which a leading man of the Senate should provide stable government by checking the people and their champions.[20] When Romans complained about a shortage of wine that led to high prices, Augustus rebuked them: "My son-in-law Agrippa has acted with enough foresight by building several aqueducts that men shall not go thirsty."[21] It would be hard to imagine Caesar ever saying that. Cato—were he not worried about a scarcity at his own table—might almost have approved.

Cato was far from forgotten in the Rome of Augustus. Though not enshrined in buildings, he was consecrated in hearts and minds. The poet Horace, who had fought with Brutus, sang of "the noble death of Cato." In an ode about a history of the civil war that a friend was writing, Horace proclaimed "all the world subdued, except for Cato's defiant soul."[22]

Vergil, in his epic *Aeneid*, has the Trojan Aeneas—an ancestor of Julius Caesar—receive a shield from the god Vulcan engraved with scenes illustrating the history of Rome, from the foundation of the city to Augustus's triumph over Cleopatra. Aeneas gazes with wonder at Romulus and Remus suckled by the she-wolf, at Horatius on the bridge, and at Gauls with golden hair and golden torques storming the Capitoline. There are high moments and low. In the deep pit of Tartarus, where criminals suffer eternal punishment, is shown Catiline, "trembling at the faces of the Furies." And then, set apart in Elysium, are the upright men, "with Cato giving laws to them."[23]

Cato became synonymous with virtue. As one early imperial writer put it, "whoever wishes to refer to a blameless and outstanding citizen just uses the name of Cato."[24] Cato's political career and especially his death were frequently recalled. In rhetoric schools, students composed speeches for the dying Cato to deliver.[25] Livy's great history of Rome is mostly lost, but later summaries suggest that he gave Cato a favorable treatment. Livy covered Cato's mission to Cyprus, his opposition to the law allowing Caesar to stand for the consulship in absentia, the great march across the African desert, the defense of Utica, and the suicide. Nobody could add to Cato's glory by praising him or lessen it by criticism, Livy said, with an obvious reference to Caesar's *Anticato* and other contributions to the war of memories that had erupted after Cato's death.[26] A slightly later historian hailed Cato as "the picture of virtue and in every way closer in his nature to the gods than to human beings."[27]

Cato was lauded—the great moments of his life summoned up before readers and listeners—but he was also sanitized. The consternation he caused colleagues and the impasses he created through his refusal to compromise were swept aside. His manipulation of senatorial procedures, his deployment of marriage alliances, and his own self-dramatizing were minimized. Historians blamed civil war on the clash between Caesar's and Pompey's desire for preeminence or on the greed and ambition of society as a whole. Some of those fighting supported Caesar, some supported Pompey. Cato alone supported the Republic—or so it was said.[28]

This Cato legend acknowledged his stature without threatening the autocracy of Augustus. In fact, the legend suited at least milder defenders of Cato as well as Augustus himself. Augustus might have appropriated Caesar's name and covered himself in Caesarian laurels, but, especially after the civil war, he also adopted a Catonian stance on good government.[29] He passed legislation against bribery and ultimately implemented a rule that candidates for office had to put down a cash pledge that they would forfeit if caught in electoral malpractice—just as Cato had done in the year 54. Augustus also increased oversight of the treasury, a favorite cause of Cato's. On his death, Augustus left a set of accounts for the whole Roman empire, which tabulated how many soldiers were under arms, what monies were in the treasury and in his own personal fund, and which taxes were outstanding. This attention to record keeping was an echo of the ledgers Cato kept in Rome and, later, Utica.

According to an anecdote, Augustus happened to be walking by the house where Cato had lived. To flatter Augustus, a man made a hostile remark about Cato's stubbornness. Augustus froze the man out. "Whoever opposes a change in the state," he said, "is a good citizen and a good man."[30] As the teller of the story shrewdly observed, the remark reflected admiration of Cato while also serving Augustus's self-interest. Augustus and his contemporaries found a way to acknowledge painful events in Rome's past while burying their contentiousness.

With a lasting end to civil war, finally the quarrel between Caesar and Cato—the contest between military domination and political freedom—seemed to have been resolved. At the heart of the resolution was the way both men were honored. In his *War Against Catiline*, written in the late 40s BC, Sallust had already pointed the way by paying tribute to both Cato and Caesar, but civil war raged when the historian wrote. Vergil's shield for Aeneas, encompassing a history of Rome from the beginning, almost seems to be a response to Sallust: Catiline glowers in hell, Cato rests with the just in Elysium, Augustus leads the ships in the final battle against Cleopatra with the star of his father in heaven shining down on the crest of his helmet.

Yet as one Caesar succeeded another after the death of Augustus—
some of whom, like Caligula, really were tyrants—the memory of
Cato nagged at consciences. Then, under the emperor Nero, who
ruled from AD 54 to 68, Cato enjoyed nothing short of a revival. It
is a remarkable episode that casts a final light on the rivalry of Cato
and Caesar and the world that emerged from it.

Nero, who came to power when just sixteen years old, initially
had to rely a great deal on his mother, Agrippina, and his tutor,
Seneca. Nero's interests lay in horse racing, acting, and singing. He
loved poetry and composed some himself, with more enthusiasm
than talent. For help and inspiration, he would invite other young
poets to the palace. Nero's patronage of the arts and his fondness
for the provocative, combined with mounting suspicion of possible
rivals and increasing repression in the later years of his rule, set the
stage for the Cato renaissance. At first, writers felt free to explore
the difficult past of Rome somewhat openly. But as they confronted
Nero's megalomania and persecutions, they saw suicide as a way
of asserting freedom. A theatrically staged death could outdo even
Nero himself.[31]

Nero's tutor and advisor Seneca, who ultimately withdrew from
politics and spent much of his time on the Bay of Naples, wrote
constantly in his final days about Cato. In a letter to a friend Seneca
held up Cato as the model of a man who could endure anything.
The very day he was defeated at elections, Cato played a game of
ball. On foot he led his army through the deserts of Africa, wearing
a heavy suit of armor, deprived of water. Whenever one of the few
springs was found, Cato sipped last. Fortune raged against Cato,
but he stood up to her on every occasion. Even "at the end, in death,
he showed that a brave man can live in defiance of Fortune, can die
in defiance of Fortune."[32]

After being implicated in a political conspiracy, Seneca took his
own life before his friends and his wife in a drawn-out scene that
was described by the historian Tacitus. First he cut his arms with a
dagger, but, as Tacitus wrote, Seneca's "old body, emaciated through

his abstemious living, allowed the blood only to escape slowly."[33] More cuts followed, and then Seneca had his doctor bring some hemlock he had kept in reserve. Finally he stepped into a scalding bath and was suffocated by steam. Throughout, Seneca made suitably uplifting remarks and even at one point called on his secretaries to take down his words for posterity.

Tacitus seems to almost mock Seneca's efforts to stage the perfect death, but his account appears to be fundamentally true. In his last years of exile, Seneca had been obsessed with death, and the example of Cato's calm and heroic end, along with that of Cato's model, Socrates, prepared Seneca for his own suicide. To die the right way allowed you to uphold your convictions and retain some autonomy. It also won you glory otherwise hard to come by in the world of the Caesars.

Another senator, Thrasea Paetus, found in Cato a model for more active political resistance to Nero. In the year AD 59, five years after becoming emperor, Nero arranged for his mother to be killed at her seaside villa. Nero's guilt was obvious, and murmurs of protest soon wafted through Rome. Nero looked to the Senate for support, and members of the body nearly fell over each other with motions for thanksgivings, annual games celebrating Nero's rescue from an alleged plot of his mother's, and the declaration of her birthday as a day of ill omen. Only Thrasea refused to go along with his colleagues and walked out of the meeting.[34]

Like Seneca, Thrasea was a student of Stoic philosophy, and, though wealthy, he practiced a sort of asceticism. He deliberately affected a sour look—like that of a schoolmaster, Nero thought. Thrasea identified with Cato, even more than Seneca had, and ended up writing a full biography of Cato that delved into Cato's politics.[35] Neronian Rome, with its stupendous architecture and lavish spectacles, might have looked very different from the city Cato had lived in, but Thrasea could see the lyre-playing, mother-slaying tyrant as the end result of the despotism Cato had warned about. And just as Cato used boycotts as a strategy of protest, Thrasea did

too. He deliberately refused to attend the emperor's new Juvenal-
ian Games. When the Senate was voting divine honors for Nero's
wife, Poppaea—after the emperor murdered her—Thrasea stayed
away, and he stayed away from Poppaea's funeral too. For three
years, Thrasea refrained from entering the Senate at all.

Finally Thrasea's protests caught up with him. A senator came to
Nero and offered to prosecute Thrasea for treason, and Nero agreed.
According to Tacitus, the prosecutor pointed out all of Thrasea's
absences; Thrasea would not even make sacrifices for the well-being
of Nero and Nero's "divine voice" (which was actually weak and
husky). "Just as once it was Gaius Caesar and Marcus Cato," the
prosecutor reportedly said, "so now it is you, Nero, and Thrasea that
the city talks about in its desire for discord."[36]

The cult of Cato was bringing back civil unrest, or at least it could
be seen as threatening to do so. After being condemned in the Senate, Thrasea took his own life with calculated bravery, emulating his
hero one final time. A crowd of men and women gathered in his
gardens, including a professor of philosophy. With the philosopher,
Thrasea discussed the nature of the soul. When a quaestor arrived
to insure that Thrasea complied with the death sentence, Thrasea
urged his friends to leave so they would incur no danger. His wife
wanted to join him in suicide, but he told her she must live on for
the sake of their daughter. Then he went out into a colonnade and
slit the arteries of his arm. As blood dripped to the ground, Thrasea
said to the quaestor, "We pour a libation to Jupiter the Deliverer."[37]

Among the fashionable young poets Nero befriended was Lucan,
a nephew of Seneca. A literary genius, Lucan won a prize in AD 60
at the new festival of the Neronia for a poem in praise of Nero. He
also achieved success as a public speaker and cultivated an interest
in Stoic philosophy. Unsurprisingly, Nero grew jealous of Lucan.
The two men had a falling out, and Nero banned Lucan from public
recital. Lucan joined a conspiracy against Nero, and after he was
caught he chose to take his own life rather than be executed. As the
blood drained out of him, Lucan is said to have recited a passage of

his poetry in which a wounded soldier died in a similar way. It was the perfect parting shot at Nero, as Cato would have appreciated.[38]

Lucan left behind an unfinished masterpiece, an epic poem on the civil war that had broken out in 49 BC. Caesar is the main protagonist of the poem, a figure of frightening energy and terror. After crossing the Rubicon, "Caesar, frantic for war, rejoices to find no passage except by shedding blood; it pleases him that the land of Italy on which he tramples supplies him with a foe.... He would rather burst a city gate than find it open to admit him."[39] For Lucan, Caesar flashes like a thunderbolt through the daytime sky, dazzling, striking fear, and spreading destruction far and wide.

Cato is also a major character in Lucan's epic, perhaps less energetic than Caesar but strong in spirit. Philosophy has made him invincible, and he will fight for freedom, even if the cause is doomed. Lucan introduces Cato by having Brutus come to him at the outbreak of war and ask if it would not be better to refrain from the crime of civil war altogether. A grey beard of mourning already hangs from Cato's stern face, but he insists on fighting. He compares himself to a father robbed of his sons by death. Cato will embrace the lifeless body of his country: "I will follow into death your name, Freedom, and your empty ghost." The sacrifice of his blood, he hopes, will pay the penalty all of Rome has incurred.

Lucan's subject is not the years-long feud between Caesar and Cato but rather the outcome of that feud, civil war. Even Cato cannot refrain from it. The madness of civil war consumes all. Romans groan when they first bare the steel, but then the sword, "discourager of justice," clings to their hands. They hate the friends they strike at; with each blow, their wavering purpose is strengthened.

Living under Nero, immersed in the story of Caesar and Cato and their final conflict, Lucan did not see Cato as simply a model, as his uncle Seneca did. Lucan grasped a larger reality: once begun, a civil war is difficult to end. To chain the beast, a society might invite in an almost equally awful jailer. People give up their own freedom or the freedom of others. They bury their history in myths.

To summon up the horror of the war's outbreak, Lucan envisions the gods filling the earth, sea, and sky with awful portents. A soothsayer is called in to consult the warm entrails of a sacrificed bull. No blood pours out of the animal, but instead a terrible, slimy liquid. An astrologer looks up at the stars and wonders:

> *And what use is it to ask the gods to end it?*
> *The peace we long for brings a master. Rome, prolong your chain*
> *of disaster without break and protract calamity*
> *for lengthy ages: only now in civil war are you free.*[40]

Only civil war can end the quarreling, but the civil war never quite dies out.

One can go beyond Lucan. The sword might counsel evil, but before civil war, bitter partisanship comes that justifies almost any deed and ravages all trust. We know that the attack is wrong, that somehow it will damage all of us, but it feels so good to strike that we find it hard to stop. And so the chain of disaster really starts.

ACKNOWLEDGMENTS

This book grew out of a course on Julius Caesar I teach at Georgetown University, where I have been honored to work for two decades now. One of the students who took the class, Grace Hanrahan, first drew my attention to the importance of Cato's opposition to Caesar. She gave me the idea for this dual biography. I thank Grace for helpful discussions, as well as another Georgetown student, Danny O'Sullivan, who commented on drafts of several chapters, and all the other great students who have sharpened my appreciation of Caesar, Cato, and the Roman Republic.

Kit Morrell and Fred Drogula generously sent me their books on Cato. Their work, which has reframed understanding of Cato and his times, helped this book enormously. For valuable discussions, both in person and online, and other support I thank friends and colleagues, especially Joel Allen, Tommaso Astarita, Doug Boin, Maya Jasanoff, Evan Jewell, Tom Kerch, Carsten Hjort Lange, Jesper Majbom Madsen, Andrew Meshnick, Kit Morrell, John Ramsey, Rob Tempio, Stefan Vranka, and Kathryn Welch.

Without Carole Sargent's ongoing friendship I could never have written this book. She has always encouraged me to try to share my ideas with the widest audience and never fails to buoy me up with her sharp wit. I often wish I worked in her field of English literature so that we could collaborate and conspire more.

Through Carole I met my agent Emma Parry. Emma not only advised and represented me; she gave me a new relish for writing Roman history. She listened to me talk about the antics of Caesar and Cato and then read what I wrote with such eagerness and insight that I was inspired to go back to my sources, where I saw so much more. Emma has been the best of mentors.

Working with the extraordinarily talented editors at Basic Books was like being on Mount Olympus. This group has superpowers. In conversations and by letter, Claire Potter helped me to turn a lumpy first draft into a richer story with deeper analysis. I thank Claire for so many smart questions and her suggestions on how to start the book and much else. Brandon Proia took what I thought was the final draft and rooted out countless obscurities. He could see the whole field of battle better than I and stepped in to the rescue where I faltered. I owe many sentences to him. Marissa Koors did brilliant work coaxing the book into final shape. She helped with the title and the cover and kept me on course in so many ways. Abby Mohr advised me on maps, art, and more. My deepest thanks to them all.

Kate Blackmer responded to an urgent request for maps and was a wonderful collaborator. Her expertise and creativity have added a lot to this book and to my understanding of Caesar and Cato's world. Likewise I am much in the debt of production editor Katie Carruthers-Busser and copy editor Kelley Blewster. Kelley has improved my writing on every page and also helped make the notes easier to use. Special thanks to Jenny Lillich for producing the index.

An anonymous reader for Oxford University Press made helpful suggestions. And for assistance in obtaining images, thanks go to John Thomassen, Jennifer Carding, and Sherri Jackson.

I gratefully acknowledge the legion of scholars, past and present, who have done so much to make the evidence for Roman history accessible while also offering many provocative interpretations. I have also gained a lot over the years from reading historical fiction on late-Republican Rome by Robert Harris, Colleen McCullough,

Steven Saylor, Rex Warner, and Thornton Wilder, among others. Novelists leap beyond the historical record, but they also pull you into the world of the Romans. Unobtrusively they offer fresh readings of evidence.

Finally, as always, I thank my family and my partner, Adam Kemerer. Even more than usual, Adam had to live through the ups and downs of the writing of this book. His love and encouragement are the greatest gift.

A NOTE ON SOURCES

The late Roman Republic is more richly attested than any other era of classical history. The sources fall into two categories. The first includes the letters, speeches, and works of literature, history, and philosophy written by participants themselves, such as Julius Caesar's commentaries on his war in Gaul and on the ensuing civil war. The second encompasses accounts of later biographers and historians. In this second group, *Parallel Lives*, by the Greek philosopher and author Plutarch, stands out; they were produced in the early second century AD. Plutarch matched Greeks with Romans in pairs—Alexander the Great with Caesar, for example— to explore questions of character. Although he wrote about great men, he wished to avoid turning his biographies into slices of history. As he tells his readers, "An offhand remark or a joke often shows more about a man's character than battles where thousands and thousands die."[1] Plutarch sought out biographically oriented sources, often those of contemporary witnesses, and as a result preserves details now otherwise lost. His biographies of Caesar, Cato, Pompey, Crassus, Cicero, and other late-Republican figures have more to say about the women in these men's lives, for instance, than the *Roman History* of Cassius Dio, written about a century later. Cassius Dio's work is important, though, for its well-informed accounts of politics.[2] Another history, Appian's *Civil Wars*, is fullest on the period after Caesar's death but has an important account of the struggle between Marius and Sulla and rising tensions before that. Also valuable is the history of the Tiberian senator Velleius Paterculus.

Plutarch's biographies provide a great deal of material for this book; a few words should be said about his *Caesar* and *Cato the Younger* in particular. Because Caesar dominated Roman politics at the end of his life, Plutarch could in fact draw on mainstream historical writing for *Caesar*, but he also found and included other anecdotal material, such as the story of Caesar's visit to the squalid Alpine village.[3] Ancient Rome swirled with rumors, gossip, and what can truly be called "urban legends." Later writers passed these stories on—and embroidered them. Caution is in order, then, about the literal veracity of Plutarch's anecdotes, even if we acknowledge that they may embody larger truths. Plutarch's entire biography of Caesar is shaped around the provocative thesis that Caesar, from the start of his political career, sought complete domination. Most individuals around him caught on too late, but there were exceptions, such as Cicero. According to Plutarch, Cicero thought Caesar's politics resembled "the smiling surface of the sea," beneath which lurked great danger.[4] The story captures the challenge that Caesar's contemporaries—as well as later biographers—faced in discerning his true intentions. Some take a less Plutarchan view than I.

Cato the Younger is a godsend for historians and biographers. This life teems, even more than *Caesar*, with personal details. Here Plutarch's main source appears to have been the biography of Cato written by the senator Thrasea Paetus, a victim of Nero who ended up committing suicide in the theatrical fashion set by Cato.[5] Thrasea Paetus, in turn, drew on an earlier biography of Cato, written soon after Cato's death by a man who knew him well, Munatius Rufus. Munatius was the Boswell to Cato's Johnson. He accompanied Cato on various travels, served as a political advisor, and then wrote a major biography. Obviously Munatius's memoir was not entirely objective, and Thrasea, in turn, perhaps added philosophical coloring to parts of it, especially the account of Cato's final days. Yet through Plutarch we can still access many reminiscences of Munatius that show Cato as far from the perfect Stoic sage.[6] There is a clear overlap with the more political Cato who constantly pops up in Cicero's contemporary letters.[7]

On Julius Caesar, in addition to Plutarch's life, there survives another ancient biography, Suetonius's *Divine Julius*. The first installment of Suetonius's twelve-part *Lives of the Caesars*, this work casts Caesar as the antimodel of a Roman emperor. In general, all later accounts of Caesar tended to do this; his dictatorship became the foil for the allegedly milder principate of his heir, Augustus. Yet a benefit accrues from Suetonius's bias. Even more than Plutarch, he dug up evidence that would shed light on Caesar's early career. Suetonius refers to and even at times quotes speeches, poems, pamphlets, and more written by enemies of Caesar.[8] While not all necessarily true, it is invaluable material—as are the snatches we get in *Divine Julius* of Caesar's eulogy for his aunt Julia, of the verses his soldiers sang at his triumphs, and of much else.[9] Suetonius captures the flavor of political attack and popular culture in Caesar and Cato's day.

Of primary sources, Caesar's accounts of his campaigns are of great importance, especially for the later chapters of this book. They tell of Caesar's wars from his own perspective. For the civil war, enough other evidence survives to show how much Caesar left out that would have been unflattering to himself, such as a mutiny of his soldiers toward the end of the year 49 BC.[10] For the war in Gaul, Caesar's narrative must be weighed against fewer other scraps of information as well as probability. As evidence of Caesar's skill in self-presentation, the commentaries speak for themselves.

Caesar abandoned his *Civil War* midway through the fighting, and he never wrote an account of his last two years in Gaul. Soon after his death, books were added to round out the story: an eighth book in the series *The Gallic War*, written by his officer Hirtius, as well as three further works on the civil war, the authorship of which is disputed (*The Alexandrian War*, *The African War*, and *The Spanish*

War).[11] This material sheds light on Caesar as a commander and the day-to-day experience of serving in his army. Also written soon after his death was Sallust's *War Against Catiline*, which offers unique details on Caesar's and Cato's involvement in the Senate's response to the conspiracy of 63 and is valuable as well for Sallust's perception of the two men and of the nature of politics in the late Republic.

In a class of their own are the multitudinous works of Cicero. Cicero, regarded as the most successful public speaker of his day, remained a powerful model of eloquence for centuries afterward. He issued written versions of his speeches, and students studied them, ensuring their survival. These are priceless both as samples of Roman oratory and as sources for political history. Also important are well-informed commentaries on five of Cicero's speeches by the ancient scholar Asconius.

Cicero had relentless literary ambition and energy. Whenever banished to the political wilderness, as he often was later in life, he produced pioneering works in Latin on moral philosophy and on the theory and practice of oratory; Caesar and, even more often, Cato appear in these.[12] Cicero was a compulsive letter writer. A corpus of around one thousand letters has been preserved, mostly those Cicero wrote but also letters to him or others, including several by Caesar and one by Cato, a precious survival.[13] Especially to his closest friend, the equestrian Atticus, a financier with conservative tendencies, Cicero sent detailed accounts of political developments when the two were separated. These provide evidence for both the day-to-day workings of politics and major episodes like the Bona Dea scandal.[14] They may be biased by Cicero's and Atticus's political views, but they are not biased by hindsight. They are perceptive on how both Caesar and Cato gained political power and how they used it.

In the main text of this book, I refrain from discussion of the sources and the specific challenges they sometimes pose. Where there are two discrepant versions of an event or problems in reconstructing chronology, I have weighed the evidence and give in my narrative the version I believe there is good reason to follow. Some scholars are more skeptical of the accounts of Caesar's and Cato's early lives than I. Endnotes indicate the ancient testimony on which I rely, as well as particular problems and alternative solutions.

Essential to my work have been major editions and translations of ancient sources, along with modern studies of Caesar and Cato, of which I single out some of the most important here. I encourage readers to dive into these excellent translations and to follow up with the modern studies for more information on episodes I have had to compress as well as alternative perspectives.

For Plutarch, Penguin Classics has issued excellent translations of the late-Republican lives, with useful annotations, in *Fall of the Roman Republic*, trans. Rex Warner, rev. ed. (London: Penguin, 2005), and *Rome in Crisis*, trans. Ian Scott-Kilvert and Christopher Pelling (London: Penguin, 2010). Christopher Pelling's *Plutarch: "Caesar"* (Oxford, UK: Oxford University Press, 2011) contains a vivid translation of this life and an infinitely helpful commentary that is typically the best starting place for any episode in Caesar's life. For *Cato*, there is Joseph Geiger, *A Commentary on Plutarch's "Cato Minor"* (PhD thesis, Oxford University, 1971), and, in Italian, *Plutarco: Focione et Cato Uticense*, ed. Barbara Scardigli (Milan: Biblioteca Universale Rizzoli, 1993).

A splendid translation of Suetonius is *Suetonius: "The Caesars,"* trans. Donna W. Hurley (Indianapolis: Hackett, 2011). Also from this publisher is the excellent *Velleius Paterculus: The Roman History*, trans. J. C. Yardley and Anthony A. Barrett (Indianapolis: Hackett, 2011).

Caesar's own writings, as well as the later books that make up the so-called "Caesarian corpus," are best accessed in the superb edition of Kurt A. Raaflaub, ed. and trans., *The Landmark Julius Caesar* (New York: Pantheon Books, 2017), which includes notes, maps, and indexes; also available are online essays by various scholars and chronologies prepared by Raaflaub and John T. Ramsey (www .landmarkcaesar.com).

A number of Cicero's most important speeches are expertly trans-lated and commented on by D. H. Berry in *Cicero: Defence Speeches* (Oxford, UK: Oxford University Press, 2000) and *Cicero: Political Speeches* (Oxford, UK: Oxford University Press, 2006). For the commentaries of Asconius, see *Asconius: Commentaries on Speeches of Cicero*, trans. R. G. Lewis (Oxford, UK: Oxford University Press, 2006), which includes the Latin text of A. C. Clark, to which it is standard to refer (e.g., p. 17C).

The Loeb Classical Library series features many fine translations. This is the best place to go for the important history of Cassius Dio, *Dio's "Roman History,"* trans. Earnest Cary, 9 vols. (Cambridge, MA: Harvard University Press, 1914–1927), as well as Appian, *Appian: "Roman History,"* trans. Brian McGing, 6 vols. (Cambridge, MA: Harvard University Press, 2019–2020). Especially rich in useful annotation is *Sallust: "The War with Catiline" and "The War with Jugurtha,"* trans. J. C. Rolfe and rev. John T. Ramsey (Cambridge, MA: Harvard University Press, 2013). Also convenient are the Loeb editions of the unsurpassed translations by D. R. Shackleton Bailey of Cicero's *Letters: Letters to Atticus*, 4 vols. (Cambridge, MA: Harvard University Press, 1999), *Letters to Friends*, 3 vols. (Cambridge, MA: Harvard University Press, 2001), and *Letters to Quintus and Brutus* (Cambridge, MA: Harvard University Press, 2002). Whenever I cite a Ciceronian letter, I include a parenthetic reference to Shackleton Bailey's renumbering (e.g., "SB 240"). Shackleton Bailey's earlier critical editions with commentaries for Cambridge University Press remain fundamental.

Of modern studies on Caesar, the most useful is still Matthias Gelzer, *Caesar: Politician and Statesman*, trans. Peter Needham (Ox-ford, UK: Blackwell, 1968); it is abundantly documented and shines with insight into Caesar's character. There are many more recent works. Undocumented, but probing, are Christian Meier, *Caesar: A Biography*, trans. David McLintock (New York: Basic Books, 1995), and, in German, Martin Jehne, *Caesar*, 4th ed. (Munich: C. H. Beck, 2008). A clear account with excellent discussion of Cae-sar's campaigns is Adrian Goldsworthy, *Caesar: Life of a Colossus*

(London: Weidenfeld & Nicolson, 2006). Tom Stevenson, *Julius Caesar and the Transformation of the Roman Republic* (Abingdon, UK: Routledge, 2015) sets Caesar in political context. Robert Morstein-Marx, *Julius Caesar and the Roman People* (Cambridge, UK: Cambridge University Press, 2021) is a thoughtful reinterpretation of major episodes in Caesar's political career.

For Cato, the fullest biographies are, in German, Rudolf Fehrle, *Cato Uticensis* (Darmstadt: Wissenschaftliche Buchgesellschaft, 1983), and, in English, Fred K. Drogula, *Cato the Younger: Life and Death at the End of the Roman Republic* (Oxford, UK: Oxford University Press, 2019). Both are invaluable, as is Susan Treggiari, *Servilia and Her Family* (Oxford, UK: Oxford University Press, 2019). A major reassessment of Cato has also been given by Kit Morrell, *Pompey, Cato, and the Governance of the Roman Empire* (Oxford, UK: Oxford University Press, 2017). Without those four books, I could never have written this one. Two older articles of enduring value, in German, are Matthias Gelzer, "Cato Uticensis," *Die Antike* 10 (1934): 59–91, reprinted in Gelzer, *Kleine Schriften* (Wiesbaden: Franz Steiner, 1963), 2: 257–285, and Adam Afzelius, "Die politische Bedeutung des jüngeren Cato," *Classica et Mediaevalia* 4 (1941): 100–203.

NOTES

Introduction: "Two Men of Extraordinary Excellence"

1. A fuller account of the Catilinarian conspiracy is given in Chapter 4. The best modern discussion is now D. H. Berry, *Cicero's "Catilinarians"* (Oxford, UK: Oxford University Press, 2020), esp. 1–56, 165–173. Key ancient sources for events narrated here are Cicero, *Against Catiline* 3–4; Sallust, *War Against Catiline*; and Plutarch, *Cicero* 17–21, *Caesar* 7.3–8.3, and *Cato the Younger* 22–24.2.

2. Sallust, *War Against Catiline* 52.5, 35. I use the translation in Josiah Osgood, *How to Stop a Conspiracy: An Ancient Guide to Saving a Republic* (Princeton, NJ: Princeton University Press, 2022).

3. Sallust, *War Against Catiline* 52.4.

4. An introduction to and translation of Sallust's work can be found in Osgood, *How to Stop a Conspiracy*. Unusually for Senate proceedings, Cicero had a team of shorthand writers taking down a full record: Plutarch, *Cato the Younger* 23.3; Cicero, *For Sulla* 42. My discussion of Sallust's work is indebted to Rudolf Fehrle, *Cato Uticensis* (Darmstadt: Wissenschaftliche Buchgesellschaft, 1983), 303–316.

5. Sallust, *War Against Catiline* 53.2, 53.5, 53.6, 54 passim.

6. Plutarch, *Cato the Younger* 51.3–4.

7. Plutarch, *Caesar* 11.2.

8. Caesar, *Civil War* 1.30.5.

9. See, e.g., Lucan, *Civil War* 1.98–157; Plutarch, *Pompey* 53.6–7. Note, too, the letter written in 50 BC by Caelius to Cicero, in Cicero's *Letters to Friends* 8.14.2 (SB 97). For a recent account of the civil war emphasizing Pompey's actions, see Luca Fezzi, *Crossing the Rubicon: Caesar's Decision and the Fate of Rome*, trans. Richard Dixon (New Haven, CT: Yale University Press, 2019).

10. Lucan, *Civil War* 1.128. One of the many contributions of Fred K. Drogula, *Cato the Younger: Life and Death at the End of the Roman Republic* (Oxford, UK: Oxford University Press, 2019), is to highlight Cato's role in causing civil war (see esp. 269–274); and see also Robert Morstein-Marx, *Julius Caesar and the Roman People* (Cambridge, UK: Cambridge University Press, 2021). Both of these authors, to varying degrees, tend to absolve Caesar, as I do not. On the legend of Cato, discussions include Lily Ross Taylor, *Party Politics in the Age of Caesar* (Berkeley: University of California Press,

1949), 162–182; Robert J. Goar, *The Legend of Cato Uticensis from the First Century BC to the Fifth Century AD* (Brussels: Latomus, 1987); and Fehrle, *Cato Uticensis*, 1–48, 279–316.

11. The impact of Rome's first civil war and its victor has started to emerge in recent research, e.g., Harriet Flower, *Roman Republics* (Princeton, NJ: Princeton University Press, 2010), 117–171; J. Alison Rosenblitt, *Rome After Sulla* (London: Bloomsbury, 2019); and Alexandra Eckert and Alexander Thein, eds., *Sulla: Politics and Reception* (Berlin: De Gruyter, 2019).

12. One example, with discussion of others, is my earlier book *Rome and the Making of a World State, 150 BCE–20 CE* (Cambridge, UK: Cambridge University Press, 2018). Here, I am more focused on tracing the origins of the political crisis that led to civil war in 49 BC. Some historians, notably Erich Gruen, *The Last Generation of the Roman Republic* (Berkeley: University of California Press, 1974), directly attribute the demise of republican government to that civil war. An excellent survey by Edward Watts, *Mortal Republic: How Rome Fell into Tyranny* (New York: Basic Books, 2018), highlights a series of damaging decisions made by politicians going back to the 130s BC.

13. For a recent discussion of polarization, which cites many relevant studies, see Ezra Klein, *Why We're Polarized* (New York: Avid Reader Press, 2020). I have learned from this book, as well as from studies of the antebellum US, especially David M. Potter, *The Impending Crisis, 1848–1861* (New York: Harper and Row, 1976), and Joanne B. Freeman, *The Field of Blood: Violence in Congress and the Road to Civil War* (New York: Farrar, Straus and Giroux, 2018).

Chapter 1. Coming of Age in Civil War

1. Julia's funeral is described in Suetonius, *Divine Julius* 6.1; and Plutarch, *Caesar* 5.1–2. These biographies, along with Velleius Paterculus 2.41–43, are the main, unfortunately brief, sources for Caesar's early life.

2. Appian, *Civil War* 1.94 (Sulla was quoting the comic playwright Aristophanes, *Knights*, 542).

3. Harriet I. Flower, *Ancestor Masks and Aristocratic Power in Roman Culture* (Oxford, UK: Clarendon Press, 1996).

4. For the history of Caesar's family and his own early life, an excellent study is Ernst Badian, "From the Iulii to Caesar," in *A Companion to Julius Caesar*, ed. Miriam Griffin (Malden, MA: Wiley-Blackwell, 2009), 11–22.

5. Suetonius, *Divine Julius* 6.1.

6. A vivid sketch of the nobles and their world is given by Susan Treggiari, *Servilia and Her Family* (Oxford, UK: Oxford University Press, 2019), 1–22. A guide to the political system is Andrew Lintott, *The Constitution of the Roman Republic* (Oxford, UK: Clarendon Press, 1999), or, more briefly, Josiah Osgood, *Rome and the Making of a World State, 150 BCE–20 CE* (Cambridge, UK: Cambridge University Press, 2018), 25–47.

7. On Aurelia, see Suetonius, *Divine Julius* 13.1; Plutarch, *Caesar* 7.2, 9.2; Cicero, *Brutus* 252; and Tacitus, *Dialogus* 28.4–6. On Caesar's father, see Suetonius, *Divine Julius* 1.1; Pliny, *Natural History* 7.181; T. Robert S. Broughton, "The Elogia of Julius Caesar's Father," *American Journal of Archaeology* 52.3 (1948): 323–330.

8. Sallust, *Jugurthine War* 85.29–30; Plutarch, *Marius* 9.2; and Flower, *Ancestor Masks*, 16–23. Plutarch's biographies (*Marius, Sulla, Pompey, Crassus*) and Sallust's *Jugurthine War*, as well as Appian's *Civil War* 1.28–106, are the main sources for the politics covered

in this chapter. Modern studies include Arthur Keaveney, *Sulla, the Last Republican* (London: Routledge, 2005); and Federico Santangelo, *Marius* (London: Bloomsbury, 2016). A well-paced introduction is Mike Duncan, *The Storm Before the Storm: The Beginning of the End of the Roman Republic* (New York: Public Affairs, 2017).

9. On the assemblies, see Lintott, *Constitution*, 40–64. Lily Ross Taylor, *Party Politics in the Age of Caesar* (Berkeley: University of California Press, 1949), 50–75, brings to life the practicalities of voting. See also her masterpiece, *Roman Voting Assemblies from the Hannibalic War to the Dictatorship of Caesar* (Ann Arbor: University of Michigan Press, 1966).

10. Read the accounts of Sallust, *Jugurthine War* 63–64, 84–86; and Plutarch, *Marius* 7–9.

11. On Marius and the army, a good discussion is Lawrence Keppie, *The Making of the Roman Army: From Republic to Empire* (Norman: University of Oklahoma Press, 1998), 57–79. For the triumph, see Mary Beard, *The Roman Triumph* (Cambridge, MA: Belknap Press of Harvard University Press, 2007); and Ida Östenberg, *Staging the World: Spoils, Captives, and Representations in the Roman Triumphal Procession* (Oxford, UK: Oxford University Press, 2009).

12. Cicero, *Brutus* 216. On young Julius Caesar's copying of Strabo, see Suetonius, *Divine Julius* 55.2.

13. Cicero, *On the Orator* 2.266. In this Ciceronian dialogue, Strabo, a major character, offers a discussion of wit.

14. The best introduction to the Porcii and Cato the Elder is Plutarch's *Cato the Elder*. I draw on this and also the excellent discussion in Fred K. Drogula, *Cato the Younger: Life and Death at the End of the Roman Republic* (Oxford, UK: Oxford University Press, 2019), 9–22.

15. Plutarch, *Cato the Younger* 1–4, is the main source for Cato's early life (not regularly cited in what follows); its rich details go back to the account of Munatius Rufus (Rudolf Fehrle, *Cato Uticensis* [Darmstadt: Wissenschaftliche Buchgesellschaft, 1983], 8–18). Drogula, *Cato the Younger*, 23–42, brings out Cato's emulation of his great-grandfather.

16. Orosius, *History Against the Pagans* 5.17.11. On Cato's father's death, see Aulus Gellius, *Attic Nights* 13.20.14.

17. See the superb reconstruction of the childhood of Cato's older half sister, Servilia, in Treggiari, *Servilia and Her Family*, 47–69.

18. Treggiari, *Servilia and Her Family*, 55.

19. Plutarch, *Cato the Younger* 3.5.

20. Plutarch, *Cato the Younger* 1.5.

21. In addition to Plutarch's account, note Valerius Maximus 3.1.2 (likely going back to Munatius); and Cicero, *Letters to Friends* 16.22.1 (SB 185).

22. Plutarch, *Cato the Younger* 2.5–6.

23. On Sulla's early life and the clash with Marius, see especially Plutarch, *Sulla* 1–10; also Plutarch, *Marius* 32–35; and Appian, *Civil War* 1.55–65.

24. Plutarch, *Marius* 34.

25. On the horrible last days of Marius, read Plutarch, *Marius* 41–46; Appian, *Civil War* 1.66–75.

26. Velleius Paterculus 2.43.1.

27. Aulus Gellius, *Attic Nights* 10.15.

28. Suetonius, *Divine Julius* 1.1.

29. The new marriage to Cornelia is dated to 84 or 83 BC by Suetonius, *Divine Julius* 1.1. There has been extensive discussion of whether Caesar was inaugurated, e.g., Badian, "From the Iulii to Caesar," 16–17; R. T. Ridley, "The Dictator's Mistake: Caesar's Escape from Sulla," *Historia* 49.2 (2000): 211–229. As often, a judicious survey and conclusions can be found in Christopher Pelling, *Plutarch: "Caesar"* (Oxford, UK: Oxford University Press, 2011), 134–136.

30. Plutarch, *Sulla* 30.1–3.

31. Plutarch, *Sulla* 31.5; François Hinard, *Les proscriptions de la Rome républicaine* (Rome: École française de Rome, 1985).

32. Plutarch, *Pompey* 6–9; also on Pompey and Sulla, see Plutarch, *Sulla* 33.3.

33. Divorce of a pregnant wife to marry another man provoked comment: a famous example was Livia's scandalous betrothal to the future emperor Augustus.

34. Suetonius, *Divine Julius* 45, describes Caesar's appearance and dress; also Plutarch, *Caesar* 17.2; and Cassius Dio 43.43. On portraits of Caesar, see Mary Beard, *The Twelve Caesars: Images of Power from the Ancient World to the Modern* (Princeton, NJ: Princeton University Press, 2021), 43–77.

35. Caesar's defiance of Sulla and what ensued is described by Suetonius, *Divine Julius* 1, 74.1; Plutarch, *Caesar* 1; and Velleius Paterculus 2.41.2.

36. For Caesar proscribed, see Ridley, "Dictator's Mistake."

37. Plutarch, *Caesar* 1.3; Suetonius, *Divine Julius* 1.3, 45.3; and Cassius Dio 43.43.4.

38. Christian Meier, *Caesar: A Biography*, trans. David McLintock (New York: Basic Books, 1995), 92.

39. Velleius Paterculus 2.43.4; Plutarch, *Caesar* 37.1; and Cassius Dio 41.18.2, 44.47.4.

40. Plutarch, *Cato the Younger* 3.1.

41. Plutarch, *Cato the Younger* 3.3; Valerius Maximus 3.1.2.

42. Plutarch, *Cato the Younger* 17.4–5.

43. Plutarch, *Cato the Younger* 3.5–4.1, 5.3–7. On his austere house, note also Lucan, *Civil War* 2.238.

44. Plutarch, *Cato the Younger* 6.3; Asconius, *Commentaries*, p. 29C; with brilliant discussion by Drogula, *Cato the Younger*, 29–31.

45. Plutarch, *Cato the Younger* 4.1. On Cato's Stoicism, see Matthias Gelzer, "Cato Uticensis," in Gelzer, *Kleine Schriften* (Wiesbaden: Franz Steiner, 1963), 2: 263–268; Adam Afzelius, "Die politische Bedeutung des jüngeren Cato," *Classica et Mediaevalia* 4 (1941): 111–117; Kit Morrell, *Pompey, Cato, and the Governance of the Roman Empire* (Oxford, UK: Oxford University Press, 2017), 100–106.

46. Plutarch, *Cato the Younger* 7. Scipio later was adopted into a great family of the plebeian nobility, the Caecilii Metelli, and was commonly referred to as Metellus Scipio. On betrothals, and all other aspects of Roman marriage, refer to the expert study of Susan Treggiari, *Roman Marriage: Iusti Coniuges from the Time of Cicero to the Time of Ulpian* (Oxford, UK: Clarendon Press, 1991).

47. Plutarch, *Cato the Younger* 7.1. Compare his chastity in Lucan, *Civil War* 2.378–380.

48. Plutarch, *Sulla* 35–37, describes the last days of Sulla, shameless to the end.

Chapter 2. Making Names for Themselves

1. Caesar's attachment to the staff of Thermus is recorded by Suetonius, *Divine Julius* 2.1.

2. On the Roman east after Sulla, see Robert Kallet-Marx, *Hegemony to Empire: The Development of the Roman* Imperium *in the East from 148 to 62 B.C.* (Berkeley: University of California Press, 1995).

3. Caesar's mission to Nicomedes is mentioned by Suetonius, *Divine Julius* 2.1, and Plutarch, *Caesar* 1.3–4. Suetonius offers an impressive collection of later stories (*Divine Julius* 49.1–3). In my article "Caesar and Nicomedes," *Classical Quarterly* 58.2 (2008): 687–691, I try to track the growth of the story.

4. Caesar's connoisseurship is described by Suetonius, *Divine Julius* 47.

5. Caesar's crown: Suetonius, *Divine Julius* 2. The privileges: Pliny, *Natural History* 16.13.

6. Suetonius, *Divine Julius* 45.2; Cassius Dio 43.43.1.

7. Suetonius, *Divine Julius* 3.

8. On Caesar and the revolt against Sulla, see Suetonius, *Divine Julius* 3. The overall picture is given by Plutarch, *Pompey* 15–16, and Appian, *Civil War* 1.105–107.

9. Cicero, *For Plancius* 64–67. This speech and *For Murena*, both defending clients of Cicero against the charge of electoral malpractice, especially illuminate the practicalities of political careers in this period.

10. The centrality of the Forum is well brought out by Fergus Millar, *The Crowd in Rome in the Late Republic* (Ann Arbor: University of Michigan Press, 2002), esp. 38–48, and Robert Morstein-Marx, *Mass Oratory and Political Power in the Late Roman Republic* (Cambridge, UK: Cambridge University Press, 2004), 34–67. On the city's developing architecture, P. J. E. Davies, *Architecture and Politics in Republican Rome* (Cambridge, UK: Cambridge University Press, 2017), is a constant guide. And see Amy Russell, *The Politics of Public Space in Republican Rome* (Cambridge, UK: Cambridge University Press, 2016). The story of the stunned crow is told by Cassius Dio 36.30.3.

11. Cicero, *For Murena* 69.

12. Plutarch, *Caesar* 4.2–4.

13. On the opportunities afforded by a criminal prosecution, see Lily Ross Taylor, *Party Politics in the Age of Caesar* (Berkeley: University of California Press, 1949), 98–118. The atmosphere of the trials is well evoked in Cicero's history of Roman oratory, *Brutus* (e.g., 200, 290).

14. Good descriptions are given by Cicero, *Brutus* 252–262, and Suetonius, *Divine Julius* 55. See also Henriette van der Blom, *Oratory and Political Career in the Late Roman Republic* (Cambridge, UK: Cambridge University Press, 2016), 146–180. Caesar's warning (Gellius, *Attic Nights* 1.10.4) comes from a two-book work he wrote on Latinity.

15. Details of Caesar's early speeches are given by Asconius, *Commentaries*, pp. 26C, 84C; Suetonius, *Divine Julius* 4.1; and Plutarch, *Caesar* 3–4.2 (chronology confused). See also Cicero, *Brutus* 317, and, for the prosecution of Antonius, Quintus Cicero, *Brief Handbook of Canvassing for Office* 8, with W. Jeffrey Tatum, *Quintus Cicero: "A Brief Handbook of Canvassing for Office"* (Oxford, UK: Oxford University Press, 2018), 191–193.

16. Cicero, a pupil of Apollonius, later paid tribute to his teacher for trying to hold back the flood of his overabundant speech (*Brutus* 316).

17. The buildup to war is discussed by Kallet-Marx, *Hegemony to Empire*, 299–302.

18. The main accounts are Velleius Paterculus 2.42; Suetonius, *Divine Julius* 4; and Plutarch, *Caesar* 1.4–2. I give a full discussion in "Caesar and the Pirates," *Greece and Rome* 57 (2010): 319–336.

19. Plutarch, *Pompey* 24, gives an indignant description, to be read with Philip de Souza, *Piracy in the Graeco-Roman World* (Cambridge, UK: Cambridge University Press, 2002).

20. Suetonius, *Divine Julius* 4.2.

21. Lily Ross Taylor's work on the circumstances and implications of Caesar's election is a triumph of historical scholarship; see especially "Caesar's Early Career," *Classical Philology* 36.2 (1941): 113–132, and "Caesar's Colleagues in the Pontifical College," *American Journal of Philology* 63.4 (1942): 385–412.

22. John North, *Roman Religion* (Oxford, UK: Oxford University Press, 2000), 21–34, is a good guide. Memberships in the colleges can be tracked in Jörg Rüpke, *Fasti sacerdotum: A Prosopography of Pagan, Jewish, and Christian Religious Officials in the City of Rome, 300 BC to AD 499* (Oxford, UK: Oxford University Press, 2008).

23. Suetonius, *Divine Julius* 5; and Plutarch, *Caesar* 5.1.

24. Valerius Maximus 2.10.8 writes that Cato had "an appearance by no means pleasant" (*minime blanda frons*), a reasonable description of the inscribed bust of Cato from Volubilis, Morocco, discovered in 1944. J. M. C. Toynbee, *Roman Historical Portraits* (Ithaca, NY: Cornell University Press, 1978), 39–41.

25. Cicero, *For Murena* 74; Plutarch, *Cato the Younger* 8.2; but cf. Cicero, *For Murena* 77. Chapters 4–8 of Plutarch's biography inform my account here.

26. Plutarch, *Cato the Younger* 4.1.

27. Fred K. Drogula, *Cato the Younger: Life and Death at the End of the Roman Republic* (Oxford, UK: Oxford University Press, 2019), 23–55, highlights Cato's skill in self-fashioning.

28. Cato's oratorical debut and style are recounted by Plutarch, *Cato the Younger* 4.2–5. Cicero gives valuable comments in *Brutus* 118–119 and *Stoic Paradoxes* 1–3. On Cato's oratory, see van der Blom, *Oratory and Political Career*, 204–247; and on the Basilica Porcia, see Lukas Thommen, "Les lieux de la plèbe et de ses tribuns dans la Rome républicaine," *Klio* 77.1 (1995): 360–364.

29. Plutarch, *Cato the Younger* 8. The war is recounted by, among others, Plutarch, *Crassus* 8–10, and Appian, *Civil War* 1.116–120.

30. Drogula, *Cato the Younger*, 36.

31. Munatius lies behind Plutarch's uniquely rich account, *Cato the Younger* 9–15. See Joseph Geiger, "Munatius Rufus and Thrasea Paetus on Cato the Younger," *Athenaeum* 57 (1979): 49–50.

32. Carlos A. Picón, *Pergamon and the Hellenistic Kingdoms of the Ancient World* (New York: Metropolitan Museum of Art, 2016), shows off the showy city. Diogenes Laertes 7.34 reveals Athenodorus's censorship.

33. Cicero, *Letters to Quintus* 1.1.19 (SB 1).

34. Stephen Mitchell, *Anatolia: Land, Men, and Gods in Asia Minor* (Oxford, UK: Clarendon Press, 1993), 1: 24–41.

35. Plutarch, *Cato the Younger* 12.5.

36. Plutarch, *Cato the Younger* 13, with Jane Bellemore, "Cato the Younger in the East in 66 B.C.," *Historia* 44.3 (1995): 376–379, on the problem of which Antioch Cato visited.

37. Caepio's death and burial is recounted by Plutarch, *Cato the Younger* 11.

38. Plutarch, *Cato the Younger* 54.7. Munatius might have been responding specifically to a charge later made by Caesar that Cato was so greedy he sifted Caepio's ashes looking for gold (*Cato the Younger* 11.4).

Chapter 3. Political Ambitions

1. Suetonius, *Divine Julius* 7.1. See also Plutarch, *Caesar* 11.3; and Cassius Dio 37.52.2.

2. Erich Gruen, *The Last Generation of the Roman Republic* (Berkeley: University of California Press, 1974), 75–81, discusses the problem. Christian Meier, *Caesar: A Biography*, trans. David McLintock (New York: Basic Books, 1995), 133–189, in my view rightly emphasizes Caesar's risk-taking in these years. For a more skeptical account of the sources than mine, see Robert Morstein-Marx, *Julius Caesar and the Roman People* (Cambridge, UK: Cambridge University Press, 2021), 33–82.

3. A good account of the restoration of the tribunate, and the aftermath, is Fergus Millar, *The Crowd in Rome in the Late Republic* (Ann Arbor: University of Michigan Press, 2002), 49–93. In this chapter I draw extensively on it as well as on Robin Seager, "The Rise of Pompey," *Cambridge Ancient History*, 2nd ed. (1994), 9: 208–228, and T. P. Wiseman, "The Senate and the *Populares*, 69–60 B.C.," *Cambridge Ancient History*, 2nd ed., 9: 327–367.

4. Quoted by Cicero (*Brutus* 217), who calls Sicinius "a foul man but quite funny" (216).

5. The best introduction is Plutarch's *Sertorius*.

6. Plutarch's *Crassus* informs my discussion throughout, as does Allen M. Ward, *Marcus Crassus and the Late Roman Republic* (Columbia: University of Missouri Press, 1977); also note Lily Ross Taylor, *Party Politics in the Age of Caesar* (Berkeley: University of California Press, 1949), 121–122, and Gruen, *Last Generation*, 66–74.

7. Taylor, *Party Politics*, 50–75, and Lily Ross Taylor, *The Voting Districts of the Roman Republic: The Thirty-Five Urban and Rural Tribes* (Rome: American Academy in Rome, 1960), 101–131, are fundamental. Henrik Mouritsen, *Politics in the Roman Republic* (Cambridge, UK: Cambridge University Press, 2017), surveys more recent work. For the census figures, see P. A. Brunt, *Italian Manpower* (Oxford, UK: Clarendon Press, 1971), 13–14.

8. Suetonius, *Divine Julius* 5. A quotation from the speech is preserved (Aulus Gellius, *Attic Nights* 13.3.5), suggesting it was published.

9. The meaning of the terms *optimates*, *boni*, and *populares* has been a battlefield in modern scholarship—and was at the time of Caesar and Cato too; these were nothing like stable political parties. A penetrating survey of the debate is Alexander Yakobson "*optimates, populares*," *Oxford Classical Dictionary*, updated August 22, 2017, https://doi .org/10.1093/acrefore/9780199381135.013.4578.

10. Cicero, *Against Catiline* 4.9.

11. For a brief sketch, see Gruen, *Last Generation*, 50–51.

12. Plutarch, *Caesar* 5.1–2; and Suetonius, *Divine Julius* 6.1. On the memory of Marius and Sulla, see Robert Morstein-Marx, *Mass Oratory and Political Power in the Late Roman Republic* (Cambridge, UK: Cambridge University Press, 2004), 110–113.

13. Cornelia's death and funeral: Plutarch, *Caesar* 5.2; and Suetonius, *Divine Julius* 6.1.

14. Suetonius, *Divine Julius* 8, with Taylor, *Voting Districts*, 123–131, on the Transpadanes.

15. Suetonius, *Divine Julius* 46–47, discusses Caesar's houses.

16. On the marriage and the affairs, see Suetonius, *Divine Julius* 6.2 and 50.1. There's an illuminating discussion in Susan Treggiari, *Servilia and Her Family* (Oxford, UK: Oxford University Press, 2019), 102–109.

17. Cicero, *For the Manilian Law* 44, 52–58; Plutarch, *Pompey* 25–26; and Cassius Dio 36.23–37.

18. Cicero, *For the Manilian Law* 60. Caesar's support is mentioned by Cassius Dio 36.43.2–4.

19. Plutarch describes Crassus's real estate empire in *Crassus* 2 and political methods in *Crassus* 3 and 7. As with many of Crassus's affairs, the origins of his association with Caesar are not well attested: Ward, *Marcus Crassus*, 120–135.

20. Cassius Dio 37.9.3.

21. Plutarch, *Crassus* 13.1; Suetonius, *Divine Julius* 11.1 (partly in error).

22. Examples of all of this can be found in Élizabeth Deniaux, "The Money and Power of Friends and Clients: Successful Aediles in Rome," in *Money and Power in the Roman Republic*, ed. Hans Beck, Martin Jehne, and John Serrati (Brussels: Éditions Latomus, 2016), 178–187.

23. The sources for Caesar's aedileship are Plutarch, *Caesar* 5.4–6; Suetonius, *Divine Julius* 10; Pliny, *Natural History* 33.53; and Cassius Dio 37.8.

24. Suetonius, *Divine Julius* 10.1.

25. Plutarch, *Caesar* 6.4.

26. Plutarch, *Cato the Younger* 46.3.

27. An invaluable source for Cato's thinking is Cicero, *Pro Murena* 58–83; and see Adam Afzelius, "Die politische Bedeutung des jüngeren Cato," *Classica et Mediaevalia* 4 (1941): 116–125.

28. The account of Cato's quaestorship comes from Plutarch, *Cato Minor* 16–18, who may exaggerate the deficiencies of others to make Cato shine: Rudolf Fehrle, *Cato Uticensis* (Darmstadt: Wissenschaftliche Buchgesellschaft, 1983), 77. A valuable profile of the civil servants is Ernst Badian, "The *Scribae* of the Roman Republic," *Klio* 71.2 (1989): 582–603.

29. Plutarch, *Lucullus* 41.2. In addition to Plutarch's life, see Arthur Keaveney, *Lucullus: A Life* (London: Routledge, 1992); and Gruen, *Last Generation*, 51–52.

30. On Lucullus's troubles, see Plutarch, *Lucullus* 33–36. Cicero, *Pro Sestio* 93, mentions the painting of the tribune Gabinius. An outstanding biography of Clodius is W. Jeffrey Tatum, *The Patrician Tribune: Publius Clodius Pulcher* (Chapel Hill: University of North Carolina Press, 1999).

31. Several years later, Lucullus publicly testified that he had learned this through his slaves (Cicero, *Pro Milone* 73; Plutarch, *Cicero* 29.4).

32. Cicero, *Academica* 2.3; Plutarch, *Lucullus* 37.1–2.

33. Fred K. Drogula, *Cato the Younger: Life and Death at the End of the Roman Republic* (Oxford, UK: Oxford University Press, 2019), 44–45. Plutarch (e.g., *Lucullus* 38.1) refers to the wife of Lucullus as a sister of Cato, but her true identity is established by Ann-Cathrin Harders, "Die verwandtschaftlichen Beziehungen der Servilia, Ehefrau des L. Licinius Lucullus: Schwester oder Nichte des Cato Uticensis?," *Historia* 56.4 (2007): 453–461.

34. Plutarch, *Cato the Younger* 17.4–5; Cassius Dio 47.6.4.

35. Suetonius, *Divine Julius* 11; Asconius, *Commentaries*, pp. 90–91C; Cassius Dio 37.10.1–3; and François Hinard, *Les proscriptions de la Rome républicaine* (Rome: École française de Rome, 1985), 204–207.

36. Plutarch, *Cato the Younger* 18.3–4, who identifies the other quaestor as Marcellus (probably Marcus Claudius Marcellus, the future consul of 51 BC).

Chapter 4. The Conspiracy of Catiline

1. In making an enemy of Cicero, Catiline sealed an awful reputation for posterity. Modern historians have sometimes tried to rehabilitate him, but unconvincingly in my view. The historian Sallust includes in *The War Against Catiline* (35) what appears to be a copy of a letter Catiline wrote in November 63 BC, in which he laid bare his pride in his ancestry, his desire to raise his standing, and his disappointment; this is key to my interpretation. I do not thoroughly document events of the conspiracy here; the major ancient sources are, in addition to Sallust, Cicero, *Against Catiline* 1–4; Asconius, *Commentaries*, pp. 82–94C; Plutarch, *Cicero* 12–24; and Cassius Dio 37.29–42. D. H. Berry, *Cicero's "Catilinarians"* (Oxford, UK: Oxford University Press, 2020), is an excellent study; also useful, and with a different take on Catiline than mine, is Gianpaolo Urso, *Catilina: Le faux populiste* (Bordeaux, FR: Ausonius, 2019). I have also been influenced by the well-informed novel of Rex Warner, *The Young Caesar* (Boston: Little, Brown and Company, 1958), and by Matthias Gelzer, *Caesar: Politician and Statesman*, trans. Peter Needham (Oxford, UK: Blackwell, 1968), 41–55. On Cicero as a "squatter," see Sallust, *War Against Catiline* 31.7.

2. See especially Cicero, *Against Catiline* 2.18–24, 3.16–17, and *For Caelius* 12–14; Sallust, *War Against Catiline* 14–16, 24.3–25.

3. Crassus's and Caesar's backing of Catiline in 64 is attested by Asconius, *Commentaries*, p. 83C. It is sometimes doubted, e.g., Urso, *Catilina*, 155–159. For a defense, see Allen M. Ward, *Marcus Crassus and the Late Roman Republic* (Columbia: University of Missouri Press, 1977), 135–151. For Orestilla, see Sallust, *War Against Catiline* 15.2, 35.3.

4. Cassius Dio 37.29.1; Cicero, *For Murena* 45–47, 67, 89; Erich Gruen, *The Last Generation of the Roman Republic* (Berkeley: University of California Press, 1974), 220–223; and Jean-Louis Ferrary, "La législation 'de ambitu', de Sulla à Auguste," in *Iuris vincula: Studi in onore di Mario Talamanca* (Naples: Jovene, 2001), 3: 172–178.

5. For Cato in the Senate, see Plutarch, *Cato the Younger* 18.1, 19.1–2; also Cicero, *On the Ends of Good and Evil* 3.7; and Valerius Maximus 8.7.2. A good discussion of senatorial oratory is John T. Ramsey, "Roman Senatorial Oratory," in *A Companion to Roman Rhetoric*, ed. William Dominik and Jon Hall (Malden, MA: Wiley-Blackwell, 2007), 122–135. On Senate procedures, see Marianne Coudry, *Le Sénat de la République romaine, de la guerre d'Hannibal à Auguste*, rev. ed. (Rome: École française, 2020).

6. Plutarch, *Cato the Younger* 20.2.

7. Cassius Dio 37.21.3–4; Velleius Paterculus 2.40.4.

8. For Cato's speech, see Plutarch, *Cato the Younger* 21.2; for his views on bribery, see Cicero, *For Murena* 74–77. For Silanus's prior run, see Cicero, *Letters to Atticus* 1.1.2 (SB 10).

9. Suetonius, *Divine Julius* 50; Plutarch, *Cato the Younger* 24.2, *Brutus* 5; and Appian, *Civil War* 2.112. The best discussion, on which I rely amply, is Susan Treggiari, *Servilia and Her Family* (Oxford, UK: Oxford University Press, 2019), 99–114.

10. Treggiari, *Servilia*, 109, 113–114.

11. Plutarch, *Cato the Younger* 24.3.

12. Cicero, *For Murena* 51.

13. Cicero, *For Murena* 50.

14. Cicero, *For Murena* 50. On the date of the elections and its implication for Catiline's plans, see the important study by John T. Ramsey, "The Date of the Consular

Elections in 63 and the Inception of Catiline's Conspiracy," *Harvard Studies in Classical Philology* 110 (2020): 213–269. On Catiline's following as an army, see Gelzer, *Caesar*, 47–48.

15. Cicero, *For Murena* 51.

16. For Cicero's breastplate and other details of the elections, see Cicero, *For Murena* 52; Plutarch, *Cicero* 14.5–6; and Cassius Dio 37.29.4–30.1. Lily Ross Taylor, *Roman Voting Assemblies from the Hannibalic War to the Dictatorship of Caesar* (Ann Arbor: University of Michigan Press, 1966), 47–58, describes the procedures.

17. Cicero, *For Murena* 13.

18. On Caesar's campaign for the position, see Plutarch, *Caesar* 7.1–3; and Suetonius, *Divine Julius* 13.

19. Cassius Dio 37.37.1–2.

20. Plutarch, *Caesar* 7.2.

21. Suetonius, *Divine Julius* 17.2.

22. Plutarch, *Cicero* 15.1–2, *Crassus* 13.3; Cassius Dio 37.31.1.

23. Sallust, *War Against Catiline* 27.4.

24. The speech is Cicero's still extant *Against Catiline* 1. On the scene in the Senate, see *Against Catiline* 1.16; for Catiline's response, see Sallust, *War Against Catiline* 31.7–9.

25. See especially Cicero, *Against Catiline* 3. Some artful omissions on how Cicero came to obtain the evidence are filled in by Sallust, *War Against Catiline* 39.6–45.

26. Sallust, *War Against Catiline* 47.4, with Gelzer, *Caesar*, 49–55.

27. Sallust, *War Against Catiline*, 48.3–9. See also Cassius Dio 37.35.1–2.

28. The effort to implicate Caesar is related most fully by Sallust, *War Against Catiline* 49; also Plutarch, *Caesar* 8.3. Other sources note suspicions of Caesar's Catilinarian sympathies: Appian, *Civil War* 2.6; Plutarch, *Cicero* 20.3–4.

29. I have given what I consider the most plausible reconstruction of the debate, but there are uncertainties. Key sources are Cicero, *Against Catiline* 4, *Letters to Atticus* 12.21.1 (SB 260); Sallust, *War Against Catiline* 50–53.1; Velleius Paterculus 2.35.1–4; Suetonius, *Divine Julius* 14; Plutarch, *Caesar* 7.4–8.2, *Cato the Younger* 22.3–24.2, *Cicero* 20.3–21; and Cassius Dio 37.36. Christopher Pelling, *Plutarch: "Caesar"* (Oxford, UK: Oxford University Press, 2011), 160–171, sets out the problems well. A different interpretation is offered by A. J. Woodman, "Cicero and Sallust: Debating Death," *Histos* 15 (2021): 1–21.

30. Suetonius, *Divine Julius* 11. Earlier in the year 63, Caesar had been able to call into question the Senate's emergency decree through the trial of Gaius Rabirius, on which see, e.g., Gelzer, *Caesar*, 45–46.

31. Sallust has put into his own words Caesar's speech and almost certainly made some modifications to it; but it ultimately is not inconsistent with Cicero, *Against Catiline* 4.7–10; Suetonius, *Divine Julius* 14.

32. Cicero, *Against Catiline* 4.11.

33. Sallust has omitted the more personal attacks Cato made on Caesar. See, e.g., Plutarch, *Cato the Younger* 23.1–2, *Caesar* 8.1, etc.

34. Plutarch, *Cato the Younger* 24.1–2, *Brutus* 5.3–4.

35. In this paragraph I draw especially on Sallust's version (*War Against Catiline* 52).

36. Cicero, *Letters to Atticus* 12.21.1 (SB 260); Sallust, *War Against Catiline* 53.1; Plutarch, *Cicero* 21.3–4; and Appian, *Civil War* 2.6.

37. Sallust, *War Against Catiline* 49.4; Plutarch, *Caesar* 8.2. And note also Suetonius, *Divine Julius* 14.2.

38. Plutarch, *Cato the Younger* 23.3; and see Cicero, *For Sulla* 42.

Chapter 5. Showdown in the Forum

1. Plutarch, *Cicero* 22.

2. The account of Metellus Nepos, Caesar, and Cato that follows is based on Cicero, *Letters to Friends* 5.1–2 (SB 1–2), and *For Sestius* 62; Suetonius, *Divine Julius* 16; Plutarch, *Cato the Younger* 26–29, and *Cicero* 23; and Cassius Dio 37.38–44. I have adopted what I consider the most convincing chronology, based especially on G. V. Sumner, "The Last Journey of L. Sergius Catilina," *Classical Philology* 58.4 (1963): 215–219.

3. Cicero, *Letters to Friends* 5.2.8 (SB 2). On the need to justify the tribunician veto, see Robert Morstein-Marx, *Mass Oratory and Political Power in the Late Roman Republic* (Cambridge, UK: Cambridge University Press, 2004), 124–126.

4. This very useful concept—not the same as "political theater" (e.g., kabuki)—is set out in an essay I draw on here: Karl-Joachim Hölkeskamp, "The Roman Republic as Theatre of Power: The Consuls as Leading Actors," in *Consuls and Res Publica: Holding High Office in the Roman Republic*, ed. Hans Beck et al. (Cambridge, UK: Cambridge University Press, 2011), 161–181.

5. Cicero, *Against Piso* 6.

6. On Nepos's background and his role in the debate over Pompey, see Erich Gruen, *The Last Generation of the Roman Republic* (Berkeley: University of California Press, 1974), 58–59, 83–85.

7. Cicero, *Letters to Friends* 5.2.6 (SB 2).

8. Morstein-Marx, *Mass Oratory*, 128–136, discusses how a politician procured the right audience. A politician's own audience was the true Roman people; another's was deemed "hirelings."

9. Plutarch, *Cato the Younger* 20.1.

10. Plutarch, *Cato the Younger* 26.1, *Caesar* 8.4, and *Moralia* 818d. For background, see Geoffrey Rickman, *The Corn Supply of Ancient Rome* (Oxford, UK: Clarendon Press, 1980), 158–173.

11. Plutarch, *Cato the Younger* 18.5.

12. Suetonius, *Divine Julius* 15.1; Cassius Dio 37.44.1–2; Cicero, *Letters to Atticus* 2.24.3 (SB 44).

13. Plutarch, *Cato the Younger* 26.4.

14. Plutarch, *Cato the Younger* 27.2–3. Munatius's account lies behind the main source for the clash with Nepos (Plutarch, *Cato the Younger* 27–29.2), with details confirmed by Cicero, *For Sestius* 62. On paraded grief, see Ramsay MacMullen, "Romans in Tears," *Classical Philology* 75.3 (1980): 254–255.

15. On the building and its uses, see Lily Ross Taylor, *Roman Voting Assemblies from the Hannibalic War to the Dictatorship of Caesar* (Ann Arbor: University of Michigan Press, 1966), 25–28, 108–109; and Morstein-Marx, *Mass Oratory*, 57–59.

16. Cato's ability to calm a turbulent assembly is noted elsewhere (e.g., Cicero, *Pro Milone* 58) and may lie behind the first simile of Vergil's *Aeneid* (1.148–153), comparing Neptune to a statesman.

17. Cicero, *On Duties* 1.112, and *Letters to Atticus* 12.4.2 (SB 240).

18. As often, it is Cassius Dio (37.43.3) who records the Senate's response. "Change of dress"—the inverse of the theater of power—is explored by Aerynn Dighton, *"Mutatio vestis*: Clothing and Political Protest in the Late Roman Republic," *Phoenix* 71.3/4 (2017): 345–369.

19. Suetonius, *Divine Julius* 16, as explained by Roman Frolov, "Better than (when) a Magistrate? Caesar's Suspension from Magisterial Functions in 62 BC," *Mnemosyne* 70.6 (2017): 977–995.

20. I draw here on Suetonius, *Divine Julius* 16; and Frolov, "Better than (when) a Magistrate?"

21. Caesar, *Civil War* 1.9.2; Suetonius, *Divine Julius* 72.

22. Cassius Dio 37.44.1–2.

23. Sallust, *War Against Catiline* 61.4. In addition to Sallust's final chapters, see Cassius Dio 37.39–41.

24. The sole source for the efforts to implicate Caesar at this time is Suetonius, *Divine Julius* 17. Vettius, whose activities as an informer would continue, is described by Cassius Dio 37.41.2–4. Of Curius, Sallust said, "The foolishness of this man was as great as his recklessness" (*War Against Catiline* 23.2).

25. Suetonius, *Divine Julius* 17.2. The president of the violence court, normally a praetor, was a lower-ranked magistrate in 62 BC.

26. Valerius Maximus 2.8.1; Lily Ross Taylor, *Party Politics in the Age of Caesar* (Berkeley: University of California Press, 1949), 127, 225 n. 35.

27. Plutarch, *Pompey* 43.1; Velleius Paterculus 2.40.2; Cassius Dio 37.44.3; and Cicero, *Letters to Friends* 5.7.1 (SB 3).

28. Plutarch, *Cato the Younger* 30.1–2, and *Pompey* 44.1–2. Cf. Cassius Dio 37.44.3. Cato's snide remark on the Mithridatic War: Cicero, *Pro Murena* 32.

29. Plutarch, *Pompey* 43.

Chapter 6. Divorces and Marriages

1. T. P. Wiseman, "The Good Goddess," in *Cinna the Poet and Other Roman Essays* (Leicester, UK: Leicester University Press, 1974), 130–137.

2. Plutarch (*Caesar* 9–10, *Cicero* 28) is the main source for Clodius's escapade. Scholars have sometimes been skeptical of Plutarch's account, especially Clodius's interest in Pompeia (overly so, in my view). A lucid account of the whole scandal is given by Philippe Moreau, *Clodiana religio: Un procès politique en 61 av. J. C.* (Paris: Les Belles Lettres, 1982). I draw on it throughout as well as W. Jeffrey Tatum, *The Patrician Tribune: Publius Clodius Pulcher* (Chapel Hill: University of North Carolina Press, 1999), 62–86.

3. The effort to bring down Clodius unfolds in Cicero's vivid letters to Atticus (1.12–16, SB 12–16).

4. This is the version of Plutarch, *Caesar* 10.6, for the occasion of which see Matthias Gelzer, *Caesar: Politician and Statesman*, trans. Peter Needham (Oxford, UK: Blackwell, 1968), 60 n. 3.

5. Cicero, *Letters to Atticus* 1.13.3 (SB 13).

6. Cicero, *Letters to Atticus* 1.14.5 (SB 14).

7. Moreau, *Clodiana religio*, 131–225, reconstructs the trial.

8. Suetonius, *Divine Julius* 18.1, with Gelzer, *Caesar*, 60–61. For the testimony of Aurelia and Julia, see Suetonius, *Divine Julius* 74.2; and *Scholia Bobiensia*, p. 89, as

quoted in *Ciceronis Orationum Scholiastae*, ed. Thomas Stangl (Hildesheim: Georg Olms, 1984).

9. Cicero, *Letters to Atticus* 1.16.5 (SB 16). The identity of Clodius's friend is uncertain since Cicero uses only a nickname; Crassus is a possibility.

10. Cicero, *Letters to Atticus* 1.16.6 (SB 16); Cassius Dio 37.46.3.

11. Plutarch, *Cato the Younger* 19.3, with Moreau, *Clodiana religio*, 232–239.

12. Cicero, *Letters to Atticus* 1.17.8 (SB 17), 2.1.8 (SB 21).

13. Cicero, *For Rabirius Postumus* 16–17, with, e.g., Erich Gruen, *The Last Generation of the Roman Republic* (Berkeley: University of California Press, 1974), 241–242, for the politics.

14. Cicero, *Letters to Atticus* 2.1.8 (SB 21).

15. Cicero, *Letters to Atticus* 2.1.8 (SB 21), translation from D. R. Shackleton Bailey, *Cicero: "Letters to Atticus"* (Cambridge, MA: Harvard University Press, 1999), 2: 133. Fred K. Drogula, *Cato the Younger* (Oxford, UK: Oxford University Press, 2019), 102–127, gives a good assessment of Cato at this time.

16. Mary Beard, *The Roman Triumph* (Cambridge, MA: Belknap Press of Harvard University Press, 2007), 7–41, gives a splendid discussion of Pompey's triumph.

17. On Lucullus's hedonism, which was redeemed by his opening up his library for scholars, see Plutarch, *Lucullus* 41–43. On Pompey's challenges, see, e.g., Gruen, *Last Generation*, 83–88; and Robin Seager, *Pompey the Great: A Political Biography*, 2nd ed. (Oxford, UK: Blackwell, 2002), 75–85.

18. Suetonius, *Divine Julius* 50.1.

19. Susan Treggiari, *Servilia and Her Family* (Oxford, UK: Oxford University Press, 2019), passim, with a good summary 251–280, highlighting the nonpolitical aspects of marriage; and see the thoughtful review by Gregory Rowe, "A Well-Behaved Woman Who Made History," *Journal of Roman Archaeology* 34 (2021): 330–336.

20. Plutarch, *Cato the Younger* 30.1–4, *Pompey* 44.2–3, with Treggiari, *Servilia*, 117–119, which informs my account.

21. Plutarch, *Cato the Younger* 30.4.

22. The whole episode is recounted by Plutarch, *Cato the Younger* 25, 52.3–5. It is variously interpreted by Treggiari, *Servilia*, 124–127, and Drogula, *Cato the Younger*, 173–175.

23. Cicero, *Letters to Atticus* 1.16.12 (SB 16). For the disgust of Cato and Servilia, see Plutarch, *Cato the Younger* 30.5, and *Pompey* 44.4.

24. Afranius's dancing is commented on by Cassius Dio (37.49.3). Dio 37.49–51 is the main source for the thwarting of Pompey; also note Cicero, *Letters to Atticus* 1.19.4 (SB 19) and Plutarch, *Cato the Younger* 31.1–2.

25. Cicero, *Letters to Atticus* 1.17.9 (SB 17), and 1.18.7 (SB 18). Cato's filibustering: Cicero, *On the Laws* 3.40; Plutarch, *Moralia* 804c; and Robert Morstein-Marx, *Julius Caesar and the Roman People* (Cambridge, UK: Cambridge University Press, 2021), 113–114. A muckraking account of the corporations the Senate relied on is Ernst Badian, *Publicans and Sinners: Private Enterprise in the Service of the Roman Republic* (Ithaca, NY: Cornell University Press, 1972).

26. On Caesar's Spanish governorship, the main sources are Cassius Dio 37.52–53 and Plutarch, *Caesar* 11–12. I discuss it in "Julius Caesar and Spanish Triumph-Hunting," in *The Roman Republican Triumph Beyond the Spectacle*, ed. Carsten Hjort Lange and Frederik Juliaan Vervaet (Rome: Edizioni Quasar, 2014), 149–162.

27. Plutarch, *Caesar* 13.1–2, *Cato the Younger* 31.2–3; Appian, *Civil War* 2.8; Cassius Dio 37.54.1–2; and Morstein-Marx, *Julius Caesar*, 109–116.

28. Suetonius, *Divine Julius* 19.1.

29. Suetonius, *Divine Julius* 19.2.

30. The pact is prominent in ancient sources (e.g., Suetonius, *Divine Julius* 19.2; Cassius Dio 37.55–58), but its nature and timing are controversial. A good guide is Christopher Pelling, *Plutarch: "Caesar"* (Oxford, UK: Oxford University Press, 2011), 188–191. On Crassus, see Badian, *Publicans and Sinners*, 99–112.

31. Cicero, *Letters to Atticus* 1.14.6 (SB 14), 2.1.10 (SB 21).

32. Valerius Maximus 6.2.7.

33. Plutarch, *Caesar* 14.5, translation modified from Pelling, *Plutarch: "Caesar,"* 87.

Chapter 7. The Consulship of Julius and Caesar

1. I follow Christian Meier, *Caesar: A Biography*, trans. David McLintock (New York: Basic Books, 1995), 204–205, in starting this chapter on Caesar's consulship with the auspice-taking and other ceremonies. My discussion of auspices draws on the major contributions of Jerzy Linderski, "The Augural Law," in *Aufstieg und Niedergang der römischen Welt* 2.16.3, ed. Hildegard Temporini and Wolfgang Haase (Berlin: De Gruyter, 1986), 2146–2312, and Lindsay G. Driediger-Murphy, *Roman Republican Augury: Freedom and Control* (New York: Oxford University Press, 2019).

2. Caesar's struggle to pass his agrarian law is recounted in the detailed narrative of his consulship by Cassius Dio 38.1–12. The consulship was a turning point in Caesar's career, and from this point on there is far more extensive secondary documentation. In this chapter I also draw on Plutarch, *Caesar* 14, *Pompey* 47–48, and *Cato the Younger* 31.4–34; Suetonius, *Divine Julius* 20–23; Appian, *Civil War* 2.9–15; and Cicero's eyewitness letters to Atticus (2.4–25 [SB 24–45]) as well as his speech *Against Vatinius*. Matthias Gelzer, *Caesar: Politician and Statesman*, trans. Peter Needham (Oxford, UK: Blackwell, 1968), 63–101, is foundational, as is Meier, *Caesar*, 204–223, and Meier, "Zur Chronologie und Politik in Caesars erstem Konsulat," *Historia* 10.1 (1961): 68–98. Robert Morstein-Marx, *Julius Caesar and the Roman People* (Cambridge, UK: Cambridge University Press, 2021), 117–191, is more sympathetic to Caesar. Guides to the chronological problems and more recent literature are Stefan G. Chrissanthos, *The Year of Julius and Caesar: 59 BC and the Transformation of the Roman Republic* (Baltimore: Johns Hopkins University Press, 2019); and Christopher Pelling, *Plutarch: "Caesar"* (Oxford, UK: Oxford University Press, 2011), 192–203.

3. The quotations in this passage are taken from Cassius Dio 38.3.2, 38.3.3, 38.4.3, 38.5.2, and 38.5.4.

4. Cassius Dio 38.6.1.

5. On this type of report, see Linderski, "Augural Law"; and Driediger-Murphy, *Roman Republican Augury*, 127–160, an important reinterpretation, which I did not entirely follow here.

6. For a different chronology of Bibulus's withdrawal (after Caesar's second agrarian law, later in the year), see Morstein-Marx, *Julius Caesar*, 142–143.

7. On the stark novelty of both sides' tactics in 59, see Meier, *Caesar*, 222–223.

8. Plutarch, *Caesar* 14.1, and *Cato the Younger* 32.1.

9. Macrobius, *Saturnalia* 2.6.1.

10. Cicero, *Against Vatinius* 5, 15, 21, 29, 38.

11. Gelzer, *Caesar*, 84–86, describes the law and its background, but I prefer the chronology of Meier, "Zur Chronologie."

12. Lily Ross Taylor, *The Voting Districts of the Roman Republic: The Thirty-Five Urban and Rural Tribes* (Rome: American Academy in Rome, 1960), 123–131.

13. Plutarch, *Cato the Younger* 33.3.

14. Alternatively, he sent notice that he was watching the skies: Driediger-Murphy, *Roman Republican Augury*, 127–160.

15. Cicero, *Letters to Atticus* 2.20.3–4, 6 (SB 40), 2.21.4 (SB 41); Suetonius, *Divine Julius* 9.2, 49.2. Lily Ross Taylor, *Party Politics in the Age of Caesar* (Berkeley: University of California Press, 1949), 136, suspects that Cato wrote the edicts, "for Bibulus is described as dull of tongue and Cato had a pungent style."

16. Cicero, *Letters to Atticus* 2.9.2 (SB 29).

17. On Curio, see, e.g., Cicero, *Letters to Atticus* 1.14.5 (SB 14), 2.8.1 (SB 28), *Brutus* 280.

18. Suetonius, *Divine Julius* 20.2.

19. Cicero, *Letters to Atticus* 2.9.1 (SB 29).

20. Plutarch, *Caesar* 14.4, *Pompey* 47.6; Suetonius, *Divine Julius* 21; and Susan Treggiari, *Servilia and Her Family* (Oxford, UK: Oxford University Press, 2019), 113, 121, 291.

21. Cicero, *Letters to Atticus* 2.17.1 (SB 37); Suetonius, *Divine Julius* 21; and Aulus Gellius, *Attic Nights* 4.10.5.

22. For the Campanian law and the Senate decree on Transalpine Gaul, see Gelzer, *Caesar*, 80–81, 87; for a different view on Transalpine Gaul, see Morstein-Marx, *Julius Caesar*, 175–179.

23. Suetonius, *Divine Julius* 22.2, translations adapted from *Suetonius: "The Caesars,"* trans. Donna W. Hurley (Indianapolis: Hackett, 2011), 13.

24. Cicero, *Letters to Atticus* 2.18.2 (SB 38).

25. Plutarch, *Caesar* 14.5, *Cato the Younger* 33.3; Suetonius, *Divine Julius* 21; Appian, *Civil War* 2.14; and Cassius Dio 38.9.1.

26. Suetonius, *Divine Julius* 50.2, with good commentary by Treggiari, *Servilia*, 121–122.

27. Cicero, *Letters to Atticus* 2.20.4 (SB 40).

28. Cicero, *Letters to Atticus* 2.19.3 (SB 39).

29. Cicero, *Letters to Atticus* 2.20.6 (SB 40), 2.21.4–5 (SB 41).

30. The main account is a spicy letter by Cicero, *Letters to Atticus* 2.24 (SB 44), with additional, not always reliable, details given by Cicero, *Against Vatinius* 24–26. See also Suetonius, *Divine Julius* 20.5; Appian, *Civil War* 2.12; and Cassius Dio 38.9.2–4. There was speculation at the time and has been ever since; Erich Gruen, *The Last Generation of the Roman Republic* (Berkeley: University of California Press, 1974), 95–96, is sober.

31. Suetonius, *Divine Julius* 23.1; Cicero, *Against Vatinius* 33–34.

32. Cassius Dio 38.12.3; Cicero, *Against Vatinius* 33–34, and *Scholia Bobiensia*, p. 150, as quoted in *Ciceronis Orationum Scholiastae*, ed. Thomas Stangl (Hildesheim: Georg Olms, 1984). See W. Jeffrey Tatum, *The Patrician Tribune: Publius Clodius Pulcher* (Chapel Hill: University of North Carolina Press, 1999), 102–149, esp. 140–141, for the aborted trial of Vatinius.

33. Tatum, *Patrician Tribune*, 150–151, 155–156; also E. Badian, "M. Porcius Cato and the Annexation and Early Administration of Cyprus," *Journal of Roman Studies* 55 (1965): 110–121.

34. Cicero, *On His House* 22, and *For Sestius* 60.

Chapter 8. Cato's Triumph

1. Cicero, *For Sestius* 59–60, 63, which makes Cato's attitude clear. Kit Morrell, *Pompey, Cato, and the Governance of the Roman Empire* (Oxford, UK: Oxford University Press, 2017), 116, rightly calls the annexation "an act of bare-faced imperialism."

2. On Ptolemy XII and his brother, see Mary Siani-Davies, *Cicero's Speech "Pro Rabirio Postumo"* (Oxford, UK: Clarendon Press, 2001), 1–38.

3. The main source for Cato's mission to Cyprus is Plutarch, *Cato the Younger* 34.2–39 (where "Canidius" should be L. Caninius Gallus). There are detailed discussions by Rudolf Fehrle, *Cato Uticensis* (Darmstadt: Wissenschaftliche Buchgesellschaft, 1983), 136–161; Fred K. Drogula, *Cato the Younger: Life and Death at the End of the Roman Republic* (Oxford, UK: Oxford University Press, 2019), 157–175; and Morrell, *Pompey, Cato*, 116–127.

4. Plutarch, *Cato the Younger* 35.4.

5. This and the following general observations are owed to James Tan, *Power and Public Finance at Rome, 264–49 BCE* (New York: Oxford University Press, 2017).

6. Cicero, *On the Response of the Haruspices* 59.

7. Brutus worked through middlemen to conceal his actions. Cicero, *Letters to Atticus* 5.21.10–13 (SB 114), 6.1.5–7 (SB 115).

8. For the quarrel, later used by Caesar in his *Anticato*, see Plutarch, *Cato the Younger* 36.3–37.

9. Pliny the Elder, *Natural History* 29.96, 34.92; Seneca, *Controversiae* 6.4.

10. In addition to Plutarch, *Cato the Younger* 39, see Velleius Paterculus 2.45.5.

11. Cassius Dio 39.22.4.

12. The major source is Cassius Dio 39.12–16, and 39.55–63, with details added by speeches of Cicero, including a defense of Ptolemy's banker, Rabirius Postumus. See Siani-Davies, *Cicero's Speech "Pro Rabirio Postumo,"* 20–30.

13. Caesar, *Gallic War* 1–2; see the next chapter for further discussion.

14. Caesar, *Gallic War* 2.35.4; Plutarch, *Caesar* 21.1.

15. This is to omit much else that was going on, such as major street violence between rival gangs of Clodius and a tribune of 57, Milo. For a vivid account, see T. P. Wiseman, "Caesar, Pompey and Rome, 59–50 B.C.," *Cambridge Ancient History*, 2nd ed. (1994), 9.368–423. Valuable studies of Caesar's position I draw on are Erich Gruen, "Pompey, the Roman Aristocracy, and the Conference of Luca," *Historia* 1 (1969): 71–108; and John T. Ramsey, "The Proconsular Years: Politics at a Distance," in *A Companion to Julius Caesar*, ed. Miriam Griffin (Malden, MA: Wiley-Blackwell, 2009), 37–56.

16. Cicero, *Brutus* 247.

17. Cicero, *Letters to Quintus* 2.5.3 (SB 9).

18. Cicero, *Letters to Quintus* 2.5.1 (SB 5).

19. Suetonius, *Divine Julius* 23.1, with the dating proposed by Ernst Badian, "The Attempt to Try Caesar," in *Polis and imperium: Studies in Honour of Edward Togo Salmon*, ed. J. A. S. Evans (Toronto: Hackert, 1974), 145–166.

20. Suetonius, *Divine Julius* 24.1; Cicero, *Letters to Atticus* 4.8A.2 (SB 82).

21. Cicero, *Letters to Friends* 1.8–9 (SB 19–20); Plutarch, *Pompey* 51.3–4, *Caesar* 21.2–3, *Crassus* 14.5–6; Suetonius, *Divine Julius* 24.1; and Appian, *Civil War* 2.17. The sources are brief and mostly from later, giving rise to extensive discussion, e.g., Allen M. Ward, *Marcus Crassus and the Late Roman Republic* (Columbia: University of Missouri Press, 1977), 253–264.

22. Cicero, *Letters to Friends* 1.9.9–12 (SB 20), *On the Consular Provinces* 28.

23. Caesar's bribes to senators and their wives are noted by Plutarch, *Caesar* 21.2, *Pompey* 51.2; and Suetonius, *Divine Julius* 23.2. For Favonius, see Plutarch, *Caesar* 21.4.

24. This is the likeliest interpretation of the various sources (Valerius Maximus 4.1.14; Plutarch, *Cato the Younger* 39.3–4; and Cassius Dio 39.23.1), but there might have been other honors offered. See Kit Morrell, "'Certain Gentlemen Say...': Cicero, Cato, and the Debate on the Validity of Clodius' Laws," in *Reading Republican Oratory: Reconstructions, Contexts, Receptions*, ed. Christa Gray et al. (Oxford, UK: Oxford University Press, 2018), 191–210.

25. Cassius Dio 39.23.2.

26. Cassius Dio 39.23.3–4.

27. The main account of Pompey and Crassus's scheme to win election is Cassius Dio 39.22–31.

28. Valerius Maximus 6.2.6.

29. For Cato and Domitius, see Plutarch, *Cato the Younger* 41.1–3, *Pompey* 52.1–2, and *Crassus* 15.1–4.

30. Plutarch, *Cato the Younger* 41.4–5; also Cassius Dio 39.31.

31. On Cato's run for praetor, see Plutarch, *Cato the Younger* 42, *Pompey* 52.2; Cassius Dio 39.32.1–2; and Livy, *Periochae* 105.

32. Cicero, *Letters to Quintus* 2.8.3 (SB 13).

33. Valerius Maximus 4.6.4; Plutarch, *Pompey* 53.3; and Cassius Dio 39.32.2.

34. On the *lex Trebonia* and Cato's opposition, see Plutarch, *Cato the Younger* 43, *Comparison of Nicias and Crassus* 2.1–2; Cassius Dio 39.33–36; and Livy, *Periochae* 105.

35. Jerzy Linderski, "The Augural Law," in *Aufstieg und Niedergang der römischen Welt* 2.16.3, ed. Hildegard Temporini and Wolfgang Haase (Berlin: De Gruyter, 1986), 2167–2168.

36. Cassius Dio 39.36.2.

37. Plutarch, *Cato the Younger* 43.5–6, in keeping with Cato's earlier warnings, as noted by Fehrle, *Cato Uticensis*, 170–171 n. 70.

Chapter 9. Gaul

1. Caesar, *Gallic War* 4.20–38, is the main source for the first British expedition. Caesar obviously narrated all of *The Gallic War* in a manner favorable to himself but appears to have adhered to a truthful outline of events; see Kathryn Welch and Anton Powell, eds., *Julius Caesar as Artful Reporter: The War Commentaries as Political Instruments* (Swansea, UK: Classical Press of Wales, 1998). Christian Goudineau, *César et la Gaule*, rev. ed. (Paris: Errance, 2000), brings in archaeology, which is also the subject of Andrew P. Fitzpatrick and Colin Haselgrove, eds., *Julius Caesar's Battle for Gaul: New Archaeological Perspectives* (Oxford, UK: Oxbow Books, 2019). Throughout this chapter I rely heavily on Kurt A. Raaflaub, ed. and trans., *The Landmark Julius Caesar* (New York: Pantheon Books, 2017), including its chronologies.

2. Caesar, *Gallic War* 4.26.5.

3. For the impact the invasion made, see Cicero, *Letters to Quintus* 2.16.4 (SB 20); Plutarch, *Caesar* 23.2–3; and Cassius Dio 39.50–53. For the pearls, see Suetonius, *Divine Julius* 47; and Pliny, *Natural History* 9.116.

4. Caesar, *Gallic War* 4.38.5, with discussion of thanksgivings by Josiah Osgood, "The Pen and the Sword: Writing and Conquest in Caesar's Gaul," *Classical Antiquity* 28.2 (2009): 339–341.

5. Plutarch, *Cato the Younger* 51.1–4, *Caesar* 22.1–3; Appian, *Celtica* fragment 18. There is an excellent treatment by Kit Morrell, "Cato, Caesar, and the Germani," *Antichthon* 49 (2015): 73–93.

6. Caesar, *Gallic War* 4.15.3, at the conclusion of his account (4.1–15).

7. On Cato and the ethics of empire, see Kit Morrell, *Pompey, Cato, and the Governance of the Roman Empire* (Oxford, UK: Oxford University Press, 2017), 98–116; also Matthias Gelzer, "Cato Uticensis," in Gelzer, *Kleine Schriften* (Wiesbaden: Franz Steiner, 1963), 2: 265–266; Adam Afzelius, "Die politische Bedeutung des jüngeren Cato," *Classica et Mediaevalia* 4 (1941): 125–133; and Rudolf Fehrle, *Cato Uticensis* (Darmstadt: Wissenschaftliche Buchgesellschaft, 1983), 176–180.

8. Plutarch, *Cato the Younger* 51.3–4.

9. Caesar, *Gallic War* 2.33.6–7. On plunder, see also Suetonius, *Divine Julius* 54.2; Osgood, "Pen and Sword," 332.

10. Suetonius, *Divine Julius* 51.

11. Cicero, *Letters to Atticus* 5.1.2 (SB 94), 5.4.3 (SB 97); Osgood, "Pen and Sword," 343.

12. On Memmius and Caesar, see Cicero, *Letters to Atticus* 4.15.7 (SB 90); Suetonius, *Divine Julius* 23.1, 49.2, 73.1.

13. For Caesar's efforts to stay in touch with politics, see Matthias Gelzer, *Caesar: Politician and Statesman*, trans. Peter Needham (Oxford, UK: Blackwell, 1968), 134–140; Osgood, "Pen and Sword"; and Robert Morstein-Marx, *Julius Caesar and the Roman People* (Cambridge, UK: Cambridge University Press, 2021), 203–219.

14. Suetonius, *Divine Julius* 28.1.

15. Cicero, *Letters to Atticus* 4.16.8 (SB 89).

16. Caesar, *Gallic War* 3.20–27, for P. Crassus in Aquitania; see also *Gallic War* 1.52.7 and, for M. Crassus, 5.46–47.2.

17. Good sketches of the most important officers are given by John T. Ramsey in Raaflaub, *Landmark Julius Caesar*, 639–676.

18. Erich Gruen, *The Last Generation of the Roman Republic* (Berkeley: University of California Press, 1974), 112–119.

19. Pliny, *Natural History* 36.48.

20. Catullus 29.1–4, 11–14. Translation from Guy Lee, trans., *Catullus: The Complete Poems* (Oxford, UK: Oxford University Press, 1990, reissued 1998), 29–31.

21. Suetonius, *Divine Julius* 73.

22. Caesar, *Gallic War* 4.17.1.

23. Caesar's feats are noted by Suetonius, *Divine Julius* 57–65; Plutarch, *Caesar* 15–17. For Oppius's reminiscence, see Plutarch, *Caesar* 17.6; Suetonius, *Divine Julius* 72.

24. Caesar, *Gallic War* 2.25.

25. Suetonius, *Divine Julius* 67.1, in a good discussion of Caesar's relations with his soldiers (65–70); on pay, see Suetonius, *Divine Julius* 26.3.

26. Plutarch, *Caesar* 15.3, with similar numbers in other sources, e.g., Pliny, *Natural History* 7.92 ("a great wrong against the human race").

27. For the campaigns of 54 and 53 BC, see Caesar, *Gallic War* 5–6.

28. Plutarch, *Caesar* 23.4, *Pompey* 53.4; Suetonius, *Divine Julius* 26.1; Cicero, *Letters to Quintus* 3.6.3 (SB 26); and Seneca, *Consolation to Marcia* 14.3.

29. Suetonius, *Divine Julius* 67.2.

30. Caesar, *Gallic War* 5.54.5.

31. Caesar's rampage in 51 BC is recorded in *Gallic War* 8.24–25 (a continuation of his commentaries by his officer A. Hirtius).

32. The last great uprising of the Gauls is the subject of the seventh book of Caesar's *Gallic War*.

33. Caesar, *Gallic War* 7.4–5; Florus 1.45.20. Vercingetorix had earlier been an ally of Caesar (Cassius Dio 40.41.1), a fact omitted by Caesar. For his emergence as a national icon in modern France, see Christian Goudineau, *Le dossier Vercingétorix* (Paris: Errance, 2001).

34. Caesar, *Gallic War* 7.56.2.

35. Plutarch, *Cato the Younger* 49.1; for the uprising as an existential crisis for Caesar, see Martin Jehne, *Caesar*, 4th ed. (Munich: C. H. Beck, 2008), 66–67.

36. Caesar described his fortifications in *Gallic War* 7.72–74. See Goudineau, *César et la Gaule*, 217–220, 304–314, for the archaeological remains, which suggest that Caesar exploited natural topography more than he indicated in his commentaries.

37. Plutarch, *Caesar* 27.5; Florus 1.45.26; and Cassius Dio 40.41.

38. Caesar, *Gallic War* 7.89.4.

39. Caesar, *Gallic War* 7.90.8.

Chapter 10. Cato's Medicines

1. Cicero, *Letters to Atticus* 4.16.6 (SB 89). This passage, along with *Letters to Atticus* 4.15.7 (SB 90) and *Letters to Quintus* 2.15.4 (SB 19), provides the main evidence for the elections, discussed by E. S. Gruen, "The Consular Elections for 53 B.C.," in *Hommages à Marcel Renard*, ed. Jacqueline Bibauw (Brussels: Latomus, 1969), 2: 311–321.

2. The medical metaphor recurs in Plutarch's *Cato the Younger* (e.g., 44.2, 47.2) and goes back to Cato's own language; on the problem as Cato saw it, see Kit Morrell, "Cato and the Courts in 54 B.C.," *Classical Quarterly* 64.2 (2014): 669–681; also Kit Morrell, *Pompey, Cato, and the Governance of the Roman Empire* (Oxford, UK: Oxford University Press, 2017), 204–218; and Adam Afzelius, "Die politische Bedeutung des jüngeren Cato," *Classica et Mediaevalia* 4 (1941): 120–133. I owe much to these studies.

3. Cicero, *Letters to Quintus* 2.15.4 (SB 19). Also, Cicero, *Letters to Atticus* 4.15.7–8 (SB 90); Plutarch, *Cato the Younger* 44.5–7.

4. Cicero, *Letters to Atticus* 4.17.3 (SB 91); Plutarch, *Cato the Younger* 44.2–3; and Morrell, "Cato and the Courts," 670–671.

5. Asconius, *Commentaries*, pp. 18–20C, 28C; Morrell, "Cato and the Courts," 673–679.

6. Plutarch, *Cato the Younger* 44.4.

7. Plutarch, *Pompey* 54.2–3.

8. Plutarch, *Pompey* 54.2–3.

9. Lily Ross Taylor, *Party Politics in the Age of Caesar* (Berkeley: University of California Press, 1949), 148; Morrell, *Pompey, Cato*, 200–201. Rudolf Fehrle, *Cato Uticensis* (Darmstadt: Wissenschaftliche Buchgesellschaft, 1983), 194–201, credits the rapprochement to Cato's maneuvering; also Fred K. Drogula, *Cato the Younger: Life and Death at the End of the Roman Republic* (Oxford, UK: Oxford University Press, 2019), 208. On the impact of Carrhae (somberly recounted by Plutarch, *Crassus* 17–33), see Morrell, *Pompey, Cato*, 177–203.

10. Suetonius, *Divine Julius* 27.1.

11. Cassius Dio 40.46.2–3, 40.56.1.

12. The most important account of Clodius and Milo is Asconius's well-informed *Commentaries* (pp. 30–56C) on Cicero's tendentious defense *For Milo*.

13. Cicero, *For Milo* 95.

14. John T. Ramsey, "How and Why Was Pompey Made Consul in 52 BC?," *Historia* 65.3 (2016): 314. Ramsey's reanalysis informs my discussion, as does Kit Morrell, "Cato, Pompey's Third Consulship, and the Politics of Milo's Trial," in *Institutions and Ideology in Republican Rome: Speech, Audience, and Decision*, ed. Henriette van der Blom, Christa Gray, and Catherine Steel (Cambridge, UK: Cambridge University Press, 2018), 165–180, which argues for more cooperation between Pompey and Cato.

15. Plutarch, *Cato the Younger* 47.2–3, *Pompey* 54.3–5, *Caesar* 28.5; Appian, *Civil War* 2.23.

16. Plutarch, *Cato the Younger* 48.1–2, *Pompey* 54.5–6.

17. Cicero, *For Milo* 13–14, with Asconius, *Commentaries*, pp. 43–45C.

18. Fehrle, *Cato Uticensis*, 213; Caesar, *Civil War* 1.32.3; Livy, *Periochae* 107; and Suetonius, *Divine Julius* 26.1. For Cato's threats, see Suetonius, *Divine Julius* 30.3.

19. Cassius Dio 40.56.1. For full discussion of this innovative law, see Morrell, *Pompey, Cato*, 214–236.

20. Plutarch, *Cato the Younger* 48.4, *Pompey* 55.1–4.

21. Plutarch, *Cato the Younger* 48.4; Valerius Maximus 6.2.5; and Cassius Dio 40.55.2.

22. Plutarch, *Cato the Younger* 49–50, is the main source for Cato's consular campaign. See also Cassius Dio 40.58; Seneca, *Letters* 104.33.

23. Marcellus is probably the friend Cato rebuked on the last day of his quaestorship. Plutarch, *Cato the Younger* 18.3–4; on his oratory, see Cicero, *Brutus* 248–250.

24. Suetonius, *Divine Julius* 28.2, 29.1; Livy, *Periochae* 108; and Cassius Dio 40.59.1.

25. Cicero, *Letters to Friends* 4.3.1–2 (SB 202). The legal questions have produced a thicket of modern discussions; valuable guides are Christopher Pelling, *Plutarch: "Caesar"* (Oxford, UK: Oxford University Press, 2011), 283–293; John T. Ramsey, "The Proconsular Years: Politics at a Distance," in *A Companion to Julius Caesar*, ed. Miriam Griffin (Malden, MA: Wiley-Blackwell, 2019), 37–56, which I follow most closely; and Robert Morstein-Marx, *Julius Caesar and the Roman People* (Cambridge, UK: Cambridge University Press, 2021), 258–320.

26. Cicero, *Letters to Atticus* 5.2.3 (SB 95), 5.11.2 (SB 104); Suetonius, *Divine Julius* 28.3; and Plutarch, *Caesar* 29.2.

27. Caelius to Cicero, *Letters to Friends* 8.4.4 (SB 81); Cicero, *Letters to Friends* 8.9.5 (SB 82).

28. Cicero, *Letters to Friends* 8.8.9 (SB 84).

29. Cicero, *Letters to Friends* 8.8.9 (SB 84).

30. Robert Morstein-Marx, "Caesar's Alleged Fear of Prosecution and His *ratio absentis* in the Approach to the Civil War," *Historia* 56.2 (2007): 159–178, and Morstein-Marx, *Julius Caesar*, 258–320, emphasize this dilemma.

31. Caesar, *Civil War* 1.9, 1.32.

32. On Caesar's investments, see Plutarch, *Caesar* 29.3; Suetonius, *Divine Julius* 26.2–3, 29.1; and Appian, *Civil War* 2.26–27. It has sometimes been suggested, despite consistent evidence, that Curio was not bought, e.g., Erich Gruen, *The Last Generation of the Roman Republic* (Berkeley: University of California Press, 1974), 470–497. Pliny, *Natural History* 36.116–120, describes Curio's dizzying theater.

33. Cicero, *Letters to Atticus* 6.2.6 (SB 116); Appian, *Civil War* 2.27.

34. Appian, *Civil War* 2.27; Hirtius, *Gallic War* 8.52.4–53 (Caesar's officer Hirtius added an eighth book to Caesar's *Gallic War*, covering the last two years of the war).

35. Plutarch, *Cato the Younger* 51.5.

36. Morrell, *Pompey, Cato*, 177–203, 234–268.

37. Cicero, *Letters to Friends* 15.3.2 (SB 103).

38. Cicero, *Letters to Friends* 15.4.14 (SB 110).

39. Caelius at *Letters to Friends* 8.11.2 (SB 91). Caesar sent a congratulatory letter to Cicero pointing out Cato's ingratitude (*Letters to Atticus* 7.1.7 [SB 124], 7.2.7 [SB 125]).

40. Cato at *Letters to Friends* 15.5 (SB 111). My translation borrows several phrases from D. R. Shackleton Bailey, *Cicero: "Letters to Friends"* (Cambridge, MA: Harvard University Press, 2001), 1: 489–491.

41. On Antony, see Plutarch, *Antony* 4–5.1; Hirtius, *Gallic War* 8.50.

42. Appian, *Civil War* 2.28; Plutarch, *Pompey* 57.

43. On the vote and its aftermath, see Appian, *Civil War* 2.30–31; Plutarch, *Pompey* 58.4–59.1, *Caesar* 30.1–2.

44. Appian, *Civil War* 2.30. On the basis of several passages in Seneca's *Letters* (e.g., 14.12, 95.69–70), it has been argued that Cato voted *for* Curio's proposal; see Helga Botermann, "Cato und die Sogenannte Schwertübergabe im Dezember 50 v. Christus," *Hermes* 117.1 (1989): 62–85. But Seneca cannot be pressed so hard, as is pointed out by Drogula, *Cato the Younger*, 256–257, who emphasizes Cato's contribution to the political breakdown.

45. This is concealed by Caesar, *Civil War* 1.8.1, but is suggested through the chronology of subsequent events. See Kurt A. Raaflaub, ed. and trans., *The Landmark Julius Caesar* (New York: Pantheon Books, 2017), 317; for a slightly different view, see Morstein-Marx, *Julius Caesar*, 640–642.

46. Caesar, *Civil War* 1.1–2; Cicero, *Letters to Friends* 16.11.2 (SB 143); Plutarch, *Caesar* 30.3–31.1 (with chronology confused); Appian, *Civil War* 2.32–33; and Cassius Dio 41.1–3.1.

47. Plutarch, *Pompey* 59.4.

48. Caesar, *Civil War* 1.4.1.

49. The most detailed, if obviously tendentious, narrative is Caesar, *Civil War* 1.3–6. For Cicero's efforts, omitted by Caesar, see Andrew Lintott, *Cicero as Evidence: A Historian's Companion* (Oxford, UK: Oxford University Press, 2008), 267–286.

50. Caesar, *Civil War* 1.7.

51. Reported by Caesar's officer Asinius Pollio: Plutarch, *Caesar* 32, *Pompey* 60.1–2; Appian, *Civil War* 2.34–35. Accounts were colored by knowledge of later events: Morstein-Marx, *Julius Caesar*, 321–335.

52. Cf. Velleius Paterculus 2.49.3.

Chapter 11. Civil War

1. Plutarch, *Cato the Younger* 52.2, *Pompey* 60.4–5. Plutarch's *Cato the Younger* is the major source for Cato in the civil war; it can be hard to see beyond its eulogy. For Caesar, we have, in addition to the usual sources, his own account, *Civil War*, biased but useful for recovering operations in detail; on it, see Richard W. Westall, *Caesar's "Civil War": Historical Reality and Fabrication* (Leiden: Brill, 2017). Modern biographies of

Cato and Caesar inform my account throughout; also very important is the reassessment of the Republican opposition to Caesar in Kathryn Welch, *Magnus Pius: Sextus Pompeius and the Transformation of the Roman Republic* (Swansea, UK: Classical Press of Wales, 2012). For a more critical view than Welch's of Pompey's actions, see Luca Fezzi, *Crossing the Rubicon: Caesar's Decision and the Fate of Rome*, trans. Richard Dixon (New Haven, CT: Yale University Press, 2019), esp. 274–278. On finance, see Bernhard Woytek, *Arma et nummi: Forschungen zur römischen Finanzgeschichte und Münzprägung der Jahre 49 bis 42 v. Chr.* (Vienna: Verlag der österreichischen Akademie der Wissenschaften, 2003).

2. Plutarch, *Cato the Younger* 52.2, *Pompey* 61.1.

3. On Cato's arrangements, see Plutarch, *Cato the Younger* 52.3–4. In his epic *Civil War*, Lucan has Marcia leave Hortensius's pyre and go straight to Cato to ask for remarriage; Cato agrees but refuses to renew the ties of the marriage bed (2.326–391).

4. Susan Treggiari, *Servilia and Her Family* (Oxford, UK: Oxford University Press, 2019), 161–182, discusses the lives of senatorial women in this period.

5. Plutarch, *Cato the Younger* 53.1; Lucan, *Civil War* 2.372–378.

6. Rudolf Fehrle, *Cato Uticensis* (Darmstadt: Wissenschaftliche Buchgesellschaft, 1983), 241–251; Welch, *Magnus Pius*, 43–62.

7. Cicero, *Letters to Atticus* 7.15.2 (SB 139), with Caesar, *Civil War* 1.6.6.

8. Cicero, *Letters to Atticus* 7.15.2 (SB 139); on the negotiations, see especially Caesar, *Civil War* 1.8–11.

9. Caesar, *Civil War* 1.11.1–2.

10. Caesar, *Civil War* 1.15–23; Cicero, *Letters to Atticus* 8.11A (SB 161A), 8.12A–D (SB 162A–D); and Welch, *Magnus Pius*, 60–61.

11. Quoted in Cicero, *Letters to Atticus* 9.7C.1 (SB 174C).

12. Quoted in Cicero, *Letters to Atticus* 9.16.2 (SB 185). My translation borrows from D. R. Shackleton Bailey, *Cicero: "Letters to Atticus"* (Cambridge, MA: Harvard University Press, 1999), 3: 91.

13. Cicero, *Letters to Atticus* 10.4.8 (SB 195), 10.8.6 (SB 199); Plutarch, *Caesar* 35.6–11; Appian, *Civil War* 2.41; Cassius Dio 41.17.1–2; Martin Jehne, *Caesar*, 4th ed. (Munich: C. H. Beck, 2008), 85; Westall, *Caesar's "Civil War,"* 57–68; and Woytek, *Arma et nummi*, 46–57.

14. Appian, *Civil War* 2.40; for Cato on Sicily, see also Cicero, *Letters to Atticus* 10.12.2 (SB 203), 10.16.3 (SB 208); Caesar, *Civil War* 1.30.4–5; Plutarch, *Cato the Younger* 53.1–3; and Cassius Dio 41.41.1.

15. Already on January 26 Cicero complained about Cato dawdling in Italy (*Letters to Atticus* 7.15.2 [SB 139]).

16. Caesar, *Civil War* 1.30.5.

17. Plutarch, *Cato the Younger* 53.3.

18. Plutarch, *Cato the Younger* 54.1–2.

19. On Cato's motion, see Plutarch, *Cato the Younger* 53.3, *Pompey* 65.1. On the Republican preparations, Plutarch, *Pompey* 64–65.1; Appian, *Civil War* 2.49–52; Cassius Dio 41.18.4–5, 41.43–44.1, and 41.52.2; and Lucan, *Civil War* 5.1–64.

20. Plutarch, *Cato the Younger* 54.3–4.

21. Suetonius, *Divine Julius* 34.2.

22. Caesar's account of the war in Spain in the latter part of *Civil War* 1 likewise reinforces his clemency.

23. Suetonius, *Divine Julius* 69; Appian, *Civil War* 2.47; and Cassius Dio 41.26–36. Caesar tellingly omits to mention the crisis in his commentaries; its gravity is emphasized by Jehne, *Caesar*, 85–87.

24. On Caesar's visit to Rome, see his own account in *Civil War* 3.1–2.1; Plutarch, *Caesar* 37.1; Appian, *Civil War* 2.48; and Cassius Dio 41.36–39.1. Caesar's comparison of his enemies to Sulla were normally implicit (e.g., they planned proscriptions, *Civil War* 3.82.3) but could be explicit (*Civil War* 1.4.2). See further Luca Grillo, *The Art of Caesar's "Bellum Civile": Literature, Ideology, and Community* (Cambridge, UK: Cambridge University Press, 2012), 151–157.

25. Caesar, *Civil War* 3.47.

26. Caesar, *Civil War* 3.47.3.

27. Suetonius, *Divine Julius* 68.2; Plutarch, *Caesar* 39.2. Westall, *Caesar's "Civil War,"* 197–236, gives an excellent account of the Macedonian campaign foregrounding Caesar's supply problems.

28. Plutarch, *Cato the Younger* 54.5–6.

29. Plutarch, *Caesar* 39.5, *Pompey* 65.1; also, e.g., Suetonius, *Divine Julius* 36.

30. Plutarch, *Cato the Younger* 54.7; cf. *Caesar* 41.1.

31. Plutarch, *Caesar* 41.1.

32. On Cato's assignment, see Plutarch, *Cato the Younger* 55.1–2, *Pompey* 67.2, *Cicero* 39.1; Cassius Dio 42.10.1.

33. Caesar, *Civil War* 3.99.4. There are different figures at Plutarch, *Caesar* 46.2; Appian, *Civil War* 2.82.

34. Plutarch, *Brutus* 5.1, 6.1–4; also Cassius Dio 41.62–63.

35. Cicero gave an eyewitness account in *On Divination* 1.68–69, 2.114; see also Plutarch, *Cato the Younger* 55.2; Cassius Dio 42.10, 42.12.3.

36. Plutarch, *Cato the Younger* 55.3, *Cicero* 39.1–2; Cassius Dio 42.10.2.

37. On Cato's actions, see Plutarch, *Cato the Younger* 56.1; Cassius Dio 42.13.2–3.

38. For the last days of Pompey, see above all Plutarch, *Pompey* 73–80. Most persuasive of the king's advisors was the rhetoric teacher Theodotus, who, after advising the murder of Pompey, smilingly added, "A dead man does not bite" (Plutarch, *Pompey* 77.4).

39. Vivid firsthand accounts of Alexandria are given by Diodorus Siculus, *Library of History* 1.50.6–7, 17.52, and Strabo, *Geography* 17.1.6–13. Archaeology has added to the picture; see, e.g., Judith McKenzie, *The Architecture of Alexandria and Egypt 300 B.C.–A.D. 700* (New Haven, CT: Yale University Press, 2011).

40. On Caesar's arrival, see especially his *Civil War* 3.106. Caesar never finished his account of the ensuing war, but after his death his *Civil War* was supplemented with additional books, including *Alexandrian War*. These pro-Caesarian accounts must be corrected by Plutarch, *Caesar* 48.2–49; Cassius Dio 42.7–9.1, 42.34–44. See further Westall, *Caesar's "Civil War,"* 271–302; Woytek, *Arma et nummi*, 155–171; and Heinz Heinen, *Kleopatra-Studien: Gesammelte Schriften zur ausgehenden Ptolemäerzeit* (Konstanz: UVK, 2009).

41. Of many books on Cleopatra, a good introduction is Duane W. Roller, *Cleopatra: A Biography* (Oxford, UK: Oxford University Press, 2010). Insightful and evocative is Stacy Schiff, *Cleopatra: A Life* (New York: Little, Brown and Company, 2010). On Cleopatra's early days of power, see the reassessment in Cecilia M. Peek, "The Expulsion of Cleopatra VII: Context, Causes, and Chronology," *Ancient Society* 38 (2008): 103–135.

42. Caesar, *Civil War* 3.108.1–3; Plutarch, *Caesar* 48.3–5; and Cassius Dio 42.34.1–2.

43. Plutarch, *Caesar* 49.1; also Cassius Dio 42.34.3–35.1 (less subtle). It was not a carpet in which Cleopatra was rolled: Christopher Pelling's *Plutarch: "Caesar"* (Oxford, UK: Oxford University Press, 2011), 385–386.

44. Cassius Dio 42.35.2–6.

45. Plutarch, *Caesar* 49.5, *Antony* 54.4; Heinen, *Kleopatra-Studien*, 154–175, 288–298; and Kathryn Welch and Mark Halsted, "Cleopatra as Pharaoh?" *Teaching History* 53.1 (2019): 10–15.

46. Suetonius, *Divine Julius* 52.1; Appian, *Civil War* 2.90; and Cecilia M. Peek, "The Queen Surveys Her Realm: The Nile Cruise of Cleopatra VII," *Classical Quarterly* 61.2 (2011): 595–607.

47. Jehne, *Caesar*, 93, judging the war Caesar's single greatest political error in his whole career; also Jehne, "Caesar und die Krise von 47 v. Chr," in *L'ultimo Cesare: Scritti, riforme, progetti, congiure*, ed. Gianpaolo Urso (Rome: L'Erma di Bretschneider, 2000), 151–173.

Chapter 12. "Even a Victor"

1. Plutarch, *Cato the Younger* 55.2. Plutarch's biography, the main source for Cato's time in Libya and the Roman province of Africa, informs this whole chapter; see also especially Cassius Dio 42.13.3–4, 42.56.2–57.4; and Appian, *Civil War* 2.87 (confused on some details). For the ongoing Republican war effort, see Kathryn Welch, *Magnus Pius: Sextus Pompeius and the Transformation of the Roman Republic* (Swansea, UK: Classical Press of Wales, 2012), 72–99.

2. According to the poet Lucan, Cato had to force his way in but took no revenge (*Civil War* 9.39–41).

3. Strabo, *Geography* 17.3.20; Josephine Crawley Quinn, "The Syrtes Between East and West," in *Money, Trade and Trade Routes in Pre-Islamic North Africa*, ed. Amelia Dowler and Elizabeth R. Galvin (London: British Museum, 2011), 11–20, with additional sources.

4. In addition to Plutarch, *Cato the Younger* 56.3–4, see, e.g., Livy, *Periochae* 112; Velleius Paterculus 2.54.3; Strabo, *Geography* 17.3.20; Seneca, *Letters* 104.33; and Lucan, *Civil War* 9.371–949 (in which Cato won't sip even a drop of water).

5. Plutarch, *Cato the Younger* 57; Cassius Dio 42.57.1–3.

6. Suetonius, *Divine Julius* 59; Plutarch, *Caesar* 52.2–3; and Cassius Dio 42.57.5; with a marvelous discussion by Jerzy Linderski, "*Q. Scipio Imperator,*" in *Roman Questions II: Selected Papers* (Stuttgart: Franz Steiner, 2007), 130–174.

7. Plutarch, *Cato the Younger* 58.4.

8. Plutarch, *Cato the Younger* 58.4.

9. *African War* 22–23; Cassius Dio 42.56.4; and Rudolf Fehrle, *Cato Uticensis* (Darmstadt: Wissenschaftliche Buchgesellschaft, 1983), 269.

10. On the motto (Suetonius, *Divine Julius* 37.2; Plutarch, *Caesar* 50.2; and Appian, *Civil War* 2.91), see Ida Östenberg, "*Veni vidi vici* and Caesar's Triumph," *Classical Quarterly* 63.2 (2013): 813–827. For fuller accounts of Caesar's movements after Alexandria until the African War, see *Alexandrian War* 65–78; Suetonius, *Divine Julius* 35–75 passim; Plutarch, *Caesar* 50–51; and Cassius Dio 42.45–55.

11. Cicero, *Philippics* 2.62.

12. Cassius Dio 42.50.4.

13. Suetonius, *Divine Julius* 70; Plutarch, *Caesar* 51.1; Appian, *Civil War* 2.92–94; Cassius Dio 42.52–55; and Stefan G. Chrissanthos, "Caesar and the Mutiny of 47 BC," *Journal of Roman Studies* 91 (2001): 63–75.

14. Suetonius, *Divine Julius* 50.2; Macrobius, *Saturnalia* 2.2.5; and Cicero, *Letters to Atticus* 14.21.3 (SB 375).

15. *African War* 1.1. This is the major source for the war, with revealing observations on Caesar's generalship. Further details are added by Plutarch, *Caesar* 52–54, *Cato the Younger* 58–73; Appian, *Civil War* 2.95–100; and Cassius Dio 43.1–13.

16. Plutarch, *Caesar* 52.4. Also, e.g., Cassius Dio 42.58.1; Suetonius, *Divine Julius* 59.

17. My account here follows *The African War*, with the excellent commentary in Kurt A. Raaflaub, ed. and trans., *The Landmark Julius Caesar* (New York: Pantheon Books, 2017), 545–604.

18. *African War* 13.1.

19. *African War* 14.3.

20. On this crucial battle, see especially *African War* 79–86. Plutarch, *Caesar* 53.3, knew of an (unconvincing) alternative tradition that had Caesar miss the battle because of "his usual sickness," i.e., epilepsy, on which see further below.

21. *African War* 85.6.

22. Plutarch, *Caesar* 53.2, reports fifty thousand dead in the Republican army.

23. M. P. Charlesworth, "The Civil War," in *Cambridge Ancient History*, 1st ed. (1932), 9: 680–690, gives an appreciation.

24. The rest of this chapter draws principally on Plutarch, *Cato the Younger* 59–73, an account full of convincing detail but framed more around philosophy than politics. For the paragraphs that follow, see in particular 59.6, 62.3, 64.5, 65.1, 66.2, and 66.3. On the number of cavalry at Utica, see *African War* 95.1–2.

25. Joseph Geiger, "Munatius Rufus and Thrasea Paetus on Cato the Younger," *Athenaeum* 57 (1979): 65–67, noting that, while there are some minor variations in the many later accounts of Cato's death (especially Seneca, *Epistles* 24.6–8; Florus 2.13.71–72; Appian, *Civil War* 2.98–99; and Cassius Dio 43.11), one well-informed source seems ultimately to lie behind them. The earliest extant account, *African War* 88, already contains much of the story in brief.

26. My account of philosophical attitudes to suicide, and Cato's own contribution, is indebted to a fascinating essay, Miriam T. Griffin, "Philosophy, Cato, and Roman Suicide," in *Politics and Philosophy at Rome: Collected Papers*, ed. Catalina Balmaceda (Oxford, UK: Oxford University Press, 2018), 402–419. Also valuable is Stanly H. Rauh, "Cato at Utica: The Emergence of a Roman Suicide Tradition," *American Journal of Philology* 139.1 (2018): 59–91.

27. Plutarch, *Cato the Younger* 71.2.

28. *African War* 90.1.

29. Plutarch, *Cato the Younger* 72.1.

30. Rauh, "Cato at Utica," shows how a tradition of honorable suicide for Romans began in the civil war of the 80s BC.

31. Cicero, *On Duties* 1.93–153 (esp. 1.112); Griffin, "Philosophy, Cato," 416; and Rauh, "Cato at Utica," 74–75.

32. Cicero, *On the Ends of Good and Evil* 3.60.

Chapter 13. Anticato

1. Cicero, *Letters to Atticus* 12.4.2 (SB 240).

2. The main source for the honors for Caesar is Cassius Dio: 42.17–20, 43.14, 43.42–45, and 44.1–11. An outstanding study of the honors, though not convincing in its main thesis, is Stefan Weinstock, *Divus Julius* (Oxford, UK: Clarendon Press, 1971). The nature of Caesar's dictatorship and his ultimate intentions have been a source of great controversy in modern scholarship. I have found Martin Jehne's work especially helpful, including *Der Staat des Dictators Caesar* (Cologne: Böhlau, 1987), and "Der Dictator und die Republik: Wurzeln, Formen und Perspektiven von Caesars Monarchie," in *Zwischen Monarchie und Republik*, ed. Bernhard Linke, Mischa Meier, and Meret Strothmann (Stuttgart: Franz Steiner, 2010), 187–211. I also rely heavily in this chapter on Jean-Louis Ferrary, "À propos des pouvoirs et des honneurs décernés à César entre 48 et 44," in *Cesare: Precursore o visionario*, ed. Gianpaolo Urso (Pisa: ETS, 2010), 9–30.

3. For the statue, see, e.g., Plutarch, *Brutus* 1.1; Suetonius, *Divine Julius* 80.3; and Cassius Dio 43.45.4.

4. Cassius Dio 42.20; Plutarch, *Caesar* 51.1.

5. Cicero, *For Marcellus* 23, told Caesar what he needed to do. For Caesar's measures, see, e.g., Suetonius, *Divine Julius* 43; Cassius Dio 43.25.2.

6. Suetonius, *Divine Julius* 43; Cassius Dio 43.14.4.

7. Ferrary, "À propos des pouvoirs," 22–24. On Caesar's plans for Parthia, see Jürgen Malitz, "Caesars Partherkrieg," *Historia* 33.1 (1984): 21–59; and, for the overall context, John Curran, "The Ambitions of Quintus Labienus 'Parthicus,'" *Antichthon* 41 (2007): 33–53.

8. Velleius Paterculus 2.56.2; Plutarch, *Caesar* 55.1–2; Suetonius, *Divine Julius* 37; Florus 2.13.88–89; Appian, *Civil War* 2.101–102; and Cassius Dio 43.19–21.2. For these triumphs and games, and Caesar's other spectacles, see Geoffrey Sumi, *Ceremony and Power: Performing Politics in Rome Between Republic and Empire* (Ann Arbor: University of Michigan Press, 2005), 47–73. On the chronology, there is good discussion in the brilliant study by John T. Ramsey and A. Lewis Licht, *The Comet of 44 B.C. and Caesar's Funeral Games* (Atlanta: Scholars Press, 1997), 179–184.

9. Suetonius, *Divine Julius* 49.4, 51.1; Cassius Dio 43.20.2; also Pliny, *Natural History* 19.144.

10. Appian, *Civil War* 2.101.

11. P. J. E. Davies, *Architecture and Politics in Republican Rome* (Cambridge, UK: Cambridge University Press, 2017), 257–266, 270–271; Richard R. Westall, "The Forum Iulium as a Representation of Imperator Caesar," *Mitteilungen des Deutschen Archäologischen Instituts, Römische Abteilung* 103 (1996): 83–118.

12. Pliny, *Natural History* 9.171, 14.97; Plutarch, *Caesar* 55.2.

13. Suetonius, *Divine Julius* 39; Plutarch, *Caesar* 55.2; Appian *Civil War* 2.102; and Cassius Dio 43.21.3–24.

14. Suetonius, *Divine Julius* 41.3; Cassius Dio 43.21.4.

15. Plutarch, *Caesar* 59.3, with full discussion of the reforms in Christopher Pelling's *Plutarch: "Caesar"* (Oxford, UK: Oxford University Press, 2011), 440–447. See also Denis Feeney, *Caesar's Calendar: Ancient Time and the Beginnings of History* (Berkeley: University of California Press, 2007), especially 193–201.

16. P. A. Brunt, *Italian Manpower* (Oxford, UK: Clarendon Press, 1971), 255–259, 319–324; Lawrence Keppie, *Colonisation and Veteran Settlement in Italy: 47–14 B.C.* (London: British School at Rome, 1983).

17. Suetonius, *Divine Julius* 52.1; Cassius Dio 43.27.3.

18. The main source is another work designed to complete Caesar's commentaries, *The Spanish War*. Kurt A. Raaflaub, ed. and trans., *The Landmark Julius Caesar* (New York: Pantheon Books, 2017), 605–637; also, Cassius Dio 43.28–41; Florus 2.13.73–87; Plutarch, *Caesar* 56; and Kathryn Welch, *Magnus Pius: Sextus Pompeius and the Transformation of the Roman Republic* (Swansea, UK: Classical Press of Wales, 2012), 99–115.

19. Suetonius, *Divine Julius* 56.5.

20. Plutarch, *Caesar* 56.3; Appian, *Civil War* 2.104.

21. See especially Cicero, *Letters to Atticus* 12.21.1 (SB 260), *Letters to Friends* 16.22.1 (SB 185). On these works, and on Caesar's reply, see most fully Hans Jürgen Tschiedel, *Caesars "Anticato": Eine Untersuchung der Testimonien und Fragmente* (Darmstadt: Wissenschaftliche Buchgesellschaft, 1981), along with helpful discussions in Rudolf Fehrle, *Cato Uticensis* (Darmstadt: Wissenschaftliche Buchgesellschaft, 1983), 279–302; Pelling, *Plutarch: "Caesar,"* 405–408; and Anthony Corbeill, *"Anticato,"* in *The Cambridge Companion to the Writings of Julius Caesar*, ed. Luca Grillo and Christopher B. Krebs (Cambridge, UK: Cambridge University Press, 2018), 215–222.

22. Cicero, *Philippics* 13.30.

23. Cicero, *Letters to Atticus* 13.46.2 (SB 338).

24. Cicero, *Letters to Atticus* 12.45.2 (SB 290).

25. Juvenal 6.336–341.

26. Plutarch, *Caesar* 3.2. For a full collection of the fragments of the work, with commentary, see Tschiedel, *Caesars "Anticato,"* 69–129.

27. Pliny, *Letters* 3.12.2–3.

28. Priscian 6.36.

29. Plutarch, *Caesar* 56.4; Cassius Dio 43.41.3–42. On civil war triumphs, see Carsten Hjort Lange, *Triumphs in the Age of Civil War: The Late Republic and the Adaptability of Triumphal Tradition* (London: Bloomsbury, 2016).

30. Cassius Dio 43.45; Ferrary, "À propos des pouvoirs," 18–22; Frederik Juliaan Vervaet, *The High Command in the Roman Republic: The Principle of the* summum imperium auspiciumque *from 509 to 19 BCE* (Stuttgart: Franz Steiner Verlag, 2014), 223–239.

31. Cassius Dio 43.45.2; Suetonius, *Divine Julius* 76.1; and Cicero, *Letters to Atticus* 13.44.1 (SB 336).

32. Cicero, *Letters to Atticus* 13.44 (SB 336), with Ramsey and Licht, *The Comet of 44 B.C.*, 19–40.

33. On the arrangements for 45, see the valuable account of Cassius Dio 43.46–48; for Balbus and Oppius, see Matthias Gelzer, *Caesar: Politician and Statesman*, trans. Peter Needham (Oxford, UK: Blackwell, 1968), 294.

34. Suetonius, *Divine Julius* 80.3.

35. Cassius Dio 43.45.1, 43.47.1.

36. See especially Cicero, *Letters to Atticus* 13.27.1 (SB 298), 13.28.2–3 (SB 299).

37. Cicero, *Letters to Atticus* 13.52 (SB 353).

38. Suetonius, *Divine Julius* 86.1; Appian, *Civil War* 2.107, 2.109. According to Suetonius, some friends of Caesar's suspected that Caesar abandoned precautions because his health was failing. There is some credible evidence of Caesar suffering at least a couple of seizures in his last years: Suetonius, *Divine Julius* 45.1; Plutarch, *Caesar* 17.2.

39. Cicero, *Letters to Friends* 7.30.2 (SB 265).

40. Appian, *Civil War* 2.110; Cassius Dio 43.51.2–6.

41. Suetonius, *Divine Julius* 79.3.

42. Suetonius, *Divine Julius* 79.2. Also, Plutarch, *Caesar* 60.1; Appian, *Civil War* 2.108. For the Ciceronian charge, see, e.g., *On Duties* 3.82; *Philippics* 2.116.

43. Ferrary, "À propos des pouvoirs," 25–30.

44. J. A. North, "Caesar at the Lupercalia," *Journal of Roman Studies* 98 (2008): 144–160; T. P. Wiseman, *Remembering the Roman People: Essays on Late-Republican Politics and Literature* (Oxford, UK: Oxford University Press, 2009), 170–175.

45. Cassius Dio 44.11.3. Along with Cassius Dio 44.11.2–3, other major sources are Cicero, *Philippics* 2.84–87; Nicolaus of Damascus, *Life of Augustus* 71–75; Plutarch, *Caesar* 61.1–4; and Appian, *Civil War* 2.109.

46. On the final conspiracy against Caesar and its immediate aftermath, see the vivid and well-informed Barry Strauss, *The Death of Caesar: The Story of History's Most Famous Assassination* (New York: Simon and Schuster, 2015). Also useful is Wiseman, *Remembering the Roman People*, 177–234, as well as standard biographical studies, including those mentioned in the next note. Major ancient sources on which I draw are Nicolaus of Damascus, *Augustus* 81–106; Suetonius, *Divine Julius* 80–89; Plutarch, *Brutus* 8–20, *Caesar* 62–69; Appian, *Civil War* 2.111–154; and Cassius Dio 44.11.4–51.

47. See especially Plutarch, *Brutus* 1. On Cassius and Brutus, see, among other works, Ulrich Gotter, *Der Diktator ist tot!: Politik in Rom zwischen den Iden des März und der Begründung des Zweiten Triumvirats* (Stuttgart: Franz Steiner, 1996), 207–232; Kathryn Tempest, *Brutus: The Noble Conspirator* (New Haven, CT: Yale University Press, 2017); Elizabeth Rawson, "Cassius and Brutus," in *Roman Culture and Society* (Oxford, UK: Clarendon Press, 1991), 488–507; and Susan Treggiari, *Servilia and Her Family* (Oxford, UK: Oxford University Press, 2019), 145–182.

48. Plutarch, *Brutus* 6–8.

49. Plutarch, *Brutus* 9.6; also, e.g., Appian, *Civil War* 2.112; Suetonius, *Divine Julius* 80.3, both with more examples of graffiti; and Robert Morstein-Marx, *Julius Caesar and the Roman People* (Cambridge, UK: Cambridge University Press, 2021), 523–528.

50. Plutarch, *Brutus* 13.3; Cicero, *Letters to Atticus* 13.22.4 (SB 329); Treggiari, *Servilia*, 175–179.

51. Plutarch, *Brutus* 12, with the brilliant interpretation of David Sedley, "The Ethics of Brutus and Cassius," *Journal of Roman Studies* 87 (1997): 41–53.

52. For the idea of "the free Republic," note especially the letter Brutus and Cassius sent to Antony in August 44: Cicero, *Letters to Friends* 11.3 (SB 336), with discussion by Louise Hodgson, *Res Publica and the Roman Republic: "Without Body or Form"* (Oxford, UK: Oxford University Press, 2017), 163–219.

53. Strauss, *Death of Caesar*, 107–154, recounts the day in detail.

Chapter 14. Requiem for a Republic

1. On the sources for Caesar's funeral, see Josiah Osgood, *Caesar's Legacy: Civil War and the Emergence of the Roman Empire* (Cambridge, UK: Cambridge University Press,

2006), 1–3. Especially important are the partly overlapping accounts of Appian, *Civil War* 2.143–147; and Plutarch, *Brutus* 20, *Antony* 14.3–4. Suetonius, *Divine Julius* 84–85, adds important details on the spectacle. For further accounts, see Barry Strauss, *The Death of Caesar: The Story of History's Most Famous Assassination* (New York: Simon and Schuster, 2015), 167–181; Harriet I. Flower, *Ancestor Masks and Aristocratic Power in Roman Culture* (Oxford, UK: Clarendon Press, 1996), 125–126; Geoffrey Sumi, *Ceremony and Power: Performing Politics in Rome Between Republic and Empire* (Ann Arbor: University of Michigan Press, 2005), 100–112; and T. P. Wiseman, *Remembering the Roman People: Essays on Late-Republican Politics and Literature* (Oxford, UK: Oxford University Press, 2009), 228–233.

2. Suetonius, *Divine Julius* 83.2; Cicero, *Philippics* 2.109; Plutarch, *Caesar* 68.1, *Brutus* 20.3; and Appian, *Civil War* 2.143.

3. The compromise is well discussed by Ulrich Gotter, *Der Diktator ist tot!: Politik in Rom zwischen den Iden des März und der Begründung des Zweiten Triumvirats* (Stuttgart: Franz Steiner, 1996), 21–25; and Kathryn Welch, *Magnus Pius: Sextus Pompeius and the Transformation of the Roman Republic* (Swansea, UK: Classical Press of Wales, 2012), 121–130.

4. Suetonius, *Divine Julius* 84.2; Appian, *Civil War* 2.146.

5. Suetonius, *Divine Julius* 85.

6. For young Cato and Favonius, see Plutarch, *Cato the Younger* 73.2, *Brutus* 49.9; Cassius Dio 47.49.4; and Suetonius, *Augustus* 13.2. The war between the Liberators, as the assassins called themselves, and the heirs of Caesar is discussed in biographies of the major actors; other accounts include Gotter, *Der Diktator ist tot!*; Osgood, *Caesar's Legacy*, 12–107; and Strauss, *Death of Caesar*, 185–228.

7. For the dedication of the temple, see Osgood, *Caesar's Legacy*, 395. On the building, see Peter White, "Julius Caesar in Augustan Rome," *Phoenix* 42.4 (1988): 338; Geoffrey S. Sumi, "Topography and Ideology: Caesar's Monument and the *Aedes Divi Iulii* in Augustan Rome," *Classical Quarterly* 61.1 (2011): 205–229.

8. I have written on the complicated series of civil wars and Augustus's final victory in *Caesar's Legacy* and also *Rome and the Making of a World State, 150 BCE–20 CE* (Cambridge, UK: Cambridge University Press, 2018), 177–258, both of which cite further studies. Especially clear narratives can be found in Adrian Goldsworthy, *Augustus: First Emperor of Rome* (New Haven, CT: Yale University Press, 2014); and J. S. Richardson, *Augustan Rome 44 BC to AD 14: The Restoration of the Republic and the Establishment of the Empire* (Edinburgh, UK: Edinburgh University Press, 2012).

9. On the games, see Cassius Dio 51.22.4–9.

10. In what follows I draw on White, "Julius Caesar in Augustan Rome."

11. Osgood, *Caesar's Legacy*, 395.

12. Cassius Dio 53.27.2–4.

13. Ovid, *Fasti* 5.545–598; *Corpus Inscriptionum Latinarum* 6.3.40954–40956; Joseph Geiger, *The First Hall of Fame: A Study of the Statues in the Forum Augustum* (Leiden: Brill, 2008).

14. White, "Julius Caesar in Augustan Rome," 339–340. The holidays appear to have gone back to a vote of the Senate in 45 BC (Appian, *Civil War* 2.106); Ida Östenberg, "Triumph and Spectacle: Victory Celebrations in the Late Republican Civil Wars," in *The Roman Republican Triumph Beyond the Spectacle*, ed. Carsten Hjort Lange and Frederik Juliaan Vervaet (Rome: Edizioni Quasar, 2014), 181–193.

15. Lawrence Keppie, *The Making of the Roman Army: From Republic to Empire* (Norman: University of Oklahoma Press, 1998), 132–144.

16. See, e.g., Cicero, *Philippics* 1.3, 5.10.

17. See especially Augustus's own account of his life, *Achievements of the Divine Augustus*, 13, 30.1, 32.3.

18. Augustus, *Achievements of the Divine Augustus* 24.2; Suetonius, *Divine Augustus* 52; and Cassius Dio 53.22.3.

19. Suetonius, *Divine Augustus* 53.3.

20. See Hannah Mitchell et al., "The Alternative Augustan Age," in *The Alternative Augustan Age*, ed. Kit Morrell, Josiah Osgood, and Kathryn Welch (New York: Oxford University Press, 2019), 1–11. Similarly, Adam Afzelius, "Die politische Bedeutung des jüngeren Cato," *Classica et Mediaevalia* 4 (1941): 190, notes the survival of the Senate and obsolescence of the Plebeian Assembly: the struggle of Cato and his associates led to defeat, but the defeat was, thanks to their tenacity, half victory. On elections, see Suetonius, *Divine Augustus* 40.2; Cassius Dio 53.21.6–7.

21. Suetonius, *Divine Augustus* 42.1.

22. Horace, *Odes* 1.12.35–36, 2.1.23–24.

23. The shield is described at Vergil, *Aeneid* 8.626–728, with quotations from 8.666–670.

24. Valerius Maximus 2.10.8.

25. Persius, *Satires* 3.44–48; Seneca the Elder, *Controversiae* 9.6.7, *Suasoriae* 6.1–2.

26. Livy fragment 45, *Periochae* 104, 107, 112–114.

27. Velleius Paterculus 2.35.2.

28. Especially by Seneca, *Letters* 95.70, 104.30.

29. See the important paper by Kit Morrell, "Augustus the Magpie," in Morrell, Osgood, and Welch, eds., *The Alternative Augustan Age*, 12–26.

30. Macrobius, *Saturnalia* 2.4.18.

31. On the Neronian principate, a good study is Miriam T. Griffin, *Nero: The End of a Dynasty* (New Haven, CT: Yale University Press, 1985). More recent approaches can be accessed in Shadi Bartsch, Kirk Freudenburg, and Cedric Littlewood, eds., *The Cambridge Companion to the Age of Nero* (Cambridge, UK: Cambridge University Press, 2017), which includes a chapter by me that I draw on here, "Nero and the Senate" (34–47). On the theatricality of suicide after Cato, see Miriam T. Griffin, "Philosophy, Cato, and Roman Suicide," in *Politics and Philosophy at Rome: Collected Papers*, ed. Catalina Balmaceda (Oxford, UK: Oxford University Press, 2018), 402–419; and Catharine Edwards, *Death in Ancient Rome* (New Haven, CT: Yale University Press, 2007), 144–160.

32. Seneca, *Letters* 104.29–33. For many further citations, see Robert J. Goar, *The Legend of Cato Uticensis from the First Century BC to the Fifth Century AD* (Brussels: Latomus, 1987), 35–41.

33. Tacitus, *Annals* 15.63.3; the whole account occupies 15.60.2–64. Thoughtful studies of Seneca's life and works are given by James Romm, *Dying Every Day: Seneca at the Court of Nero* (New York: Knopf, 2014), and Emily Wilson, *The Greatest Empire: A Life of Seneca* (New York: Oxford University Press, 2014).

34. The main source for Thrasea is Tacitus, who drew on a memoir by a friend of Thrasea's, Arulenus Rusticus, which might have been patterned on Thrasea's life of Cato (Tacitus, *Agricola* 2.1; Suetonius, *Domitian* 10.2–3). Relevant passages for my account are Tacitus, *Annals* 14.12.1, 14.49, 15.23.4, 16.21–35.

35. Plutarch, *Cato the Younger* 25.1, 37.1.

36. Tacitus, *Annals* 16.22.2.

37. Tacitus, *Annals* 16.35.1.

38. Suetonius, *Lucan*; Tacitus, *Annals* 15.49.3, 15.70. A good introduction to the poet can be found in the fine translation *Lucan: "Civil War,"* trans. Susan H. Braund (Oxford, UK: Oxford University Press, 1992), xiii–l.

39. Lucan, *Civil War* 2.439–461 (selections), as translated by *Lucan: "The Civil War,"* trans. J. D. Duff (Cambridge, MA: Harvard University Press, 1928), 89–91. What follows draws on these passages: 1.151–157, 2.302–303, 2.312–313, 4.247–252 (with quotation from 4.248).

40. Lucan, *Civil War* 1.669–672, translation from Braund, trans., *Lucan: "Civil War,"* 20.

A Note on Sources

1. Plutarch, *Alexander* 1.2.

2. Josiah Osgood and Christopher Baron, eds., *Cassius Dio and the Late Roman Republic* (Leiden: Brill, 2019).

3. Plutarch, *Caesar* 11.2.

4. Plutarch, *Caesar* 4.4.

5. See Plutarch, *Cato the Younger* 25.1, 37.1, with Joseph Geiger, "Munatius Rufus and Thrasea Paetus on Cato the Younger," *Athenaeum* 57 (1979): 48–72.

6. E.g., Plutarch, *Cato the Younger* 7, 11, 36–37.

7. E.g., Cicero, *Letters to Atticus* 1.18.7 (SB 18), 2.1.8 (SB 21).

8. E.g., Suetonius, *Divine Julius* 9, 20.2, 49–50.

9. Suetonius, *Divine Julius* 6.1, 49.3, 51, 80.2.

10. Suetonius, *Divine Julius* 69; Appian, *Civil War* 2.47; and Cassius Dio 41.26–36.

11. A helpful discussion is given by Jan Felix Gaertner, "The *Corpus Caesarianum*," in *The Cambridge Companion to the Writings of Julius Caesar*, ed. Luca Grillo and Christopher B. Krebs (Cambridge, UK: Cambridge University Press, 2018), 263–276.

12. Caesar is attacked in Cicero's treatise *On Obligations*, written in late 44 BC (e.g., 1.26, 1.43, 3.82–83).

13. Letters from Caesar include *Letters to Atticus* 9.6A (SB 172A), 9.7C (SB 174C), and 9.16 (SB 185). The letter from Cato is *Letters to Friends* 15.5 (SB 111).

14. On the Bona Dea scandal, see Cicero, *Letters to Atticus* 1.12–16 (SB 12–16).

INDEX

Josiah Osgood is a professor of classics at Georgetown University and holds a PhD from Yale University. A winner of the Rome Prize, he is the author of five books on Roman history and the translator and editor of *How to Be a Bad Emperor*, a 2020 edition of Suetonius's *Lives of the Caesars*. He lives in Washington, DC.